Tourism in Actio

TEN CASE STUDIES IN TOURISM

John Ward

Stanley Thornes (Publishers) Ltd

First published in 1991 by:
Stanley Thornes (Publishers) Ltd
Old Station Drive
Leckhampton
CHELTENHAM GL53 0DN
England

British Library Cataloguing-in-Publication Data

Ward, John
    Tourism in action: Ten case studies in tourism.
    I. Title
    338.407

    ISBN 0–7487–1180–5

Typeset by Tech-Set, Gateshead, Tyne & Wear
Printed and bound in Great Britain at The Bath Press, Avon

Contents

Introduction

In setting out to write this book I had a number of objectives:

♦ to stimulate an interest in the workings of the tourist industry
♦ to introduce a complex activity, namely tourism, which is hard to define, in an approachable way
♦ to demonstrate why tourism is perceived as such an important growth industry
♦ to offer some views from participants in the industry and observers of it about future developments and future issues which the industry is likely to face
♦ to provide some real contexts for studying economic and industrial issues affecting the tourist industry.

There are a number of books already available which provide a general introduction to tourism. These are invaluable in providing an overview, but I hope that the case studies in this book will demonstrate how the principles are put into practice.

Each case study features a different sector or aspect of tourism in operation. They explore how organisations begin, develop and change. Ideas about marketing, customer relations, and education and training are given real contexts, although many of the conclusions are equally valid for other industries.

Tourism development often seems to be driven by economics and politics, yet some of the case studies highlight the need to be aware of the environmental and social impact of tourism.

The case studies should have a broad appeal. Some are very straightforward; others, such as the travel office study with its explanation of financial issues, are more complex. Similarly, the exercises cover both oral and written tasks and vary from those requiring rapid responses to those which could be developed into extended assignments.

No doubt the book will be put to many different uses, but I hope it will be successful in:

♦ providing additional knowledge and resources
♦ illustrating the development and impact of tourism
♦ analysing a range of destinations more fully
♦ offering suggestions for written and oral assignments for a range of tourism courses
♦ providing a source of class background reading while the tutor is supervising group work
♦ providing supplementary reading for programmes of careers education
♦ supporting studies in Geography, Economics, Technology, Business Studies, Leisure, and Food Service.

The book will be a particularly useful resource for the following courses:

GCSE in Travel and Tourism
BTEC National in Travel and Tourism
BTEC First and National Courses in Leisure and Business
City and Guilds:
    480 Introduction to Tourism in the UK
    499 The Travel Industry in Britain
    481 Recreation and Leisure Industries

A Note on Key Terms

Key terms are highlighted in the text in bold print. They include both terms used in tourism and vocabulary relevant to a particular case study. Definitions can be found at the end of each section in which key terms appear.

1 *Bloomsbury Crest Hotel*

Introduction

A traveller to Edinburgh wrote in 1783:

> ... there was no such place as an hotel: the word was not known, or only intelligible to French scholars.

Certainly the word 'hotel' was originally a French one, meaning a large residence, either privately owned or housing an important public official. In the eighteenth century most travel in England was by road, and inns and ale-houses were used where overnight stops were necessary.

By the early nineteenth century the word hotel was in more common use and was defined as 'a genteel inn'. Travellers to spa towns like Bath would generally have stayed in private houses, and it took the establishment of steamboat services to coastal resorts to create a demand for hotels outside the major urban centres like London and Manchester.

A former railway hotel, St Pancras

However, it was the expansion of the railways in the middle decades of the nineteenth century which really stimulated hotel development. The railway companies themselves played a major part in this, constructing large hotels adjacent to most of the major railway termini. These were frequented initially by the well-off, as they were the people who could afford to travel. Such travellers, many of them accustomed to employing domestic servants, expected the hotels to provide service in addition to a room to sleep in. At first the only services provided were cleaning and the provision of food, but later hotels developed **room service**, **valet service** and a range of leisure services.

Today a hotel can be defined as a building providing sleeping facilities in private rooms, and catering facilities, usually in a restaurant or communal dining room, for paying guests.

Hotels are most frequently located in urban centres, along major road and rail routes, close to airports and near major visitor attractions.

Hotel Facilities and Services

In a small hotel, meals will probably be served in a dining room and will often consist of a set menu with little choice available. Large hotels may have more than one restaurant, offering everything from snacks to meals from an **à la carte** menu. Large hotels will probably also offer to provide meals in the bedrooms as part of their room service.

Facilities such as a television or a kettle are likely to be found in the bedrooms of larger hotels. Hotel chains will often try to encourage customer loyalty by guaranteeing a similar provision of facilities in all the group's hotels. For example, Crest hotels, who owned the Bloomsbury Crest until 1990, offered the following standard facilities in all their bedrooms:

- **ensuite bathrooms**
- colour television and radio
- telephone
- hospitality tray
- trouser press.

The **Crown classification** scheme means that people intending to stay in hotels which belong to the scheme will have a very precise knowledge of the facilities they can expect in each room.

Public Areas

A small independent hotel is likely to offer shared facilities such as a bar and a television lounge. A larger hotel will have to accommodate a range of needs for a greater number of guests. This may include the provision of leisure facilities, such as a swimming pool or exercise centre, or services such as laundry provision or the booking of theatre tickets.

Special Room Categories

However, these facilities might be regarded as usual in most large hotels and so companies such as Crest introduced additional facilities in their rooms. Crest developed four room categories and the different facilities that were available in each category illustrate how hotels are continually seeking to attract particular **market segments**. Executive Bedrooms included extras such as remote-control television, bathrobes, hair dryers and a small refrigerated drinks cabinet. Business Study Rooms had desks, safes and a small reference library. Lady Crest Rooms were generally sited in the most secure part of the hotel and contained hair dryers, irons and ironing boards, make-up mirrors and magazines.

No-Smoking Rooms, as the name suggests, guaranteed guests an environment free of tobacco smoke.

Business Facilities

At one time hotels were merely used as accommodation by business travellers. They might have used residents' lounges as meeting places, but would have had to find other premises in which to work effectively. To meet this need, hotels have developed business centres. These offer a range of services including fax, telex, photocopying, copy typing, message handling, onward reservations, postal services, courier services, car rental, film developing, travel advice and florist services.

A business centre

As more and more companies send employees on external training courses hotels respond by providing training centres capable of accommodating large numbers of delegates. These may be constructed with movable partitions so that exhibitions can be mounted or buffet meals provided within the same area. Smaller meeting rooms may also be available for delegates wishing to work in groups. In addition to suitable furniture, meeting rooms are generally equipped with pencils, paper, flip charts and soft drinks. Resources such as television and video are available if required.

Leisure Facilities

Many hotel visitors will be seeking relaxation as well as or instead of working, and larger hotels have developed facilities to meet this need. Popular leisure facilities include swimming pools, **saunas**, **solariums**, games rooms and fitness rooms.

Key Terms

room service – food, drinks and services supplied to individual hotel rooms.

valet service – assistance with clothing and appearance.

à la carte – a menu on which each item is separately priced.

ensuite bathroom – a private bathroom with a connecting door to a hotel bedroom.

Crown classification – a system of grading the level of furnishings and facilities to be found in a hotel.

market segment – a group of potential customers who share a common characteristic such as the age group to which they belong.

sauna – a room producing dry or moist heat to invigorate the body.

solarium – artificial tanning facilities.

◇ *Exercise* ◇

The Bloomsbury Crest Hotel is situated in the heart of London. Many of the Bloomsbury Crest's visitors are Americans.

You have been asked by the Crest company to develop six themed rooms, for which a higher tariff will be charged in exchange for added facilities and atmosphere.

What suggestions can you make to be included in the decor, facilities and design of one of the following themed rooms ?

- The New York Room
- The California Room
- The Las Vegas Room
- The Texas Room
- The Boston Room
- The Florida Room.

Staffing Requirements

Hotels are **labour intensive**. This means that the wages and salaries of their staff account for a large proportion of their costs. The reason for this is that the range of services provided by hotels is largely dependent on people. Although a certain amount of information can be conveyed by technology, hotel guests expect a friendly, personal service. Many of the tasks within a hotel, such as bed-making or meal preparation, can only be done by hand. In areas such as reception guests will need a prompt service, and in a large hotel this will require more than one member of staff. The larger hotels, especially those with visitors arriving from abroad, will have to maintain a 24-hour service with receptionists, telephonists, cleaners, porters and a night manager on duty.

A chef will do many tasks by hand

The Extent of Hotel Use in Britain

Hotels have never been used by more than a quarter of British **domestic holiday-makers**. They have had to face competition from cheaper forms of accommodation such as caravans, self-catering apartments, campsites and chalets, as well as the most common location of holiday accommodation – the home of a friend or relative.

Hotel Ownership

The building and purchase of hotels by large companies is a continuing trend, although smaller hotels are often privately owned. A hotel chain, a group of hotels owned by the same company, is able to negotiate reduced rates for food supplies and redecoration. Large companies are more likely to be able to finance developments on prime sites close to major attractions and facilities. They are more likely to be able to afford to use television and the press for nationwide advertising campaigns. They are also able to invest in automated reservations systems and high-quality training programmes.

Key Terms

labour intensive – dependent on a large number of staff to provide goods or services.

domestic holiday-makers – people taking holidays in their own country.

◇ *Exercise* ◇

Study the table and graph:

Table 1 Accommodation of British Tourists in England, 1989

	Trips %	Nights %	Amount spent %
Hotel/Motel/ Guesthouse	23	19	38
Paying guest in:			
farmhouse	–	1	1
other private house/B & B	3	2	3
Self catering in rented:			
flat/apartment	2	4	4
house/chalet/villa/ bungalow	3	6	6
hostel/university/ school	2	2	2
Friends/relatives' homes	49	42	24
Own second home/ timeshare	1	1	1
Holiday camp/village:			
self catering	2	2	3
serviced	1	1	2
Camping	4	4	3
Caravan:			
towed	4	6	5
static owned	3	3	2
static not owned	3	5	5
Boat(s)	1	1	1
Sleeper cab of lorry/ truck	1	1	1
Other transit	1	–	–
Total commercial accommodation	44	49	69
Total non-commercial accommodation	58	51	31
Total serviced	27	23	43
Total self catering	17	27	26

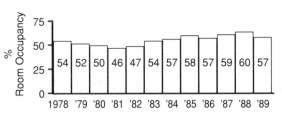

In 1988, the average duration of stay was 2.3 nights, 18% of arrivals at English hotels were from overseas.

Figure 1   English hotel occupancy

1 What is the difference between room occupancy and bed occupancy?

2 Why might Figure 1 not give a very accurate picture of how successful the hotel and catering sector had been during the period 1978–89?

3 If the Minister for Tourism were making a speech about the future of the hotel and catering sector, how might he or she use the information in Table 1 to suggest the best way ahead?

The Bloomsbury Crest

Twenty years ago Sir Robert McAlpine's construction company erected the building now known as the Bloomsbury Crest. The company leased the hotel to Center Hotels. Crest Hotels took over the site in 1979, ten years after the company had opened its first hotel.

Over the years Crest introduced a number of changes, particularly to the range of rooms available and the facilities offered in them. They increased the number and quality of restaurant and business facilities. In February 1988 a major **refurbishment** was started, taking a year to complete. The number of bedrooms was increased from 243 to 284 and an entire new floor was built, housing **suites** and executive rooms.

The Bloomsbury Crest Hotel, front entrance

Crest Hotels Limited

When Crest was sold to Forte plc in 1990, it operated 51 hotels in the United Kingdom, five in Amsterdam and one in each of the centres of Antwerp, Bologna, Florence, Brussels, The Hague and Madrid. Two other hotels were in the process of construction. All of these hotels were classified as three-star or above.

Like other companies, Crest Hotels had a need to make the public aware that they were all part of the same company, so that people would choose to stay in their hotels rather than those of their competitors. They did this largely through advertising, but the use of the company logo on all brochures, advertisements and communications was another means of establishing the company identity.

The Crest Hotels' logo

CREST HOTELS

All the hotels in the group reflected local and regional differences. Restaurants or bars were sometimes named after local places or characters or events from local history. Individuality was also expressed in a number of other ways. For example, a particular hotel might set up a themed promotion, such as a Parisian week, during which there would be French **cuisine**.

The size and style of the hotels within the group varied considerably. The Unicorn Crest Hotel in Stow-on-the-Wold is a seventeenth-century stone building with just 20 bedrooms, while the Regent Crest Hotel is a modern building in the West End of London with 320 bedrooms. However, the main differences were largely determined by whether the majority of guests were business people, conference delegates or tourists because this affected the kind of facilities and services available.

Key Terms

refurbishment – giving a new appearance by alterations, decoration, etc.

suite – several linked rooms acting as a single accommodation unit.

cuisine – a style of cooking.

◇ *Exercise* ◇

Forte plc have constructed a new hotel close to where you live.

a) What names could you provide for the following in order to give them a local flavour:

- a formal restaurant serving à la carte meals?
- a small café area offering light meals?
- a bar and lounge area?
- a fitness centre?

b) Draw a rough design for a page of a brochure about the new hotel, featuring the four facilities listed here under the names you have given them.

Setting Standards

The Head Office of Crest Hotels was located in Banbury, Oxfordshire. One of its functions was to set standards for all of the hotels in the group. These covered issues such as appropriate appearance and dress, the way reports were presented and the necessity of providing vegetarian and diabetic meals. Crest also laid down standards of service and customer care.

Marketing

Marketing and advertising activities illustrate the relationship which existed between individual hotels and the group. The main purpose of any Crest advertising campaign was to raise awareness of the Crest **brand**. Before an advertising campaign was planned there would be some discussion of whom it was to be aimed at. In most cases this would either be the business traveller or potential weekend customers. However, on occasions a more specific audience, such as female business travellers, was targeted.

The fact that all Crest hotels had similar star ratings made it easier to mount a national advertising campaign because many of the facilities and qualities featured in Crest's advertising could be found in all their hotels. The Head Office managed the planning and printing of leaflets and brochures, and individual hotels then ordered as many as they thought they would require for local use.

Sales

The Head Office also laid down some specific sales activities which should take place. Each hotel was required to identify potential local customers and to make contact with them directly or through advertising and **mail shots**. Individual hotels were able to make their own decisions about which times of year were most appropriate for them to mount local sales drives.

A business meeting room in the Bloomsbury Crest Hotel

The Boulevard Restaurant in the Bloomsbury Crest Hotel

Change of Ownership

The Bloomsbury Crest was, prior to May 1990, part of Crest Hotels Limited, which was a subsidiary company of Bass plc. The hotel sector saw a number of takeovers and changes of ownership in the 1980s, often involving international companies with a variety of interests in addition to hotel operations. Bass plc were perhaps best known for their brewing interests. They own Bass Charrington, Tennants, and Mitchells and Butlers, as well as other drinks organisations such as Britvic, Corona, Hedges and Butler, and Mouton Cadet. When Bass plc acquired Holiday Inns International in 1990 they decided to sell the major part of the Crest organisation to Forte plc in order to concentrate on the single, larger and more international brand name, Holiday Inns.

The new owners of the Bloomsbury Crest, Forte plc, may well adopt different styles of marketing, sales and regulation of individual hotels, but these functions will still be controlled centrally. The change of ownership will not have a radical effect on many of the hotel's established practices, apart perhaps from changes in suppliers.

Key Terms

brand – goods or services sold under a single name or trademark.

mail shot – advertising material sent through the post.

◇ *Exercise* ◇

The towns listed below show the locations of the Forte Crest Hotels in the United Kingdom:

Aylesbury	Gloucester	Newcastle-upon-Tyne
Basildon	Grimsby	Nottingham
Belfast	Guildford	Plymouth
Bexley	Heathrow	Portsmouth
Birmingham	Hull	Preston
Brighouse	Leeds/Bradford	Rochester
Bristol	Lincoln	Runcorn
Cardiff	Liverpool	Sheffield
Coventry	London, Bloomsbury	Southampton
Exeter	London, Regents Park	Swansea
Farnborough	London, St James'	Swindon
Gatwick	Luton	Winchester
Glasgow	Manchester Airport	
Glasgow Airport	Milton Keynes	

Use a road atlas to check where each location is.

The Forte group has budgeted for four regional sales conferences, at which every Crest hotel is to be represented.

Choose **four** Forte Crest hotels to host these conferences, explaining the reasons for your choices and listing the venues which each of the representatives should attend.

The Location of the Bloomsbury Crest

The location of a hotel is the most important factor in attracting people to stay in it. A hotel in the middle of an industrial estate or at the end of a long, narrow lane may have difficulty in attracting customers. The location of the Bloomsbury Crest in Coram Street in the centre of London makes it ideal for visiting the West End or conducting business in London. It is very close to Russell Square tube station, which makes access to other parts of London relatively easy. It is also within a few minutes' walk of Euston, from where British Rail runs services to the Midlands, the North of England and Scotland.

Many visitors to the hotel are from overseas and find its location ideal for a number of activities. Knightsbridge, and in particular Harrods, can be reached easily on the Piccadilly Line, as can Covent Garden with its distinctive shops and its street performers.

The hotel is also close to theatres, museums, historical landmarks and parks. A theatre booking service is available in the hotel, run in association with a theatre ticket agency. Events such as the Chelsea Flower Show, the Trooping of the Colour, and the Wimbledon Lawn Tennis Championships have attracted overseas visitors for many years, and Crest Hotels included a calendar of major London events in their 'Welcome Breaks' London brochure.

Covent Garden

West End theatres

◇ *Exercise* ◇

Find a street map of London and locate Coram Street, where the Bloomsbury Crest is to be found.

Work in pairs and take it in turns to act as the hotel's hall porter and a hotel guest asking for directions to the following places:

a) The British Museum in Great Russell Street

b) Euston Station
c) Lincoln's Inn
d) King's Cross Station
e) Endell Street Baths
f) The Opera House in Bow Street
g) the beginning of Oxford Street at St Giles Circus.

Employment and Training

Working in a hotel may have the disadvantage of unsocial hours, but many people enjoy working in what is often a lively environment. In a large hotel it is the task of the personnel manager to recruit and train all those working in the hotel. It may be necessary to contact an employment agency if staff with specific skills are being sought. The company may advertise for staff both nationally and, more commonly, locally. Other staff may be recommended by a friend or relative already working in the hotel, or they may simply walk into the building seeking employment.

◇ *Exercise* ◇

On the following page you will see a chart showing the staff structure at the Bloomsbury Crest Hotel.

Which member of staff do you think would be called on to deal with the following situations, and whose help might they request?

a) an individual shower unit fails to work
b) a major food supplier telephones to say that because of a health scare they cannot deliver any beef for at least two weeks
c) a guest complains of verbal abuse from a cleaner

d) a firm's secretary telephones to enquire about holding a sales conference in the hotel
e) Head Office requests a report on the profitability of a themed food week held in the hotel
f) the behaviour of a party of guests in the bar becomes sufficiently boisterous to cause annoyance to others.

Company Guidelines on Training

Well-trained staff are clearly essential to the smooth running of a good hotel. The Crest company set out guidelines which helped to establish training priorities. The individual hotels in the group used these to devise a training plan. They then kept records of all the training they had provided.

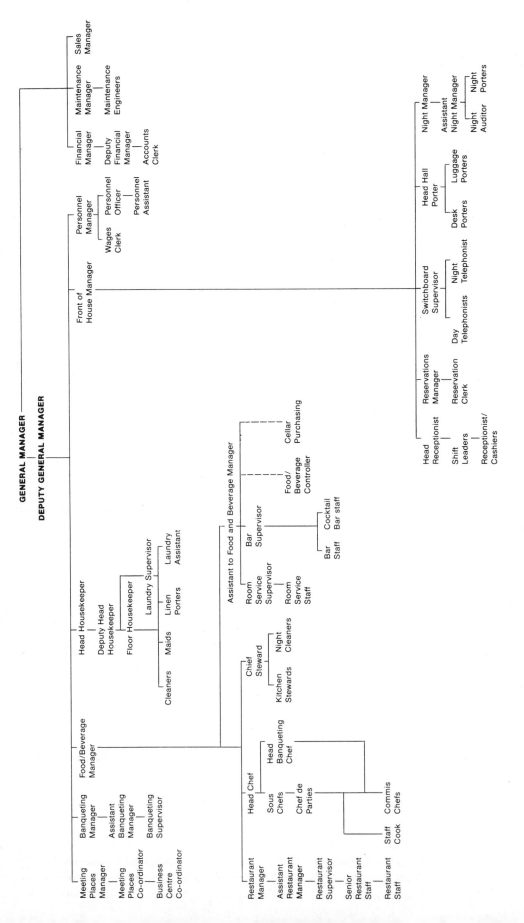

The staff structure at the Bloomsbury Crest Hotel

◇ *Exercise* ◇

Match up the following departments within the Bloomsbury Crest Hotel with the descriptions of their responsibilities. Then check your answers by looking at page 24.

Department	Description
1 Front office (concierge)	a) dealing with all things that break down; day-to-day decorating
2 Front office (reception)	b) providing food for restaurants, room service, staff canteen, banqueting
3 Housekeeping	c) recording all financial transactions in the hotel; dealing with all wages
4 Room service	d) organising recruitment of staff; training; staff counselling; helping to sort out grievances
5 Kitchen	e) helping guests with enquiries about bookings, cash, currency
6 Switchboard	f) organising meetings and functions, including catering arrangements
7 Reservations	g) helping guests with newspapers, keys, luggage, messages, etc.
8 Maintenance	h) dealing with all banqueting operations; room layout, menus, etc.
9 Personnel	i) dealing with all bookings made by people wishing to stay in the hotel
10 Meeting Places	j) supplying food and other requests to rooms; stocking mini-bars
11 Banqueting	k) dealing with incoming calls; early morning calls; bleep system; back door security
12 Accounts	l) dealing with laundry; tidying rooms; supplying irons, boards, extra bedding

How many of the above services do you think you would find in a ten-room hotel?

Three partners plan to open and run a ten-bedroom hotel. Devise a plan by which they might divide up their responsibilities, while at the same time ensuring that the day-to-day running of the hotel went smoothly.

Induction Training

New employees at the Bloomsbury Crest, at whatever level they were employed, were given **induction training** about the hotel, the group and their policies. Soon after appointment they were assessed and a joint agreement was reached about their training needs. Despite the change of ownership, training is still seen as a continuous process because there are always new skills, new techniques and more up-to-date knowledge to be acquired. The training schemes themselves have to receive company approval and, once staff have been selected to go on such courses, they must be released from their duties.

Job Descriptions

In order to help individuals to assess their own responsibilities, each employee is provided with a job description. These descriptions serve a greater purpose than simply reminding people of what they are supposed to be doing. They allow everyone in the organisation to assess how effectively it is running, whether communications are working successfully, and whether some individuals are over-burdened or under-employed. They can be used to help individuals to identify their strengths and weaknesses, their training needs and their possible future career paths. One of the job descriptions is shown below.

Key Term

induction training – training introducing employees to a company.

BLOOMSBURY CREST HOTEL

JOB DESCRIPTION

JOB TITLE: COOK/COMMIS
RESPONSIBLE TO: CHEF DE PARTIE
TERMS: AS PER CONTRACT OF EMPLOYMENT
UNIFORM: COOK'S WHITES

PURPOSE AND SCOPE OF POSITION

To prepare food within the section efficiently and to the highest standards achievable as directed by the Chef de Partie.

DUTIES AND RESPONSIBILITIES

1 GENERAL

a Being responsible for ensuring that the food is prepared to the highest standards within the Company guidelines as stated in the Standards Manual.

b Producing food as directed by the Chef de Partie and presenting it at the times required.

c Being fully aware of all items on the menu which are the responsibility of the section and of their recipes and quantities.

d Working in close liaison with all sections within the kitchen to ensure efficient service.

e Attending instruction or lectures/meetings as laid down by the Head Chef or Sous Chef.

f Working to the rotas laid down by the Chef de Partie.

g Being alert for any opportunities to improve the profitability, economy and efficiency of the department and reporting such ideas to the Head Chef or the Chef de Partie.

2 HYGIENE

a Maintaining a high standard of hygiene both personally and in the preparation of food, as laid down by the Food Hygiene Regulations and by Company standards as stated in the Standards Manual, and co-operating generally with the Hygiene Officer.

b Reporting any hygiene problems to the Chef de Partie or the Sous Chef in his absence.

c Being responsible for ensuring that there is NO cross-contamination of foods.

d Reporting to the Chef de Partie, or a Sous Chef in his absence, any pest sightings.

3 HEALTH AND SAFETY

a Knowing the Health and Safety Policy and being personally responsible regarding the health and safety of other persons at work.

b Reporting any defects in machinery and equipment immediately to the Chef de Partie, or Sous Chef in his absence, with special regard to:

    i) Slicers, ovens, mixers, steamers

    ii) Trolleys

c Being alert to unsafe practices such as dangerous stacking, and reporting them to the Chef de Partie, or a Sous Chef in his absence, so that these practices can be superseded by safe procedures.

d Knowing the Fire Procedure and, in particular, the procedures for fighting kitchen fires. Co-operating generally with the Fire Officer.

e Knowing the First Aid Procedure.

4 SECURITY

a Co-operating with the Management in maintaining security.

b Being responsible in co-operation with the Management for the prevention of theft of food and other Company property.

c Detecting undesirable and suspicious characters in the kitchen areas and either taking action or reporting to the Duty Manager, Head Chef or Chef de Partie as appropriate.

d Knowing the Bomb Procedure.

◇ *Exercise* ◇

All of the following food and beverages appear on the various menus available in the Bloomsbury Crest:

Starters
Terrine of chicken liver pâté (with brioche)
Asparagus mousse
Avocado pear (on lime and walnut mayonnaise)
Smoked salmon roulade

Soups
Crab bisque
Beef consommé
Traditional minestrone

Fish
Darne of salmon (with hollandaise sauce)
Fillets of sea bass en croûte (with orange fondue butter)

Main courses
Lasagne verdi
Pork escalope calvados
Duckling with Cointreau
Boeuf bourguignon
Fricassée of chicken

Vegetables
Cauliflower florets
Broccoli
Courgettes

Potatoes
Château potatoes
Croquette potatoes
Boulangère potatoes
Noisette potatoes

Desserts
Chocolate mousse with Grand-Marnier
Soufflé Vesuvius
Profiteroles
Black Forest Gâteau

White wines
Muscadet
Mâcon Villages
Orvieto
Liebfraumilch

Red wines
Beaujolais
Rioja
Chianti
Valpolicella

Devise a training programme which would enable those waiting at tables to pronounce these names clearly and confidently.

Divide into pairs, with one person taking the role of trainer and the other the role of employee. Use the training programme you have devised to try and improve your partner's ability to pronounce the words correctly.

Discuss how effective your training programme was and how you might improve it in the light of your experience of trying to test it.

The Use of Technology

In a large hotel there are many tasks involving information and communications which can be performed much more rapidly and efficiently by using technological hardware.

All rooms in the Bloomsbury Crest are equipped with telephones. At one time the switchboard operator would have had to note how many units had been used in each guest's outgoing telephone calls, and the cost would be written manually onto their bill. Calls are now recorded automatically and included as an item on a computerised bill.

In the past reservations were recorded on a system known as Whitney Racks. These racks held different coloured squares, each colour representing a different kind of room. Details of reservations were displayed on a board which had to be constantly updated. The process was extremely time-consuming because it involved three separate activities. First the details of reservations had to be entered in a book. This information was then collated and entered onto the Whitney Rack. Finally, a summary chart of all reservations was put onto a colour-coded magnetic board which was used to indicate which accommodation was still available. A computer now handles all reservations in a fraction of the time that the old system would have taken, as well as enabling much more efficient storage of records and information.

A switchboard operator at the Bloomsbury Crest Hotel

The Restaurant and Housekeeping Managers need up-to-date information to complete their duties. The Restaurant Manager must know how much stock to order and how much food to prepare, while the Housekeeping Manager will need to know that a sufficient number of staff are available to clean and service all the rooms required. The number of guests and the number of occupied rooms have to be counted each day. The housekeeper who has completed the servicing of an individual room simply keys a code into the telephone. This connects it automatically to a central computer system which changes the status of the room from unserviced to **serviced**.

Key Term

serviced accommodation – accommodation where catering and cleaning services are provided.

◇ *Exercise* ◇

1 One area which might appear to offer less scope for the use of information technology than others is the kitchen.

The Food and Beverage Manager, working closely with the Head Chef, will probably have all of the following responsibilities:

♦ ordering food
♦ working out its cost and the prices on the menu
♦ deciding on portion sizes
♦ assessing ingredients for their nutritional, aesthetic and flavour value
♦ ensuring that the menus offer a variety of dishes, including those catering for particular needs such as vegetarian diets
♦ carrying out stock control and re-ordering.

a) How might the system of menu planning be computerised?
b) Which decisions could be based on the evidence of a computerised system of menu planning?

2 One of the Bloomsbury Crest's buffet menus offers:

Chicken drumsticks
Goujons of plaice
Mini sausage rolls
Assorted cocktail sandwiches
Cheese and pineapple sticks
Eggs stuffed with mayonnaise
Selection of quiches
Mushrooms with dips
Assorted Danish pastries

Imagine that this particular menu is ordered approximately 80 times during one year and that the number of guests varies between 30 and 50. What are the various ways in which the use of a computer could benefit this particular service?

Health and Safety

All hotels have a responsibility to look after the health, welfare and safety of employees, guests and visitors. The Health and Safety at Work Act 1974 placed the following responsibilities on all employers:

♦ to provide and maintain plant and systems of work that are, so far as is reasonably practicable, safe and without risks to health.
♦ to make arrangements to ensure, as far as is reasonably practicable, safety and the absence of risks to health in connection with the use, handling, storage and transport of articles and substances.
♦ to provide such information, instruction, training and supervision as will ensure, so far as is reasonably practicable, the health and safety of its employees.
♦ to maintain any place of work under its control in a condition which is, so far as is reasonably practicable, safe and without risks to health, and to provide and maintain safe means of access and egress.
♦ to provide and maintain a working environment which is, so far as is reasonably practicable, safe and without risks to health, and which is adequate as far as statutory welfare facilities and arrangements are concerned.

Safety Handbook

Crest Hotels had their own health and safety policy. Each new employee was given a handbook covering subjects such as personal hygiene, the use of equipment, emergency routes and exits, hazardous materials, fire training, kitchen safety and safety signs. Employees were required to return a signed statement that they had read and understood the company guidelines on health and safety at work.

Hygiene

Much of the advice about personal hygiene was common sense and related to cleanliness, tying long hair back, and wearing appropriate clothing correctly. As hotels provide food for so many people, it is vital that illnesses or cuts and sores among staff handling food are identified and treated early.

Hazards

Hotels are full of potential hazards such as electrical appliances, chemical fluids for cleaning, hoists and lifts, and sharp kitchen implements. Large kitchens can be particularly dangerous. Machinery used for chopping, mincing, mixing and waste disposal needs to be handled with care. For example, anyone cleaning such machinery would need to be absolutely certain that the power source had been disconnected. Cooking frequently demands the use of boiling liquids which need to be handled with great care, especially in a confined space. Where gas appliances are used in kitchens there should be checks that pilot lights are on and that there have been no leaks.

Hazard warning signs

Accident book

The Bloomsbury Crest is legally required to keep an accident book, and employees must report all accidents as well as any potential hazards. One member of the hotel management team has a specific responsibility for health and safety, and will receive and act on the information provided.

◇ *Exercise* ◇

Look at the extract below, taken from the Crest *Health and Safety at Work – an Employers' Handbook.*

Clear Exits and Routes

Be careful of damaged floor coverings and steps, you could trip over them.

Don't abandon boxes or equipment in corridors, and watch out for wire or string trailing from packaging.

Move any obstacles immediately.

Never prop open fire doors. Move anything that blocks a fire exit. It could save vital seconds in the event of an emergency.

The requirements of the Health and Safety at Work Act 1974 include the phrase 'as far as is reasonably practicable'. If you were planning a training session covering health and safety, what examples would you use to get participants to think about whether any kind of obstruction to routes and exits was sometimes necessary, and what rules should be applied to such special circumstances?

Looking to the Future

Many people employed in hotels would see the future solely in terms of trying to keep occupancy rates as high as possible. A number of factors may affect what happens to the Bloomsbury Crest in the next few years.

The King's Cross Development

There are plans for a major new development at nearby King's Cross, to include offices, housing, shops and hotels. This will create a potential new market, but it may also establish further hotel competition. The scheme depends on the establishment of an international rail terminal linked to the Channel Tunnel. British Rail owns 30 acres of derelict land in the area but the development scheme has met with opposition, in particular to its requirement that listed buildings such as The Great Northern Hotel be pulled down. However, the greatest uncertainty relates to the building of the Channel Tunnel link itself, which cannot go ahead until it has been approved by Parliament, a process which has already been postponed twice.

Changing Patterns of Travel in Europe

Both the Channel Tunnel and the increasing co-operation within the European Community are likely to affect London hotels. It seems likely that there will be changes in patterns of European travel as well as in the European **labour market**. Overland journey times to London will be considerably reduced and it will be easier to work in another country within the Community.

Population Changes

Demographic trends mean that the proportion of young people within the British population as a whole will fall. As hotels have traditionally attracted staff from the younger age groups, in some regions of Britain they will face increasing competition from other employers attracting school leavers. Some hotels may decide to provide child care facilities to enable mothers with young children to return to work.

Future Business Travel

Looking further ahead, hotels will have to be aware of what the latest research shows about the needs of business travellers. It will be important to know about the technology which they rely on to keep in communication, about new areas of prosperity, and about the changes in the travelling habits of the families of business people.

Key Terms

labour market – all those available for or seeking employment.
demographic trends – changes in population distribution.

◇ *Exercise* ◇

Forte plc is planning a campaign to enable them to meet the challenges of the 1990s.
  Write a memorandum to be circulated to all hotel managers suggesting some of the possible focuses of this campaign and requesting their own observations, advice and comments.

◇ *Discussion points* ◇

1 Why might companies choose to send employees to hotels for training courses rather than holding them on their own premises?

2 What possible reasons can you suggest to explain why only a quarter of British domestic holiday-makers stay in hotels?

3 Why do you think marketing campaigns developed on behalf of hotel chains rarely target children and young people?

4 What do you think a personnel officer is likely to discuss on their first meeting with a new recruit to the staff of a large hotel?

5 Do you think some fashions and hairstyles are unsuitable for people intending to work in a hotel?

6 What effects do you think population changes will have on employment patterns in the future?

Answers to the exercise on page 15 are:

1 (g), **2** (e), **3** (l), **4** (j), **5** (b), **6** (k), **7** (i), **8** (a), **9** (d), **10** (f), **11** (h), **12** (c).

2 *Intasun – A Tour Operator*

Introduction

A tour operator plans and markets holidays. This will involve selecting destinations, organising travel and accommodation, and providing customer services. The operator will produce brochures advertising the range of holidays available and will set a price for each one. The majority of these holidays are sold through travel agents' offices, but some companies sell directly to the public.

Operating **package holidays** is a complex matter. Transport has to be arranged well in advance and times checked carefully so that transfers between aircraft, ferries and coaches do not involve long delays. Accommodation has to be checked to see that the advertised facilities are available and that the quality is appropriate to the type of holiday being planned. Many people book their holidays several months in advance so that they can be certain of their preferred destination, so brochures and other advertising materials have to be ready in time for them to make informed choices.

The First Tour Operations

The rapid expansion of the railway system in Britain in the 1830s brought seaside resorts like Brighton and events such as the Great

One of the tour operating staff at work

Exhibition of 1851 within reach of a much greater number of travellers. Excursions organised by people like Thomas Cook quickly became popular.

The Growth of Package Holidays

Package holidays have been the biggest growth area in tour operation until relatively recently. They were popular with holiday-makers because the **charter flights** enabled people to travel to warmer climates much more cheaply than if they were using **scheduled flights**. Initially such packages concentrated on destinations like Spain but other parts of the Mediterranean coast soon followed. As flight times were reduced and people grew interested in resorts outside Europe, North Africa and Florida began to attract growing numbers of charter flights. In the late 1980s **long haul** destinations such as Thailand were included in the range of package holidays on offer. The search for new destinations led to the rapid growth of tourism in countries such as Turkey, Goa, and the Gambia.

How Package Holidays Affected Tour Operators

Airlines encouraged the growth of package tours because they enabled them to fill empty seats by offering reduced fares to tour operators buying tickets in bulk. The tour operators profited by an extension to the traditional holiday season, with skiing and winter sun holidays filling a previously quiet period. However, fierce competition between operators meant that the profit on each package holiday sold was small and by the late 1980s smaller operators began to find it difficult to survive. Bigger companies could negotiate better rates for hotels and other accommodation because of the quantity of business which they were able to generate. A series of mergers and takeovers meant that, although by 1989 there were over six hundred tour operators in Britain, 58 per cent of all package holidays purchased were bought either from Thomson (who also own Horizon) or the International Leisure Group (to which Intasun belonged). Ten years earlier the market share of these two companies had been a mere 18 per cent. Some smaller operators became specialists, offering tours to less well-known destinations or concentrating on holidays likely to appeal strongly to a particular **market segment**, for example overland trekking.

Key Terms

package holiday (sometimes called an inclusive tour by charter) – a holiday booking which includes the cost of travel and accommodation and sometimes food and services as well.

charter flights – flights booked for a special purpose such as transporting holiday-makers to a specific destination.

scheduled flights – flights which run according to an airline's regular timetable.

long haul – requiring a long aeroplane flight, usually in excess of eight hours.

market segment – a group of potential customers who share a common characteristic such as the age group to which they belong.

◇ *Exercise* ◇

A tour operator decides to organise coach tours of European capital cities. The operator plans to run six coaches each day and intends to offer all of the following places in England as pick-up points:

Birmingham	Manchester
Darlington	Newcastle
Gravesend	Nottingham
Leeds	Ramsgate
Leicester	Rochester
Liverpool	Sheffield
London	Stoke
Luton	Wolverhampton

All the tours will cross the Channel from Ramsgate on a service which will require coaches to check in at 17.00 hours. The operator hopes to attract a similar amount of business from each of the points of departure, except for London, Birmingham and Manchester which are expected to attract approximately twice as many customers as the others.

Use an up-to-date motorway map to plan routes for the six coaches which would enable them to serve all the pick-up points and, as far as possible, allow an adequate number of seats for travellers from each one.

Estimate the time each of the six journeys would take, including stops, and work out pick-up times for travellers from each of the starting points.

A good road atlas should provide both motorway maps and a chart showing the distances between each of the chosen pick-up points.

The Economics of Tour Operations

The two biggest costs in putting a holiday package together are the costs of accommodation in the chosen resort and the seat on the aircraft.

Finding Suitable Accommodation

Negotiations with overseas property owners begin approximately 14–16 months before the start of the holiday season. One way of organising negotiations is to provide a contracting executive with a 'bed brief' for each destination which will outline the number of beds required in each hotel or the number of apartments needed in each resort. The contractor will seek to secure this accommodation at the best possible price. The rate is often determined by the size of the company because the greater number of rooms which a large company can guarantee to fill will enable them to negotiate lower rates than smaller companies. In some instances contractors will have a long-standing relationship with property owners, which makes negotiation easier.

*Two examples of
overseas accommodation
used by Intasun*

Agreeing a Contract for Accommodation

There are three main methods of contracting beds. In the first method, beds are contracted as *guaranteed property*. This means that the contractor agrees a price for a specified number of beds per night for the whole summer season. The property owner benefits from this method because payment by the tour operator is guaranteed, regardless of whether or not the beds are filled. The tour operator benefits by being able to negotiate better rates because of the block bookings. The system is generally used only for self-catering apartments or hotels in destinations where the demand for rooms is likely to exceed the supply. Tour operators can lose money through this system, particularly if beds remain unoccupied during the low season.

If beds are contracted as *non-guaranteed property*, the tour operator will pay the owner only if the room or apartment is filled. The contractor will negotiate with the property owner to take an agreed number of rooms or apartments. If these rooms are sold, the company is guaranteed their use, but if they remain unsold a release date is agreed. After this date the owner will accept other bookings for the accommodation.

The third method of negotiating beds tends to be used only if sales are going well and extra beds are required. When this happens a contractor may negotiate for extra rooms during the holiday season. This tends to be the most expensive way of contracting rooms unless the holiday season has up to that point been so poor that there is a room surplus.

Purchasing Aircraft Seats

Package tours generally make use of charter flights. Flight costs are calculated on the basis of an 85 per cent occupancy of the aircraft. Generally the cost of aviation fuel and any fuel surcharges are incorporated into the initial cost of the holiday so that the first price quoted to clients remains unaltered. Scheduled flights are occasionally used for city breaks, ski holidays or some of the more expensive long-haul tours, largely because fewer passengers are involved than in the summer, but also because these holidays have been deliberately developed to use up spare capacity on specific scheduled routes.

Additional Holiday Costs

Airports will charge taxes for all flights arriving and departing, as well as making handling charges to cover services such as baggage movement. The tour operator will also have to pay whatever **commissions** have been agreed with the United Kingdom travel agents who sell the holidays. Some holidays have specific additional costs to the operator, such as agreements with car hire companies, complimentary food packs, and flight supplements for seats on daytime scheduled flights. The final cost which must be built into the holiday price is the tour operator's **profit margin**. This will generally be in the form of a lump sum added to the overall cost of the holiday, and will vary according to the destination involved.

Compensation

The operator may have other financial obligations. If flights are not on time, they may agree to provide light refreshments and meals. In the event of a serious delay, the operator may offer clients who have purchased company insurance a full refund or cash compensation. They may also offer compensation for airport departure changes, resort changes or changes of accommodation.

Over-estimating Demand

Forecasting the demand for holidays is a difficult process because accommodation and flights have to be booked 18 months in advance. Once contracts have been made it can be difficult to renegotiate them. If the holiday demand proves to be substantially smaller than had been predicted, as in the summer of 1991, contracts may be cancelled. Thus, if two flights departing for the same destination on the same day are less than half full, one flight will be cancelled and the passengers consolidated onto the remaining flight. Consolidation for a summer season flight is generally not possible after January as large cancellation fees would then be payable to the airlines concerned. The tour operator would in any case have to pay for any seats on the flight which remained unsold. Whether or not failure to fill accommodation incurs expense for the tour operator would largely depend on whether the contract was guaranteed or non-guaranteed.

Under-estimating Demand

Increased demand is generally less of a problem to a large tour operator. In such cases extra flights can usually be arranged, as long as sufficient additional accommodation of the required quality is available. Such an imbalance between supply and demand is less likely to happen between November and May. The market for winter holidays is very much smaller, and passengers are often those in higher income brackets, able to afford second holidays.

Key Terms

commission – a sum paid by a tour operator to a travel agent, usually a percentage of the value of each of the tour operator's holidays which the agent sells.

profit margin – the percentage of the selling price not accounted for by any costs.

◇ *Exercise* ◇

Look at the table of prices for four Intasun holidays in Austria, which the company had planned to offer to clients in summer 1991.

Basic Holiday Prices per person in £'s

	Rosenhof				Alpenrose				Seewinkl				Seerose			
Board	BB				BB				HB				HB			
Holiday Code	Q39003				Q39004				Q39001				Q39006			
Accommodation	Twin				Twin				Twin				Twin			
No of nights	7	10	11	14	7	10	11	14	7	10	11	14	7	10	11	14
13 May-23 May	199	235	242	253	197	227	233	241	293	365	385	434	278	343	361	403
24 May-30 May	219	247	258	269	214	238	245	252	309	376	396	445	295	354	372	414
31 May-13 Jun	215	258	268	281	202	241	247	255	299	378	398	447	283	356	374	417
14 Jun-4 Jul	231	274	283	299	211	246	257	266	347	434	483	543	292	362	391	437
5 Jul-18 Jul	244	279	288	304	232	261	269	281	371	461	488	559	323	391	416	464
19 Jul-1 Aug	246	287	296	312	235	271	278	289	374	469	496	567	327	403	423	474
2 Aug-22 Aug	243	283	289	305	233	268	274	285	371	467	494	565	325	401	418	467
23 Aug-29 Aug	244	271	279	293	232	255	258	268	377	461	488	559	316	376	385	432
30 Aug-12 Sep	229	262	265	277	219	246	252	259	346	429	429	489	299	362	379	422
13 Sep-19 Sep	206	241	248	258	199	233	239	247	297	369	389	439	281	348	366	409
20 Sep-26 Sep	199	238	245	255	198	229	236	243	293	367	387	436	278	345	-	-
27 Sep-30 Sep	-	-	-	-	196	228	-	-	-	-	-	-	-	-	-	-
Supplements per person per night	Single room £3.00(£3.30) Balcony £1.40				Shower & WC £2.20 (£3.10)				Lakeview £3.10							

(Departures on or between)

Supps in brackets apply to nights in hotel, Rosenhof 24 Jun-18 Aug, Alpenrose 8 Jul-25 Aug.

FLIGHTS TO AUSTRIA
(All resorts except Seefeld)
Salzburg Airport

Flight Code	No. of Nights	Day	Date of Departure	Take-off Time	Return Landing	Flight Supp.
From Gatwick Airport				Flying time: 1hr 50 mins		
01Q90	7&14	Thu	17 May-27 Sep	14.50	20.15	**Nil**
01Q94	7&14	Sun	13 May-30 Sep	07.20	19.20	**£16**
01Q90	10	Thu	17 May-27 Sep	14.50	19.20 Sun	**Nil**
01Q94	11	Sun	13 May-23 Sep	07.20	20.15 Thu	**Nil**
From Manchester Airport				Flying time: 2hrs 5 mins		
20Q90	7&14	Thu	17 May-27 Sep	07.25	20.50	**£14**
20Q92	7&14	Sun	13 May-30 Sep	16.35	21.30	**£29**
20Q90	10	Thu	17 May-27 Sep	07.25	21.30 Sun	**£14**
20Q92	11	Sun	13 May-23 Sep	16.35	20.20 Thu	**£14**
From Birmingham Airport				Flying time: 2hrs		
21Q90	7&14	Thu	17 May-27 Sep	15.00	14.00	**£10**
From Belfast Airport				Flying time: 2hrs 20 mins		
30Q90	7&14	Sun	27 May-16 Sep	14.00	12.40	**£42**

Destination	Reductions per child		
	1st Child		2nd Child
	7 nights	10-14 nights	All durations
Austria	£40	£80	£20

Now look at the table giving information about flights and flight supplements.

Calculate the cost of the following holidays:

a) a holiday for two adults wishing to fly from Manchester Airport and stay for 11 nights at the Hotel Seewinkl, commencing on 16 June.

b) a holiday for two adults and three children wishing to fly from Belfast Airport and stay at the Hotel Seerose for 14 nights, commencing on 27 May.

c) a holiday for a single person wishing to fly from Birmingham Airport and stay at the Hotel Rosenhof, where they want a room with a balcony for 7 nights commencing on 1 August. (Answers are on page 48.)

Tour Operators and the Law

Compensation schemes are increasingly used to satisfy clients who may have suffered inconvenience or disappointment.

The Trades Descriptions Act 1968

This Act is the best known piece of legislation affecting the holiday industry. It states that it is a criminal offence for any person in the course of trade or business 'to make a statement which he knows to be false' or 'recklessly to make a statement which is false.' This means that it is vitally important for overseas representatives to pass on all information about hotels and facilities, particularly if they have changed in any way since brochures advertising the resort were published.

The kind of brochure claims which might lead to disputes would include descriptions of properties as 'quiet' when they were within earshot of restaurants or discos, or descriptions of beaches as 'sandy' when in fact they were shingle. The company would be liable even if the failure to supply what was promised was only temporary, as in the case of a swimming pool being out of action for a week while it was being cleaned.

The Consumer Protection Act 1987

This Act makes it an offence to mislead consumers about the price of goods for sale. It applies wherever the prices are quoted, whether it be in a brochure, on a television advertisement or over the telephone. If a company advertises free tennis for customers travelling to a particular hotel, they must be sure that no charge is made for hiring balls and rackets. The Act insists that the total sum to be paid by the consumer should always be quoted as the price. Any additional costs, such as holiday insurance, must always be quoted when bookings are made.

The Unfair Contract Terms Act 1977

This Act ensures that tour operators do not commit customers to unreasonable agreements. For example, a company could not include a clause in a holiday contract which said that they were not liable for any death or personal injury resulting from negligence.

◇ *Exercise* ◇

Read the booking agreement from the Intasun Tunisia brochure below.
a) Make a list of the things the customer agrees to on the left-hand side of a sheet of paper. On the right-hand side list the things the company agrees to.

b) Can you suggest any other questions about booking a holiday which this agreement does not appear to cover?

2. BOOKING YOUR HOLIDAY

Once you book your holiday with us this brochure forms the basis of the agreement between Intasun and you and your party. Set out below are further details of your and our obligations once the booking has been made. When you book your holiday your agreement will be with ILG Travel Limited t/a Intasun Holidays and some of the questions you might have about booking are answered below.

a. How is the agreement made?
Your party leader must sign the Booking Form accepting the conditions of this agreement. The holiday contract incorporates all of the information contained in this brochure. If you are booking a late offer holiday any information or conditions set out in the late offer documents are also part of your contract and if in doubt you should check with your Travel Agent. The agreement or contract is concluded only when the Booking Allocation is despatched to you or your travel agent after receipt and acceptance of your booking. Any money paid by you to your travel agent in respect of the holiday is held by the travel agent on your behalf until the Booking Allocation is despatched. Thereafter, any money held by the travel agent is held on Intasun's behalf. You must check the Booking Allocation carefully and raise any queries immediately. This agreement is governed by English Law and exclusive jurisdiction is conferred on the English Courts.

b. When do I pay?
You pay the deposit immediately in all cases and if you book within 8 weeks of departure, the total cost of your holiday. Approximately ten weeks before departure, you will receive a Final Invoice showing the total cost of your holiday. This must be paid not later than eight weeks before your departure date. No further reminder is sent to you and, if the balance remains unpaid by then, we reserve the right to cancel your booking and to make a cancellation charge as shown in paragraph 2 h.

c. Is my money safe?
Yes!! We are members of the Association of British Travel Agents (ABTA membership number 3691X) and so your money is fully protected by their guaranteed bonding system. In addition, all charter flights used by us are licensed by the Civil Aviation Authority (CAA) under Air Travel Organisers Licence (ATOL) 1960.

d. Can the price of my holiday go up?
Definitely not! The price of your holiday is fully guaranteed and will not be subject to any surcharges.

e. What is included in the price of my holiday?
All Holidays
★ Accommodation. The holiday price, unless otherwise stated, applies to each of 2 adults sharing a room (see note below about apartments). Accommodation will be confirmed on your Booking Allocation.
★ Meal Arrangements. If you book full board you will receive breakfast, lunch and dinner. If you book half board, breakfast and dinner are provided.
★ Services of an Intasun Resort Representative.
★ Local Taxes and Normal Service Charges.
★ Services of the Gordon T Gopher Club representative at specified hotels.

Air holidays
★ **Return flights.** Some flights have no supplement. Others carry a supplement – check flight pages for full details.
★ **Airport tax and security charges**
★ **Free luggage allowance.** Usually 20kgs (44lbs) per person (excluding infants) unless indicated otherwise on your air ticket. Golf clubs may be carried within this allowance provided we are notified in advance.
★ **Transport between destination airport and your hotel or apartment** (except when car hire has been booked at the destination airport).

ABTA Code of Conduct

A new Code of Conduct drawn up by the Association of British Travel Agents (ABTA) came into effect from May 1990. This requires tour operators to accept responsibility for any deficiencies of their own staff and of the services and suppliers they use. The Code also requires tour operators to provide assistance in the event of illness or injury to clients, regardless of whether or not these were directly the result of an activity forming part of the holiday arrangement.

In the event of complaints from customers, the ABTA Code of Conduct sets time limits within which the tour operators should have investigated the complaint and provided compensation where this was appropriate. The overall aim of the ABTA Code is to improve the public image of the tourism industry.

The Emergence of Intasun as a Tour Operator

The Early Years

In 1971 Harry Goodman, who eventually became the Chairman of the International Leisure Group, formed a company called Vacation Apartments Limited. The following year this company bought three travel agents in South London with the intention of using them as a base from which to establish the company as a tour operator. Despite an early lack of capital the company, which became known as Intasun, sent its first passengers abroad in the summer of 1972.

Five thousand passengers went in that first year. The company brochure, published half in colour and half in black and white, featured five destinations – Majorca, the Costa Blanca, the Costa Brava, the Costa del Sol and Rimini. The story goes that the money ran out half-way through printing what was intended to be an all-colour brochure and so it had to be completed in black and white. The passengers were booked on British Airtours flights using Comet B4 aircraft. The original cost to Intasun per seat worked out at a mere £9 return.

The original team of four reservations agents hand-wrote bookings onto charts. They would then use blue stickers to indicate that a flight was nearly full and red stickers to show that all seats on it had been sold. Harry Goodman would support his small team by answering the phone and making reservations, concealing his identity under the pseudonym George.

The Price War of the 1970s

By 1973 fierce competition between smaller tour operators was leading to a price-cutting war, as a result of which many companies such as Clarksons went out of business. Harry Goodman visited all the resorts which Clarksons had featured and signed contracts with all the hotels and apartments which they had used. He then persuaded charter airlines to sell extra seats on any available aircraft to Intasun. Within days of the Clarksons collapse, Intasun began selling this extra capacity. So successful was this operation that the number of passengers travelling with Intasun rose to 80,000 in 1973.

Bonding Arrangements

One result of the Clarksons collapse was that thousands of clients who had paid for holidays found themselves with no company to take them and no means of getting their money back. No bonding arrangement or guarantees existed in those days, so that if a travel company went bankrupt holidays were cancelled and no money was recoverable. The government was forced to take action to avoid this situation occurring again. They imposed a 2 per cent levy on the cost of each holiday. This money, known as a bond, was held by the Association of British Travel Agents (ABTA) and was used to refund clients the cost of their holiday if a tour operator went out of business. Two years later this bonding arrangement was taken over by ABTA, all of whose members are now covered by the bond.

Air Europe

The next few years saw a steady increase in the number of passengers travelling with Intasun. As the company grew larger, they began to have some difficulty in securing the number of aircraft seats they required for the holidays they were offering. As many charter airlines were also tour operators, they were in direct competition with Intasun and would obviously secure seats for their own clients before those of Intasun. The only solution seemed to be for Intasun to establish its own charter airline operation. Air Europe began operating in 1979.

Florida

Intasun made another significant step forward with the introduction of a holiday programme to Florida in summer 1981. Traditionally Florida had been a winter sun destination attracting mainly North American and Canadian visitors. Its high summer temperatures and its humidity were considered deterrents to summer visitors, but the presence of Disneyland in Orlando represented a major year-round attraction. Intasun was the first British tour operator to exploit this on a significant scale. They contracted eleven DC10s, each with the capacity to carry 390 passengers, to provide a holiday service between Manchester and Orlando.

International exchange rates contributed to the rapid success of the Florida programme. Because the US dollar/sterling exchange rate was so favourable at that time (£1 : $2.40), the cost of each holiday was kept very low. At £149 for seven nights and £199 for 14 nights' bed and breakfast in a mid-range hotel, the cost in the first year was little more than the price of a Spanish holiday.

Computerised Reservations Systems

In 1980 all Intasun's reservation, administration and management information systems were computerised. Up to that time all reservations had been handled over the telephone, by Intasun reservations agents, using a paper system known as T-charts.

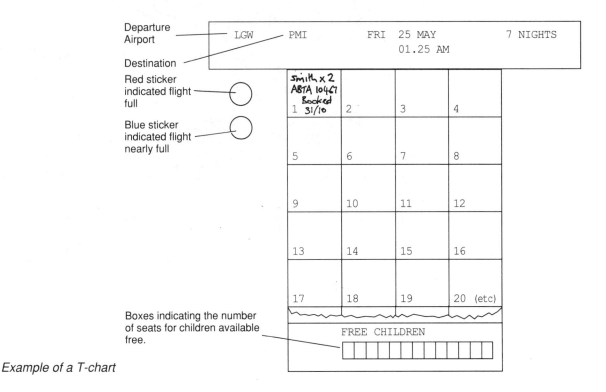

Departure Airport
Destination
Red sticker indicated flight full
Blue sticker indicated flight nearly full
Boxes indicating the number of seats for children available free.

Example of a T-chart

These charts each represented individual flights. They would show the departure airport, the destination, the duration of the holiday, and the time and date of the departure. Each chart contained a series of numbered boxes which represented seats on the plane. The reservations agents wrote the details of each booking onto these until each flight was fully booked. Initial entries were made in pencil and were inked in once the bookings had been confirmed. Four days were allowed for confirmation and, if this was not received within that time, the pencil booking details would be erased. The details required by the airlines and hotels were typed manually from the information written on the T-charts. Eventually it required 20 staff to manage this typing task alone and clearly, with 400,000 passengers a year being carried, computerisation had become absolutely essential.

From 1980 all information relating to Intasun bookings was held on computer. The touch of a button would reveal whether seats were available on specific flights, whether particular hotels were available, and what the cost of flights and accommodation would be. All the information which the airlines and hotels required could be generated automatically. As soon as a booking was made, information stored in the computer was updated so that availability of flights and hotel rooms could be assessed accurately.

The computerised office

Company Expansion

In the early 1980s the travel industry was made up of numerous small operators. Intasun took a conscious decision to expand, largely by means of undercutting the prices of their competitors. In the years between 1983 and 1987 Intasun more than doubled the number of passengers they carried and Thomsons, Intasun's biggest rival, followed suit and began to cut their prices. Though neither company made much profit from tour operations during this period they did succeed in their aim, which was to increase their share of the market.

Further Development

In 1985 the group changed its name to the International Leisure Group (ILG). By this time the group had acquired interests in an airline, hotels, and a range of holiday companies catering for different age groups and interests. People associated the name Intasun with a single brand of holidays and the group wished its name to reflect more accurately the diverse nature of its activities. Long-haul destinations such as India, Mexico, the Caribbean and the Far East were added to the Intasun range of available holidays. Low-cost accommodation programmes were extended to include Greece and Turkey and, most importantly, Air Europe scheduled services were increasingly used for shorter city break holidays. It was the expansion of the scheduled air services which was eventually to lead to the company's collapse in early 1991.

The Range of Holidays Operated by Intasun

By 1990 Intasun was carrying in excess of one and a half million passengers a year. They were able to sustain these numbers in part through very competitive pricing, but the range of products they offered was also an important factor in attracting people with a wide range of ages, backgrounds and interests.

Summer Package Holidays

The *Summersun* brochure carried the main bulk of the summer package holidays. Over 120 European destinations were featured with many, though not all, of them located on the Mediterranean coast. A choice of accommodation was available, ranging from self-catering apartments to four-star hotels. In order to meet what was seen as a growing demand for more flexibility this brochure featured many two-centre holidays which enabled holiday-makers to gain a wider experience of the country they were visiting.

The Gordon the Gopher club

These summer package holidays attracted many families with young children, and many Intasun destinations offered children's clubs. These clubs, using an invented cartoon character known as Gordon the Gopher as a theme, provided activities to entertain children and to give their parents a rest. The clubs were split into three separate age groups and, in addition to the provision of activity packs and free T-shirts, put on discos, birthday parties, video evenings and supervised play activities.

Flight-only Holidays

As passengers began to look for more independence, Intasun's *Skyworld* brochure grew in popularity. *Skyworld* offered the chance to buy charter flight tickets on a 'seat only' basis. This enabled people who wanted to organise their own accommodation, or to stay with friends or relatives, to take advantage of the fact that charter flights are considerably cheaper than scheduled flights. Other people wishing to take advantage of this arrangement were those who had purchased a second home abroad or who belonged to **time-share schemes**.

Luxury or Simplicity?

Some of Intasun's brochures were aimed at particular market segments. The *Quality Choice* brochure offered more expensive hotels with considerable flexibility in length of stay and choice of flights. Much emphasis was placed on comfort and style. Intasun provided special offers for honeymoon couples, including sparkling wine, flowers and candle-lit dinners, in the hope that this would encourage return visits. In contrast to the *Quality Choice* brochure, Intasun gave both its Greek and Turkish brochures the title *Plain and Simple*. These brochures stressed that accommodation could be basic, sometimes with shared bathroom and toilet facilities and with only very basic cooking facilities. It was not in the company's interests for clients to arrive unprepared for differences in culture, transport or sanitation and so the brochures warned of plumbing differences, of possible water shortages and of the unreliability of transport timetables in some places.

Long-haul Holidays

The growing market for long-haul travel was reflected in Intasun's *Far and Away* brochure, which featured destinations as far apart as Thailand, Acapulco, Barbados, Jamaica, the Dominican Republic and Goa. The brochure gave information about local customs and traditions and there was advice about what was considered respectful behaviour. Visitors to Thailand, for example, were advised that 'a strong Buddhist influence means respectful dress is required in the many holy places. Don't pose for photos in front of Buddhas. Showing emotion openly (e.g. anger) is frowned upon ...'. Tours and trips were available in each of these destinations and could be included as part of a holiday package.

Coach Travel

The cost of flying still remains beyond the reach of some travellers, while others simply do not like it as a means of transport. Intasun provided an express coach service linking more than 80 pick-up points in the United Kingdom with destinations in the South of France, Spain, Italy and Yugoslavia. The coaches were designed to make travelling long distances as comfortable as possible, with reclining seats, toilet facilities and non-smoking areas. A host or hostess served drinks and snacks, and there was music and video entertainment. This service attracted people with children and so a child fare discount system was operated.

Intasun's Coach Europe service

Ski Holidays

Being able to use a resort all year round has advantages for a tour operator, particularly when accommodation contracts are negotiated. In this respect some parts of Intasun's *Skiscene* brochure and their *Lakes and Mountains* brochure were complementary. The ski resorts attracted summer holiday-makers who enjoyed mountain scenery. Resorts in Austria, Switzerland, Italy and France particularly attracted people who enjoyed active pursuits such as walking, climbing, biking, tennis or sailing, while the less active could simply enjoy the wonderful views.

Cruising

Cruising gives tourists the opportunity to visit a range of places of interest without having to move any baggage. The Intasun *Cruise and*

Stay brochure offered a choice of transport, ranging from a luxury yacht to a small liner. Most cruises stopped at Mediterranean ports, but it was also possible to cruise around the Black Sea calling at Varna in Bulgaria and Odessa and Yalta in the USSR.

Special Offers

Tour operators lose money whenever flights and accommodation they have contracted to fill remain empty. Brochures such as Intasun's *Pick and Choose* were intended to reduce the frequency of this happening. The brochure offered a limited choice of holidays at discounted prices. Departure times and dates were also limited and, although the destination was specified, the accommodation was not. This enabled Intasun to use up unbooked accommodation and to match accommodation contracts to numbers of bookings more precisely.

Key Term

time-share schemes – holiday accommodation sold to various buyers, who each occupy the accommodation for a unit of time every year.

◇ *Exercise* ◇

1 It was very important that everyone contributing to the Intasun brochures agreed on a definition of each type of accommodation.

Match each of the eight types of accommodation listed below with its definition. (Answers are on page 48)

a) Chalet
b) Studio
c) Apartment
d) Hotel
e) Aparthotel
f) Caravan
g) Villa
h) Pension/Taverna/Gasthof

i) A building with a combination of apartment or studio accommodation and hotel rooms with normal hotel facilities
ii) An establishment which is locally categorized as an hotel, offering sleeping accommodation and meals
iii) A detached/semi-detached house or bungalow, usually with its own private land, pool, bedroom(s), bath/shower room and kitchen
iv) A house or small guest house offering sleeping accommodation
v) Permanent unit of accommodation usually with cooking facilities, shower, WC, hot and cold running water
vi) One living/dining/sleeping room with kitchen or kitchenette area and bath or shower room. There are no proper separate bedrooms
vii) Mobile unit of accommodation with cooking facilities
viii) Comprises of a living/dining area with a kitchen or kitchenette area and a bath or shower room plus at least one separate bedroom with four walls and a proper door to give complete privacy.

2 Now work out suitable and precise definitions for each of the following brochure terms:

balcony, sea view, terrace, patio, garden, kitchen, kitchenette, bathroom, shower room.

How Intasun Marketed its Holidays

Company marketing staff are involved in assessing customer needs, persuading them to buy a particular product and ensuring that the company makes a profit in the process. Market research, advertising, press and public relations and sales are all key elements in marketing.

Market Research

Questionnaires were completed by Intasun clients. They were asked about brochures, travel agents, the quality of hotels and the resort they had visited, the Intasun representatives and their future holiday booking thoughts. The responses to these questionnaires were analysed in order to give what is known as a **geo-demographic breakdown** of the clients who favoured each product. This meant that the sales of each holiday or flight could be analysed according to the number of purchasers from particular geographical regions. Clients were also analysed according to their age, their family size and the type of area or housing in which they lived.

All responses to questionnaires were held on a database. This information could be sorted and listed according to a wide range of criteria. For example, if Intasun had wanted to discuss the type of clients who booked a *Far and Away* holiday, they could examine the average age of clients, how long they had been away for, where they had booked the holiday, and the average number of people per party.

The database served an additional marketing purpose, being used to send direct mail targeted at a particular segment of the market. If, for example, the *Golden Days* brochure had featured a special offer, the database could have produced a mailing list consisting of questionnaire respondents who had either been on a previous *Golden Days* holiday or who were over 55 years of age.

Advertising

Intasun advertised both on television and in the national newspapers. The individual brand name, Intasun, was thought more likely to attract holiday-makers than the company name, International Leisure Group.

With so many holiday brand names in the tourist industry, each company seeks to find an image which can be easily identified with the product. When the Intasun company was established, they decided to use a stylised image of a woman with long flowing blonde hair. This image appeared on all Intasun brochures, booking slips, acknowledgement slips and tickets.

The design of the Intasun Girl, as she became known within the company, was originated in the early 1970s. In the following years the style of her face changed along with current fashions. In 1985 the company reverted to the use of holiday photographs on their *Summer Sun* brochures and only the head of the Intasun Girl was featured.

An Intasun brochure

Press and Public Relations

Although Intasun had its own Press Office, most of its contact with the media was made through a public relations (PR) company. The Press Office would provide the information for press releases about new products or significant events concerning Intasun but the PR agency would actually write the text of the press release. The contract with the agency gave them the responsibility of ensuring that Intasun had a wide coverage in the local and national press, as well as in specialist travel and tourism publications.

The Press Office dealt with any enquiries from the press. If stories or allegations which journalists intended to run seemed likely to be damaging to the company's reputation, the Press Office had to ensure that the company's comments were fairly represented.

In the rare event of a natural disaster affecting Intasun clients the Press Office would set up an immediate hot-line. When hundreds of Intasun passengers were stranded by a hurricane in the Caribbean in 1989, the Press Office kept an up-to-date record of developments so that friends and relatives were as well-informed as possible.

Sales

Intasun's sales force was largely occupied in promoting the company's products to travel agents. The results of market research indicated particular parts of the country where Intasun were much more successful than their competitors. Joint marketing campaigns, on a shared cost basis, were carried out with selected independent and **multiple retailers**. The ILG marketing database was used to identify towns and regions with the greatest selling potential. Then the company's Sales and Marketing Services Unit selected the most suitable postcode sectors within these regions for generating business through direct mail advertising.

Key Terms

geo-demographic breakdown – an analysis of a group of people based on the region in which they live.

multiple retailer – a company with outlets selling direct to the public in a wide variety of locations.

◇ *Exercise* ◇

Competitions are often used to encourage people to sample new products. The example below was designed to encourage people to book their holidays with Intasun.

YOUR HOT SPOTS ENTRY FORM

Book before 10th November 1990 and you could be a millionaire before Christmas

To take part all you have to do is book an Intasun holiday for Summer '91 before 10 November 1990. You can choose any Intasun holiday you like from the Intasun 1991 range of brochures which includes Intasun Florida, Far and Away, Summersun, Greece, Turkey, Lakes and Mountains, Express Coach, Quality Choice, Cyprus, Tunisia, Israel, Yugoslavia, France, Camping and Skyworld. Remember this competition is only valid for holidays departing from March 21st to October 31st 1991.

WHAT TO DO

When you book your Intasun holiday ask your travel agent to confirm receipt of your deposit by dating your entry form, filling in your Intasun holiday booking reference number together with the travel agent's name and branch address.

HOW TO ENTER

Twelve Intasun holiday destinations are listed on the entry form. A panel of judges, including meteorological experts have estimated what they believe to be the maximum likely temperature in the shade in each destination on 21st June 1991.

All you have to do, using your own skill and judgement, is to estimate the temperatures forecast by our panel of judges for each destination. To help you we've given you the range of maximum temperatures in the shade actually recorded for each destination over the last 5 years. Further details of destination temperatures are obtainable from your local library in publications such as the World Weather Guide, Berlitz and Fodor Travel Guides, various atlasses and of course our Intasun holiday brochures. And you can have up to 3 tries at winning! If you book your Intasun holiday in September you have 3 attempts at winning £1,000,000. If you book your Intasun holiday in October or before 10 November 1990 you have 2 attempts at winning £1,000,000. So book early!

£1,000,000 ISN'T ALL YOU CAN WIN!

Estimate all 12 maximum temperatures correctly 'in any one line' of your entry form and you will win £1,000,000 (or a share of £1,000,000 if there is more than one winning entry). You could be on holiday for life! BUT if you correctly estimate only 10 or 11 of 12 in any one column

we'll deduct £250 from the cost of your holiday! If you correctly estimate 8 or 9 out of 12 we'll take £100 off the cost of your holiday! And if you correctly estimate any 6 or 7 (just half!) out of 12 we'll give you a discount of £50 off the cost of your holiday! Enter today and you might be cutting the cost of your holiday!

A STEP BY STEP WINNER'S GUIDE

1. Book your Intasun holiday with your local travel agent and pay your deposit in full.
2. Ask your travel agent to fill in the date, holiday booking reference number and agency name and branch address on your entry form. Your entry is now valid.
3. Complete the competition entry form overleaf estimating the maximum temperature in the shade on 21 June 1991 for each of the 12 destinations listed as calculated by our panel of judges. NB. You may enter 3 columns if you book in September but only 2 columns if you book between October 1st and 10 November.
4. Send your completed entry form to the address below. The last

date for sending off your entry is 10 November 1990. All entries must be received by 16 November 1990.

5. Sit back and look forward to your Intasun holiday – who knows, you might be a millionaire by the time you go on it!

Range of maximum temperatures actually recorded in the shade for each destination over the past 5 years.

Palma	25°C – 34°C
Dubrovnik	19°C – 29°C
Ibiza	25°C – 30°C
Luqa	25°C – 30°C
Corfu	25°C – 28°C
Tenerife	24°C – 27°C
Orlando	30°C – 35°C
Bangkok	31°C – 34°C
Heraklion	25°C – 35°C
Limassol	27°C – 31°C
Torremolinos	26°C – 30°C
Faro	21°C – 30°C

1 Which parts of the advertisement were designed to encourage a specific reaction from readers?

2 Design a suitable entry form for the competition.

3 Discuss how the front cover of the competition leaflet might have been made sufficiently eye-catching for casual visitors to pick it up in a travel agency.

Maintaining Good Customer Relations

Whether or not Intasun's clients became repeat customers was likely to hinge on the quality of their holiday experience. The response of company staff to requests for help and information, as well as their ability to create a friendly atmosphere, were seen as key factors. Staff were trained to meet these demands. Questionnaires were then used to evaluate how holiday-makers felt about the quality of service they had received.

Training

The majority of Intasun staff were based overseas and so were given initial training in the United Kingdom before they departed. An overseas representative, for example, would undergo a six-day course covering their role and responsibilities. The course provided background knowledge of the company, its brochures and booking procedures. The representatives would learn how to conduct welcoming meetings and make presentations about the company's additional services. It was particularly important that they understood the company's legal responsibilities and duties, and were aware of emergency procedures. They were taught the requirements of airports, and the baggage and transfer procedures. In order that the company could monitor its service in individual resorts, they learnt how to complete reports to be returned to the United Kingdom.

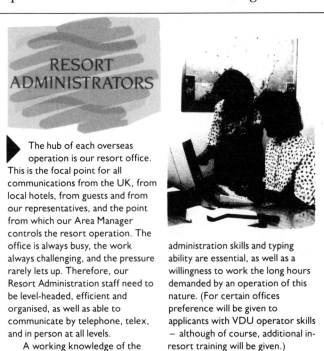

RESORT ADMINISTRATORS

▶ The hub of each overseas operation is our resort office. This is the focal point for all communications from the UK, from local hotels, from guests and from our representatives, and the point from which our Area Manager controls the resort operation. The office is always busy, the work always challenging, and the pressure rarely lets up. Therefore, our Resort Administration staff need to be level-headed, efficient and organised, as well as able to communicate by telephone, telex, and in person at all levels.

A working knowledge of the relevant European language together with competent administration skills and typing ability are essential, as well as a willingness to work the long hours demanded by an operation of this nature. (For certain offices preference will be given to applicants with VDU operator skills – although of course, additional in-resort training will be given.)

The minimum age for these positions is eighteen.

The role of resort administrators

Customer Questionnaires

Questionnaires are a valuable means of recording customers' impressions in more detail. As customers are unlikely to complete lengthy questionnaires, Intasun tried to keep questionnaires concise. While representatives were encouraged to give occasional gentle reminders to clients about returning questionnaires, they were warned not to be too insistent. Clients who had had problems on holidays were not avoided when questionnaires were distributed because these were the people most likely to highlight areas that Intasun would need to improve if their custom was to be retained.

◊ *Exercise* ◊

This extract is from an Intasun questionnaire given to customers on their short City Breaks holidays:

SECTION 5 - HOLIDAY OVERALL

Q1 Overall did your holiday live up to your expectations?   YES ☐   NO ☐

Q2 How likely are you to choose:

	Definitely	Probably	Possibly	Not Likely
Intasun City Breaks again?	☐	☐	☐	☐
This resort again?	☐	☐	☐	☐
This accommodation again?	☐	☐	☐	☐

Q3 Have you had a City Break type holiday abroad before?   YES ☐   NO ☐

If yes, have you been on holiday before to:-

This country?	YES ☐	NO ☐
This resort?	YES ☐	NO ☐
This accommodation?	YES ☐	NO ☐

Q4 How many times have you travelled with Intasun City Breaks previously?
Never ☐   1 ☐   2 ☐   3 ☐   4+ ☐

Q5 With which holiday company did you take your last overseas City Break holiday?

Intasun City Breaks	☐	Cresta	☐
Kirker	☐	Ultimate City Breaks	☐
Time Off	☐	Osprey	☐
Thomson City Breaks	☐	Pegasus Cities	☐
Travelscene	☐	Quo Vadis	☐
Paris Travel Service	☐	NSR	☐
Belgium Travel Service	☐	GTF Germany	☐
Scantours	☐	Sovereign	☐
Airtours Paris	☐	Swiss Travel Service	☐
American Express	☐	Other	☐

Q6 How does this holiday compare with your last overseas City Breaks holiday?
Better ☐   The same ☐   Not as good ☐

SECTION 6 - HOLIDAY CHOICE

Q1 Which travel agent did you book through?

Name _____

Town _____

Or did you book direct with your tour operator?   YES ☐   NO ☐

Q2 When choosing this holiday, how important were the following points?

	Important	Relevant	Unimportant
Holiday available for date required	☐	☐	☐
Previous holiday with same operator	☐	☐	☐
Recommendation of travel agent	☐	☐	☐
Recommendation of friends	☐	☐	☐
Reputation of Intasun for quality and reliability	☐	☐	☐
Low price/value for money	☐	☐	☐
Childrens' cheap price/offers	☐	☐	☐
Similar holiday unavailable with another tour operator	☐	☐	☐
Convenient local departure point	☐	☐	☐
Suitability of resort for children	☐	☐	☐
Chosen accommodation available	☐	☐	☐

Q3 Was this your first choice of holiday?   YES ☐   NO ☐

Q4 How many overseas holidays have you taken in the last 12 months including this one?
1 ☐   2 ☐   3 ☐   4 ☐   5 or more ☐

1 How do you think the company would have used information collected from each of the responses?

2 Make a list of other questions which you think might have been included in the first four sections of the questionnaire, covering holiday details, the brochure, the travel, the accommodation and services.

The Collapse of the International Leisure Group

The tour operations side of the International Leisure Group's activities would probably have survived the economic difficulties which the travel industry faced early in 1991. However, the high interest costs resulting from Air Europe's purchase of new aircraft, combined with the falling demand for seats on scheduled flights, led to the collapse of the company in March 1991.

The number of passengers booking holidays and airline flights in the early part of 1991 was considerably lower than had been predicted. The two major causes were the Gulf War and a period of recession. The war came at a time when many people traditionally book their summer holidays and it increased fears that British aircraft would be vulnerable to terrorist attacks. The recession considerably reduced the spending power of many families. Intasun had relied heavily on inexpensive holidays to destinations like Spain, and demand for this type of package fell more rapidly than that for other holidays.

Liquidation

The crisis within the company was brought to a head when city banks, concerned about mounting debts, decided to repossess some of Air Europe's aircraft, thus stranding some holiday-makers and preventing others from departing. It quickly became clear that the ILG could no longer continue operating, and the company was put into the hands of administrators. They attempted unsuccessfully to sell some of the travel brands within the group, including Intasun. However, any purchaser would have had to begin operating without any income from the holidays Intasun had already sold. At the same time they would have had to provide substantial funds for new bonding arrangements.

Factors Affecting Forward Planning for Other Tour Operators

Tour operators must always consider three things when planning for the future. They need to know:

♦ when different population groups will choose to go on holiday
♦ what will determine their destination choice
♦ what they will want to do when they get there.

Timing of Holidays

School holidays have always had a strong influence on when families with children take their main holidays. Any move to alter these, for example by the introduction of a four-term school year, would affect the package holiday market. The traditional pattern of a single two-week summer holiday is a thing of the past for many people. Second and third holidays, taken out of season, are increasingly popular. The increasing proportion of retired people in the population, with plenty of leisure time, is likely to reinforce the trend to extend the holiday season.

New Destinations

Another factor encouraging people to travel in the winter months is the opening up of winter sun destinations, such as the Gambia, to charter flights. This may have a long-term effect on traditional Mediterranean resorts because more tourists may seek the novelty of long-haul destinations. Some Mediterranean resorts may adopt new marketing strategies in an attempt to capture more people seeking a short break holiday.

Changing Lifestyles

After many years of advertisements featuring seaside holidays as healthy and relaxing, recently people have expressed concern about the adverse effects of sunbathing and of exposure to sea pollutants. Public campaigns aimed at encouraging healthy lifestyles have emphasised the importance of diet and exercise. Tour operators will need to look at the extent of this interest in healthy living and whether it will ultimately lead to a move away from traditional sun spots to destinations where more physical activities are encouraged.

Cultural Interests

Although an empty beach and a luxury hotel with numerous facilities is still many people's ideal, European cities are becoming more alert to the fact that history, art and architecture can offer an equally desirable form of escape for others. The rapid changes in Eastern Europe, for example, have encouraged more people to visit that part of the world and have stimulated an interest in the cultures of the people who live there. No doubt the opening of the Channel Tunnel will reinforce this interest, in addition to having some effect on the preferred means and routes of travel to Europe.

The Impact of Tourism

Concerns about the impact of tourism cannot be overlooked by the tour operators of the future. Most operators now stress the need for quality and the need to protect what draws people to visit destinations in the first place. Many companies now include information and advice in their brochures aimed at encouraging their clients to be sensitive to the feelings of the host communities of the places they are visiting.

◇ *Exercise* ◇

Holiday complexes like Center Parcs have been designed to have a minimum impact on their surrounding environments. Many activities which might normally take place on a public beach are enclosed within a simulated environment.

Discuss the degree to which simulated holiday environments could be extended.

Draw up plans for a simulated holiday environment which might provide much of the enjoyment to be had in an actual destination which is currently under pressure from an increasing number of visiting tourists.

◇ *Discussion points* ◇

1 Use an atlas to discuss whether you think the development of new long-haul tourist flights will continue, and which routes might be seen as having the greatest potential.

2 How easy is it for people booking holidays to assess the precise quality of the accommodation they will stay in?

3 Should airlines have to pay more compensation for some causes of flight delay than for others?

4 Which aspects of a tourist destination may prove hard to describe with complete accuracy in a brochure?

5 Why do you think Disneyland, despite its distance from Europe, has attracted so many British visitors?

6 What factors should be taken into account in choosing the name of a company?

7 Why do you think Intasun developed holidays by coach rather than by rail?

8 Do you think questionnaires produce accurate and reliable information?

9 If you had only a limited income, would you rate holidays as more or less important than buying fashionable clothes, going out in the evenings, buying presents, smoking and drinking, or decorating your home?

Answers to the exercise on page 31 are:

a) £994, b) £2,160, (if the third child gets a £20 reduction), c) £288.90.

Answers to the exercise on page 40 are:

a) (v), b) (vi), c) (viii), d) (ii), e) (i), f) (vii), g) (iii), h) (iv).

3 *Thames and Chilterns Tourist Board*

Introduction

In the early 1970s the English Tourist Board set up twelve regional tourist boards. These boards were to work with **local authorities** and the commercial sector to promote regional tourism development. They were given the responsibility of planning local tourism strategies and of seeking ways of encouraging local authorities and businesses to carry them out.

The regional boards spend much of their time promoting the regions both in Britain and, with the help of the British Tourist Authority, abroad. The production of brochures and guides, the organisation of special events and representation at exhibitions and **trade fairs** are mostly conducted on a commercial basis. Individual companies and local authorities may sponsor an exhibition stand, while local advertisements will largely pay for the production of brochures and guides. In the case of the Thames and Chilterns Tourist Board, annual turnover in 1989 was almost £1 million, about two-thirds of which was spent on marketing. Marketing activities include laying on press visits for domestic and overseas journalists, arranging **familiarisation trips** for travel agents and tour operators, and planning media campaigns.

The regional tourist boards administer the **Crown classification** scheme for hotels within their own regions. They are in charge of granting approval for new holiday parks and holiday homes, and grading them according to the standard of facilities offered. The regional boards are also involved in encouraging the development and upgrading of selected hotel and accommodation schemes, renovation of historic buildings and monuments, and monitoring new attractions.

Another function of the regional tourist boards is to co-ordinate the establishment and work of the local tourist information centres. From time to time, they may also be involved in the planning of special events. For example, 1992 marks the fiftieth anniversary of the arrival in Britain of the United States Eighth Air Force. Many of the airmen were based in East Anglia, and to mark this occasion the East Anglia Tourist Board intends to aid US services charities and to encourage permanent reminders of the link with the US airmen around the region. The Northumbria Tourist Board formed a strong link with the management company of the National Garden Festival when it was sited in Gateshead in 1990.

Key Terms

local authorities – groups of people elected to carry out local government, e.g. a town or a county council.

trade fair – an exhibition attended by companies representing a particular sector of the economy.

familiarisation trip – a visit enabling tourism employees to gain first-hand knowledge of a destination.

Crown classification – a system of grading the level of furnishings and facilities to be found in a hotel.

◇ *Exercises* ◇

England's Regional Tourist Boards

1 Use the outline map of the regional tourist boards and a more detailed map of England to work out in which of the regional tourist board areas each of the following can be found:

Oxford, Chester, Norwich, Windermere, Stratford-upon-Avon, Lincoln, Newquay, Brighton, Ventnor, Scarborough, Lindisfarne, Kensington.

2 Use brochures, regional guides or reference books to work out the regions in which these tourist attractions can be found:

a) the Norfolk Broads, b) Leeds Castle, c) Chatsworth House, d) Sellafield, e) Dartmoor, f) the New Forest, g) the Dales, h) the Malvern Hills, i) Beamish Museum, j) Blenheim Palace, k) Wigan Pier, l) The National Maritime Museum.

Marketing

Many people think of advertising when the term 'marketing' is used, yet marketing amounts to rather more than that. It can include:

♦ researching customer needs
♦ persuading people to buy
♦ ensuring that the products or services that people want are available at the right time and at the right price.

Regional tourist boards become involved in a wide range of marketing activities.

Brochures and Publications

Most boards produce publications featuring historic houses, places to visit, and conference facilities within their region. In addition, smaller areas within the regions may produce brochures featuring their own particular attractions and facilities. They also often publish separate accommodation guides.

When marketing abroad it is important to give some idea about the geography of the region. For this reason the Thames and Chilterns Tourist Board often describes itself in publications intended for the overseas market as being 'on London's doorstep'.

Travel Fairs

Travel fairs fall into two main categories. There are those organised for the travel trade, attended by tour operators, travel agents and handling agents. They offer the opportunity for boards to negotiate package holidays and tours within their own region for overseas visitors. Other fairs are public, and at these the boards aim to interest the travelling public in visiting hotels and tourist attractions in their region.

A TCTB stand at a travel fair

Mounting a stand at a major fair can be expensive. However, some of these costs are generally met by companies sharing the stand with the tourist board. Usually these companies represent tourism interests within the region, such as castles or safari parks. Local authorities might also share the stand with the tourist board. Whether a board attends a particular travel fair will depend on the cost of being represented, the degree of financial support from co-exhibitors and an estimate of how many people are likely to visit the fair.

◇ *Exercise* ◇

St Albans Borough Council intend to share a Thames and Chilterns Tourist Board stand at a weekend travel fair for the public in the north of England. On the basis of previous years' figures, it is expected that between two and three thousand people will attend over the two days.

Read the following information giving details of some of the attractions in St Albans.

St Albans

As Verulamium, St Albans was one of the leading cities of the Roman Empire. Named after the first Christian martyr in Britain, Alban, who was executed about AD209, St Albans developed around the magnificent Cathedral and Abbey Church of St Alban.

Around the field from the abbey gateway stands the Old Fighting Cocks Inn, whose triangular shape derives from its use in the past as a cockpit. The city streets, notably Fishpool Street and George Street, contain some beautiful old houses, many of them excellently restored, some dating back to the 15th C.

Cathedral and Abbey Church of St Alban

Open: *daily May–Sept until 6.45, Oct–Apr until 5.45. Tel: St Albans (0727) 60780.*
Though originally built by the Saxons on the supposed site of St Alban's execution, the abbey we see today is Norman with 12th- and 13th-C. additions, making it the second-longest church in England. It became a cathedral in 1877. The magnificent new Laporte rose window was unveiled in the north transept last year by H.R.H. The Princess of Wales. The Chapter House was opened in 1982 and houses the shop and Refectory café.

The massive abbey gateway, once the main entrance to the Benedictine monastery, is now all that remains of the buildings to the south.

Museum of St Albans

Open: *Mon–Sat 10–5, Sun, B.H. 2–5. Tel: St Albans (0727) 56679.*
This recently redesigned local history museum in Hatfield Road tells the story of St Albans from the dissolution of the monasteries to the present. It also houses a nationally recognized collection of local craft tools displayed in reconstructed workshops.

Clock Tower

Open: *Good Fri–mid Sept, Sat, Sun, B.H. Mon 10.30–5. Tel: St Albans (0727) 60984.*
At the Market Cross in the High Street stands a five-storey, 15th-C. flint and rubble clock tower. There are fine views from the roof, a small exhibition of local history and the 1866 clockworks can be seen.

Gardens of the Rose

Open: *16 June–21 Oct, Mon–Sat 9–5, Sun, B.H. Mon 10–6. Tel: St Albans (0727) 50461.*
South of St Albans in Chiswell Green Lane are the world-renowned Royal National Rose Society's gardens. Thirty thousand roses of 1,700 varieties are displayed in 12 acres. Especially interesting are the trial grounds where new varieties, submitted by leading hybridists from all over the world, undergo field trials. Each year in July there is a major festival to coincide with the best of the rose flowerings.

Verulamium Museum

Open: *Apr–Oct, Mon–Sat 10–5.30, Sun 2–5.30; Oct–Feb closes at 4. Tel: St Albans (0727) 66100.*
Relics of the city's past are found in the Verulamium Museum, including late Iron Age and Roman material, superb mosaics and a wide range of pottery. New exhibitions showing 400 years of domestic life in Verulamium open at Easter. In the nearby park is the hypocaust – one room of the bath wing of a Roman town house. Large sections of the Roman wall can also still be seen in the park which has a lake, children's amusements, sports facilities and views of the cathedral.

Verulamium Roman Theatre

Open: *daily 10–5 (dusk in winter). Closed Christmas and Boxing Day.*
West of St Albans in the grounds of the Gorhambury Estate is the Roman theatre, unique in Britain in having a raised stage, unlike an amphitheatre. Not discovered until 1847, the theatre is thought to have been built around AD 150 and is the only completely exposed Roman theatre in Britain.

Cathedral and Abbey Church of St Alban

Prepare some notes to take to a meeting on the planning of this stand. You should consider:

♦ how the stand is to be arranged (a sketch may help)
♦ what resources should be available
♦ how transport of the stand is to be organised
♦ what the main aims of the people staffing the stand should be
♦ what the major costs of being represented will be
♦ how the individual attractions can be best represented.

The Classification of Accommodation

In Britain for many years hotels were only classified if they chose to participate in a voluntary scheme, such as those operated by the motoring organisations, the AA and the RAC. However, the regional tourist boards now operate a national classification and grading scheme for all types of serviced tourist accommodation. This also operates on a voluntary basis. The classification of hotels and guesthouses is based on a scheme first used in Scotland, awarding a number of crowns to represent the range of facilities provided. The classifications run from 'Listed' up to Five Crowns. In each category requirements for the bedrooms, bathrooms, toilets and other facilities are listed by the English Tourist Board and must be provided if the classification is to be awarded. The example below shows the detailed requirements which Listed establishments must satisfy.

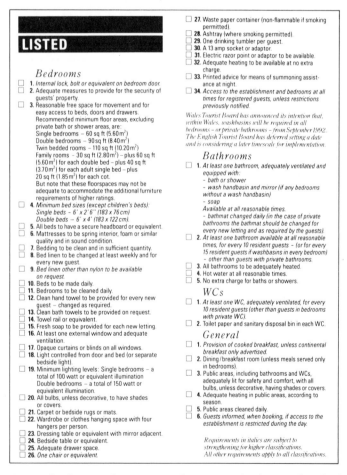

LISTED

Bedrooms

1. *Internal lock, bolt or equivalent on bedroom door.*
2. Adequate measures to provide for the security of guests' property.
3. Reasonable free space for movement and for easy access to beds, doors and drawers. Recommended minimum floor areas, excluding private bath or shower areas, are:
   Single bedrooms – 60 sq ft (5.60 m²)
   Double bedrooms – 90 sq ft (8.40 m²)
   Twin bedded rooms – 110 sq ft (10.20 m²)
   Family rooms – 30 sq ft (2.80 m²) – plus 60 sq ft (5.60 m²) for each double bed – plus 40 sq ft (3.70 m²) for each adult single bed – plus 20 sq ft (1.85 m²) for each cot.
   But note that these floorspaces may not be adequate to accommodate the additional furniture requirements of higher ratings.
4. *Minimum bed sizes (except children's beds):*
   Single beds – 6' x 2' 6" (183 x 76 cm).
   Double beds – 6' x 4' (183 x 122 cm).
5. All beds to have a secure headboard or equivalent.
6. Mattresses to be spring interior, foam or similar quality and in sound condition.
7. Bedding to be clean and in sufficient quantity.
8. Bed linen to be changed at least weekly and for every new guest.
9. *Bed linen other than nylon to be available on request.*
10. Beds to be made daily.
11. Bedrooms to be cleaned daily.
12. Clean hand towel to be provided for every new guest – changed as required.
13. Clean bath towels to be provided on request.
14. Towel rail or equivalent.
15. Fresh soap to be provided for each new letting.
16. At least one external window and adequate ventilation.
17. Opaque curtains or blinds on all windows.
18. Light controlled from door and bed (or separate bedside light).
19. Minimum lighting levels: Single bedrooms – a total of 100 watt or equivalent illumination Double bedrooms – a total of 150 watt or equivalent illumination.
20. All bulbs, unless decorative, to have shades or covers.
21. Carpet or bedside rugs or mats.
22. Wardrobe or clothes hanging space with four hangers per person.
23. Dressing table or equivalent with mirror adjacent.
24. Bedside table or equivalent.
25. Adequate drawer space.
26. *One chair or equivalent.*

27. Waste paper container (non-flammable if smoking permitted).
28. Ashtray (where smoking permitted).
29. One drinking tumbler per guest.
30. A 13 amp socket or adaptor.
31. Electric razor point or adaptor to be available.
32. Adequate heating to be available at no extra charge.
33. Printed advice for means of summoning assistance at night.
34. *Access to the establishment and bedrooms at all times for registered guests, unless restrictions previously notified.*

Wales Tourist Board has announced its intention that, within Wales, washbasins will be required in all bedrooms – or private bathrooms – from September 1992. The English Tourist Board has deferred setting a date and is considering a later timescale for implementation.

Bathrooms

1. At least one bathroom, adequately ventilated and equipped with:
   - bath or shower
   - wash handbasin and mirror (if any bedrooms without a wash handbasin)
   - soap
   Available at all reasonable times.
   - *bathmat changed daily (in the case of private bathrooms the bathmat should be changed for every new letting and as required by the guests).*
2. At least one bathroom available at all reasonable times, for every 10 resident guests – (or for every 15 resident guests if washbasins in every bedroom) – other than guests with private bathrooms.
3. All bathrooms to be adequately heated.
4. Hot water at all reasonable times.
5. No extra charge for baths or showers.

WCs

1. At least one WC, adequately ventilated, for every 10 resident guests (other than guests in bedrooms with private WC).
2. Toilet paper and sanitary disposal bin in each WC.

General

1. *Provision of cooked breakfast, unless continental breakfast only advertised.*
2. *Dining / breakfast room (unless meals served only in bedrooms).*
3. Public areas, including bathrooms and WCs, adequately lit for safety and comfort, with all bulbs, unless decorative, having shades or covers.
4. Adequate heating in public areas, according to season.
5. Public areas cleaned daily.
6. *Guests informed, when booking, if access to the establishment is restricted during the day.*

Requirements in italics are subject to strengthening for higher classifications. All other requirements apply to all classifications.

The aim of this voluntary scheme, which is funded by the government and which by 1990 included 16,000 participants, is to enable visitors to judge their chosen accommodation objectively. Certain minimum standards apply to all accommodation in the scheme. For example, all accommodation must comply with the requirements of the Fire Precautions Act, 1971 and have **public liability insurance**. It should be clean and suitable for use as accommodation. If visitors opt for accommodation which is involved in the grading scheme they will also get an indication of the quality of these facilities and services.

Key Term

public liability insurance – insurance paid by the owner of the accommodation which will compensate a member of the public for any injury suffered in using it.

◇ *Exercise* ◇

Study the list of accommodation in Bedfordshire.

HOTELS, GUEST HOUSES, FARMHOUSES, INNS, B&B

Establishment Name & Address	Crown Classification	Bedroom Numbers and Facilities	Prices (£) MIN	MAX
Moore Place, The Square, **Aspley Guise**, Nr. Woburn, MK17 8DW ☎ (0908) 282000	♛♛♛♛♛	18 35 1F 54 ⬚ ♿ ☡ ♀ 🅲 🅿 SB 🏛 ☼ ⟟	75.00 85.00	80.00 95.00
Barns Hotel, Cardington Road, **Bedford**, MK44 3SA ☎ (0234) 270044		47 2F 49 ♿ ☡ 🅲 🅿 SB 🏛 ⟟	55.00 65.00	—
Bedford Moat House, St. Mary's Street, **Bedford**, MK42 0AR ☎ (0234) 55131		31 48 21F 100 ♿ ☡ 🅲 🅿 SB ⟟	57.50 75.00	— —
Bedford Swan Hotel, The Embankment, **Bedford**, MK40 1RW ☎ (0234) 46565	♛♛♛♛♛	31 53 2F 86 ☡ ♀ 🅲 🅿 SB ✸ 🏛 ☼ ⟟	— —	59.00 69.00
Kimbolton Hotel, 78 Clapham Road, **Bedford**, MK41 7PN ☎ (0234) 54854	♛♛♛	9 5 14 ☡3 ♀ 🅲 🅿 SB ⟟	23.00 34.50	33.75 43.70
The Knife and Cleaver, Houghton Conquest, **Bedford**, MK45 3LA ☎ (0234) 740387	♛♛	6 6 ☡ ♀ 🅲 🅿 🏛 ⟟	32.00 40.00	32.00 40.00
The Queens Head Hotel, 2 Rushden Road, Milton Ernest, **Bedford**, MK44 1RV ☎ (0234) 272822	♛♛♛♛	2 11 14 ♿ ☡ ♀ 🅲 🅿 SB 🏛 ⟟	49.00 66.00	52.50 68.00
Woodlands Manor, Green Lane, Clapham, **Bedford**, MK41 6EP ☎ (0234) 63281		4 25 29 ☡7 ♀ 🅲 🅿 SB ✸ 🏛 ⟟	42.00 56.00	59.75 89.50
Stratton House Hotel, London Road, **Biggleswade**, SG18 8EO ☎ (0767) 312442 & 314540	♛♛♛	14 16 5F 29 ☡ ♀ 🅲 🅿 SB 🏛 ⟟	28.00 45.00	40.00 50.00
Cranfield Conference Centre, Wharley End, **Cranfield**, MK43 0HG ☎ (0234) 751077		106 6 112 ♿ ☡ ♀ 🅲 🅿 ☼ ⟟	48.00 58.00	—
Highwayman Hotel, London Road, **Dunstable**, LU6 3DX ☎ (0582) 661999	♛♛♛♛	24 14 38 ☡ ♀ 🅲 🅿 SB ⟟	43.00 53.00	—
Old Palace Lodge Hotel, Church Street, **Dunstable**, LU5 5LL ☎ (0582) 662201	♛♛♛♛♛	5 44 0F 49 ☡ ♀ 🅲 🅿 SB ✸ 🏛 ⟟	59.50 65.00	—
Priory Guest House, 30 Priory Road, **Dunstable**, LU5 4HR ☎ (0582) 661900	♛♛	2 5 1F ☡ 🅿	16.00 28.00	—

Key to Symbols

	No. of single rooms
	No. of double/twin rooms
F	No. of family rooms
⬚	No. of en-suite bathrooms
♿	Disabled access
☡	Children welcome (min. age if any)
♀	Liquor licence
🅲	Credit cards accepted
🅿	Parking
SB	Short breaks
✸	Christmas/New Year breaks
🏛	Building of historic interest
	Four-poster beds
☼	Leisure/sports facilities
⟟	Conference facilities

Now choose the most appropriate place(s) to stay for each of the following:

a) a company requiring a high standard of accommodation and conference facilities for 35 employees

b) a family of four intending to stay for one night and with a maximum budget of £90

c) a couple wishing to take a Christmas break in a hotel room with a four-poster bed

d) a disabled guest requiring a single room in Bedford

e) a family with three children seeking a short break in a hotel with leisure facilities.

Assessment of the Quality of Accommodation

The Crown classifications indicate facilities and services but do not indicate standards of provision. Therefore the English Tourist Board also introduced a system listing three levels of quality – Approved, Commended and Highly Commended. These descriptions indicate the places which offer higher quality standards of accommodation and service for their guests than the minimum required to obtain a classification. Thus, a One-Crown guesthouse may have limited facilities but may be Commended because of the high standard of what it does offer.

Fees and Inspections

Establishments participating in the scheme pay an annual fee, which covers the cost of inspections and enables them to display their English Tourist Board classification and, where appropriate, grading. Those establishments seeking a grading as well as a classification are assessed by inspectors on the basis of the services and facilities they offer, as well as their efficiency, warmth of welcome, the quality of their fittings, furnishings and decor, and the standard and presentation of meals. Whether an establishment is Approved, Commended or Highly Commended is dependent on the number of items on the inspector's checklist which are judged 'poor', 'good' or 'excellent'. To achieve a Highly Commended grading at least 60 per cent of the aspects inspected must be judged 'excellent' with the remainder all being considered 'good'. A hotel may be designated 'Two Crown, Commended' but it would not be permitted to use the quality description without also referring to the Crown classification.

Access for all

Establishments can also display a logo indicating that they are suitable for handicapped guests if they satisfy a number of specific requirements. These include ramp provision, a reasonably wide entrance, and sufficient space to allow safe and easy access to all facilities a visitor may wish to use.

MINIMUM REQUIREMENTS FOR DISABLED PEOPLE

This symbol is used in English Tourist Board publications to indicate those establishments which may be suitable for physically handicapped guests. The minimum requirements are:

■ At least one entrance must have no steps or be equipped with a ramp whose gradient does not exceed 1:12. The entrance door must have a clear opening width of at least 80 cm.

■ Where provided, the following accommodation must either be on the ground floor or accessible by lift (NB where access to a specified area involves step(s), a ramp with a gradient of no more than 1:12 must be provided): – Reception; Restaurant/Dining room; Lounge; Bar; TV Lounge; public WC; and at least one bedroom served EITHER by a private bath/shower and WC en suite, OR by public facilities on the same floor.

■ A lift giving access to any of the above must have clear gate opening of at least 80 cm; the lift must be at least 140 cm deep, and 110 cm wide.

■ Doors giving access to any of the above areas (including bath/WC facilities) must have at least 75 cm clear opening width.

■ In bedrooms, private or public bathrooms and WCs used by disabled people, there must be a clear space immediately adjacent to the bed, bath or WC with a width of at least 75 cm. In bedrooms, there must be a turning space of 120 cm x 120 cm (in bathrooms and WCs: 110 cm x 70 cm) clear of the line of the door-swing.

If you would like to know more about catering for disabled guests, please write to or ring the Holiday Care Service, PO Box 20, Horley, Surrey, RH6 9UY (Tel. 0293 774535) for free advice.

Different Types of Accommodation

The classification system divides accommodation up into a number of types – hotels, guesthouses, motels, inns, bed and breakfast accommodation and farmhouses. A voluntary classification and grading scheme has also been introduced for self-catering accommodation. Over 10,000 holiday homes in England are inspected and given a Key classification which denotes the facilities and equipment provided. Observation of such things as warmth of welcome and atmosphere, as well as the quality of furnishings, fittings and equipment leads to a quality commendation which may be either Approved, Commended or Highly Commended. The quality commendation is not dependent on the Key classification, so that a One Key holiday home can be Highly Commended.

Table 1   Requirements for Key classifications

One Key	Clean and comfortable, adequate heating, lighting and seating, TV, cooker, fridge and full range of crockery and cutlery.
Two Key	Colour TV, easy chairs or sofas for all occupants, fridge with ice-maker, bedside units or shelves, heating in all rooms.
Three Key	Dressing tables, bedside lights, linen and towels available, vacuum cleaner, iron and ironing board.
Four Key	All sleeping in beds or bunks, supplementary lighting in living areas, more kitchen equipment, use of an automatic washing machine and tumble drier.
Five Key	Automatically-controlled heating, own washing machine and tumble drier, bath and shower, telephone, dishwasher, microwave and fridge freezer.

A similar system is applied to caravan and camping parks choosing to participate. They are inspected and classified according to the quality of the facilities provided.

◇ *Exercise* ◇

Work out a classification system for camping and caravan sites, using a similar system to the Crown and Key classifications.

Choose a suitable symbol, for example a trailer, and write descriptions of the facilities you would expect to be provided for each of the levels of classification, from one to five.

Tourist Information Centres

There would be little point in attracting visitors to a region if, once there, they could find nothing of interest to do or see. An important function of the regional tourist boards is to develop and support Tourist Information Centres.

*Tourist Information
Centre, High Wycombe*

Tourist Information Centres stock brochures, maps, guides and books about the surrounding area. They will have access to local transport and accommodation information, including timetables and prices. They are usually staffed by people with good local knowledge. These people may have studied for qualifications such as the City and Guilds Certificate of Tourist Information Centre Competence. This involves study of the work and structure of the English Tourist Board, timetable reading and regional geography. The British Tourist Authority produced an induction training programme in 1989 for people about to begin work in tourism. This covered a range of issues including the importance of local knowledge. Employees working in tourist information should know the whereabouts of taxis, bus stops, stations, car parks, hotels, shops, leisure centres, medical facilities, restaurants and religious centres. Familiarity with reference books such as telephone directories, **trade directories**, street maps, timetables and local entertainment guides is also important.

Giving directions is a service which all staff should be able to provide effectively. The induction programme offers the following advice on the subject:

Giving directions is not always simple, particularly when they are given to people from overseas. Over short distances, it is often better actually to accompany the tourist, if time is available for this.

A sketch map or photocopied street plan is worth a thousand words, especially if the route required is highlighted on it. This is the most effective way of giving directions for a complicated route involving several streets, for example.

When it is not possible, or appropriate, to issue a map, then staff should give directions as simply as possible, using the shortest (but safest) route.

Some tips for staff:

■ mention any landmarks en route
■ give the enquirer some idea of how far away their destination is
■ say approximately how long it will take to reach it
■ caution the tourist against any busy roads or trouble spots
■ check that the directions have been understood
■ make sure that the tourist leaves with the impression that you have done as much as possible to help.

Sometimes there may be too few tourists in a particular locality to warrant the development of an Information Centre, but nevertheless there remains a need for some tourist information. The simplest solution is to put up Tourist Information Points, giving maps and directions to places of interest.

Key Term

trade directory – a directory listing local companies, often in alphabetical order.

◊ *Exercises* ◊

1 Working in pairs, role play a conversation between a visitor to your locality and a Tourist Information Centre officer. The visitor must first decide what information they require.

2 The map below shows the districts covered by the Tourist Information Centres in Buckinghamshire:

Aylesbury TIC
County Hall
Walton Street
Bucks HP20 1UA
Tel: 0296 395000

High Wycombe TIC
6 The Corn Market
High Wycombe
Bucks HP11 2B4
Tel: 0494 461000

Milton Keynes TIC
Saxon Court
502 Avebury Bvd
Bucks MK9 3HS
Tel: 0908 691995

Marlow TIC
Court Garden Complex
Pound Lane
Marlow SL7 2AE
Tel: 06284 3597

Wendover TIC
Clock Tower
High Street
Bucks HP22 6DU
Tel: 0296 623056/624161

1 **Aylesbury, Buckingham & District**
2 **Amersham, Chesham & District**
3 **Milton Keynes & District**
4 **High Wycombe & District**
5 **Beaconsfield & South Bucks**

Divide into five groups. Each group writes a letter to a different Tourist Information Centre in Buckinghamshire, requesting information about places of interest within the district.

In your group prepare a report, briefly outlining the content of what you received from the TIC and giving your view about the quality and presentation of the information.

Come out of your groups to compare the five information packs. Were they similar? Did you think they were helpful? Do you think you would now like to visit Buckinghamshire? Why?

Development of the Thames and Chilterns Tourist Board

The Thames and Chilterns Tourist Board appointed its first Director in 1972. In its first year of operation he worked from the study of his house in north-west London, with the assistance of a secretary who came in three days a week. Their first permanent headquarters were in what had formerly been a seed shop in Abingdon, Oxfordshire. Staff were recruited, and in 1974 a property in Market Place, Abingdon, was purchased and remained the home of the Board until 1988.

Relationship with Local Authorities

Many local authorities within the region took several years to accept that there could be some economic value in supporting tourism and the efforts of the regional board. It was not until the early 1980s that the county authorities in the Thames and Chilterns region became seriously involved in promoting tourism.

Central Role of the ETB/BTA

However, during the mid-1980s the role of the regional boards and their relationship with the English Tourist Board changed. In 1983 the government announced the results of a wide-ranging review of tourism. This resulted in the establishment in 1985 of a joint English Tourist Board/British Tourist Authority headquarters, with departments specialising in personnel, administration, finance, research and training.

Government Departments and Tourism

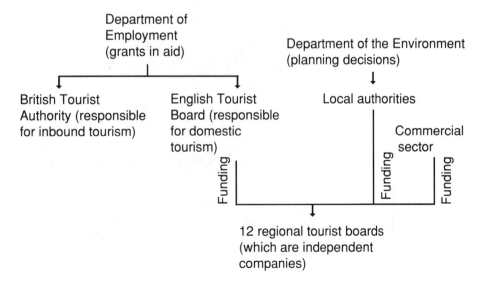

Note:
Every government department is likely to have an impact on tourism. Other departments most likely to affect the tourist industry are the Department of Transport, and the Department of Education and Science (who are able to promote education and training in areas related to tourism).

Government Support for Tourism

A report produced by the Department of Employment in 1985 called *Pleasure, Leisure and Jobs* attempted to tackle the problem of unemployment and signalled increasing government support for tourism. At the same time the regional boards were being encouraged to take on more responsibility for developing local accommodation facilities.

A Vision for England

In 1987 the English Tourist Board produced a major report called *Tourism – a Vision for England* in which they outlined their strategy for a five-year period. One of the major objectives stated in this report was to stimulate investment, both private and public, in tourism and leisure. This would clearly require regional tourist boards to work very closely with local authorities and leading representatives of the **private sector**.

The Mount House

In September 1988 the Thames and Chilterns Tourist Board moved to new premises in Witney. The Mount House is an attractive old house with an estimated market value of over £485,000. The building has about 492 square metres (5,300 square feet) of office space, very large areas of storage space, a modern telecommunications system and attractive grounds. Its size is an indication of how much the work of the Board has expanded since its beginnings.

The Mount House

Key Term

private sector – the part of the economy owned and operated by private individuals and firms, as opposed to the public sector which is financed and managed by the government.

◇ *Exercise* ◇

One of the roles of the Thames and Chilterns Tourist Board is to co-ordinate the marketing interests of each of the counties in the region.

Below are four brochure extracts, each describing the ease with which conference delegates could get to suitable venues in four of the counties in the region.

*H*ertfordshire provides the perfect location for any conference. Bordering on London and serviced by major road, rail and air links with the rest of the country, accessibility has to be the main attraction of the county to any conference organiser. The M1, M25 and A1(M) make travelling by car easy, the proximity of Stansted, Luton and Heathrow airports extends Hertfordshire's reputation for accessibility to the overseas visitor, and the recent Thameslink with Gatwick and the South coast completes the picture of the county as the ideal business destination.

ROAD, RAIL AND AIR LINKS

By road:
Berkshire is well served by the national motorway network, in particular the M4, M3 and M25. There are excellent public transport express coach links with London.

By rail:
Intercity links with London and all major UK departure points.
Passenger Information: Reading (0734) 595911 (British Rail)

By air:
Within easy travelling distance of Heathrow and Gatwick airports.

AIR
The county boasts its own international airport at Luton, close to Junction 10 of the M1 motorway and good rail links. Heathrow Airport is only a short journey away and Gatwick Airport can be easily reached thanks to the British Rail Thameslink service.

ROAD
The M1 motorway in the West of the county and the A1 Great North Road in the East along with their links to the M25 London orbital route mean that London, the South-East, the Midlands and the Anglian region are within travelling distance.

RAIL
Bedfordshire is fortunate to have good rail services. Luton and Bedford are on Network Southeast Thameslink line which connects to London Kings Cross (Thameslink) and to Gatwick Airport, Brighton and Sevenoaks. The Great Northern Electrics line runs to and from London, Leeds, York and the North East passing through Sandy and Biggleswade. Leighton Buzzard is on the Northampton line linking London Euston to Milton Keynes, Birmingham and the North-West.

A network of good roads affords fast and convenient access to Buckinghamshire – particularly from London via the M25/M40 in the south and the M1 in the north. By rail the county is also easily accessible – the north being served by the Intercity Northampton Line which links London with Milton Keynes in a matter of 45 minutes; and the south being served by the Chiltern Line, and the London Underground Metropolitan Line which runs out to Chesham. Delegates travelling by air will find that Buckinghamshire conference venues are convenient to both Heathrow and Luton Airports – most venues being within an hour's drive of either airport.

Devise a single page of a brochure which would effectively show why the Thames and Chilterns area as a whole is an accessible region in which to hold conferences, regardless of where delegates may be travelling from.

The Finances of the Thames and Chilterns Tourist Board

Until February 1989 the regional boards administered a government grants scheme, set up under section four of the 1969 Development of Tourism Act. This enabled the Thames and Chilterns Tourist Board to put sums of £10,000 and £8,000 towards the development of Tourist Information Centres in St Albans and High Wycombe during 1988–9. However, after a recent government review of tourism, this scheme has now been suspended.

Apart from money raised from its own publishing and training activities, the Thames and Chilterns Tourist Board receives income from commercial members from the private sector and local authority members, as well as an annual grant from the English Tourist Board. The Thames and Chilterns Tourist Board is registered as a company. Among other requirements, this means that annual financial statements must be audited and published.

How the Board Spends its Income

The major expenses of the Board include producing publicity materials, administration, an advice and information service, research, and the purchase of fixed assets such as buildings or equipment.

Costs of Publicity

An example of the publicity material produced by the Board is the brochure called 'London's Country', which stresses the proximity of the region to the capital. The high costs of this 32-page colour publication, inflated by the fact that it is translated into five European languages, are largely met by charging fees to the companies and organisations represented in it.

'Churches of the Thames and Chilterns' is a much smaller publication, and the contents are to some extent determined by the cost. The smaller villages and towns in the region contain over a hundred parish churches, yet only a selection could be included. A limit also had to be set on the number of photographs which could be included.

Exhibition and Trade Fair Costs

The venue, the size of the stand, the number of staff required and the duration of the event will all affect the cost of taking part in trade fairs and exhibitions. Regional boards have to set these costs against what they estimate to be the likely gains. Thus, though it may be costly for the Thames and Chilterns Tourist Board to set up a stand at the five-day Ireland Holiday Fair, over 40,000 people visit this event. As over 1.3 million visits are made to Britain from Ireland each year, the Board is confident that it can attract more of these tourists to come to the Thames and Chilterns region.

Costs of Tourist Information Centres

Within the Thames and Chilterns region there are 39 Information Centres, and the Tourist Board has been instrumental in getting many of these established. The Board has in the past funded the provision of equipment such as answering machines, especially for centres which have limited opening hours during the winter months.

Main Attractions of the Thames and Chilterns Region

The Thames and Chilterns region covers five counties to the north and west of London. The region is dominated by the River Thames, the Chiltern Hills and the city of Oxford.

The Thames Valley

The Thames flows close to the walls of Windsor Castle, the home of English kings and queens since William the Conqueror. It passes through attractive towns like Cookham, Marlow and Henley, well known for its international rowing **regatta**.

Key Term

regatta – an event featuring a series of boat races.

◇ *Exercise* ◇

Look at the six advertisements taken from the Thames and Chilterns Tourist Board's 1990 publication *Where to Go:*

RIVER TRIPS

Large range of public sailings in fully weatherproof boats

Vessels available for private hire: Riverboat shuffles, weddings, receptions and all types of social functions.

FRENCH BROTHERS AND WINDSOR BOATS
The Runnymede Boathouse
Windsor Road, Old Windsor
also at The Promenade, Barry Avenue,
Central Windsor
Tel: (0753) 851900/862933

RIVER THAMES CRUISES

Mid-May to Mid-September. Daily Public Passenger Boat Services, calling at such places as

OXFORD, ABINGDON, READING, HENLEY, MARLOW, COOKHAM, MAIDENHEAD, WINDSOR, RUNNYMEDE & STAINES

Boats for 12–200 passengers also available for Private Charter day or evening with bar, food and music if required.

SALTER BROS LTD Folly Bridge, Oxford
 Tel. Oxford 0865 243421

Hobbs & Sons Ltd.
of Henley

- PARTY BOAT HIRE
- SELF-DRIVE DAY BOAT HIRE
- HOLIDAY CABIN CRUISER HIRE
- MARINE SALES
- CHANDLERY AND FUEL SALES
- MOORINGS AND STORAGE OF BOATS

PHONE: HENLEY 572035
(ESTABLISHED 1870)

KENNET HORSE BOAT Co.

Horsedrawn and Motor Barge Day-Trips. Step back in time with a relaxing trip through beautiful Berkshire countryside. Freshly made tea and coffee and licensed bar. Friendly crew and warm welcome. Book now for Spring and Summer.

PUBLIC TRIPS   Brochure from: **PRIVATE CHARTER**
32, West Mills, Newbury, RG14 5HU
Tel: (0635) 44154

Yes   **TEL (043 871) 4528**

ARCTURUS

CANAL BOAT TRIPS

EASTER TO OCTOBER SUNDAYS & BANK HOLS
2.30 p.m. and 4.00 p.m. as required
also TUESDAYS and THURSDAYS
in AUGUST at 2.00 p.m. and 3.30 p.m.

CASSIOBURY PARK WATFORD
M25 J20/Hunton Bri/A411/Langley Way/Park
The Trip **from Ironbridge Lock** includes one of the most beautiful stretches of the canal

BEAM ENDS

Old Toms, Northside
Steeple Aston, OXFORD
Tel. 0869 40212

An individual, spacious and most comfortable room, with en suite facilities, on the first floor of a restored 18th century stone barn. Own access and parking. Just off A423 between Banbury – 9 miles and Oxford – 14 miles.

Brochure available.
Families accommodated.

If possible, plan a trip to one of these attractions, or a similar attraction in your own locality. Select an advertisement and write a letter giving full details of your booking. You should also ask for any additional information which you think you may need in order to plan your trip.

On your return write an account of what happened.

The Chilterns

The Chiltern Hills form an attractive, often wooded stretch of countryside stretching from Bedfordshire, across Buckinghamshire into South Oxfordshire and Berkshire. They are traversed by numerous footpaths, including the Ridgeway which stretches for 85 miles from Ivinghoe in Buckinghamshire, through Goring on Thames, to Avebury in Wiltshire. A number of historic country houses are found within these hills, including Waddesdon Manor, Hughenden Manor, Claydon House and the Prime Minister's country residence, Chequers.

Other Attractions in the Region

The region also includes the city of Oxford, the Roman bath and museum at St Albans, the famous racecourses at Ascot and Newbury and the safari parks at Woburn and Windsor.

The Thames and Chilterns Tourist Board markets the whole region, but also assists individual counties in promoting their own separate images. Thus Berkshire is described as 'Beautiful Berkshire – the Royal County', while Hertfordshire's recent publications describe it as 'England's best-kept secret.'

◇ *Exercise* ◇

Read the descriptions of Bedfordshire, Buckinghamshire and Oxfordshire opposite.

1 Think up a slogan which seems to you to represent the attractions of each county most effectively.

2 Use the information provided and appropriate brochures, guides or reference books to help you to prepare the script for a five-minute slot on a television holiday programme featuring one of the counties.

Tourists in Oxford

Most visitors to the Thames and Chilterns region finish up in Oxford sooner or later. Oxford is the home of one of the world's best-known universities. The 35 colleges which make up the university are a major attraction, with their chapels, **quadrangles** and gardens. There are over six hundred listed buildings in the city centre, as well as museums, galleries, gardens and riverside meadows.

Bedfordshire

Bedfordshire is a county of great natural beauty, from the high point of the Dunstable Downs in the south to the River Great Ouse winding its way gently through the north. It is a beauty that is very accessible to visitors, as many country parks, nature reserves, riverside walks and grand estates are open to the public. Many of the open spaces are under the care of North Bedfordshire Borough Council and Bedfordshire County Council which have provided extra amenities for visitors.

The area has many historic connections — prehistoric man, the Saxons, Romans and Normans have all left their mark. The 4,000-year-old Icknield Way and Roman Watling Street both cross the county.

Bedfordshire's most famous son is probably John Bunyan, the 17th-C. Nonconformist preacher and author. He was born at Harrowden and was imprisoned for his beliefs for many years in Bedford County Gaol.

Among the many stately homes to visit in the county are two of England's finest – Woburn Abbey and Luton Hoo. Woburn is also the home of the famous Wild Animal Kingdom and Safari Park, and the Wild Animal Park at Whipsnade is well known for its breeding of endangered species.

Buckinghamshire

Buckinghamshire has rightly been called the Queen of the Home Counties. From the Ouse and the Grand Union Canal in the north to the Thames in the south and the beechwoods of the Chiltern Hills in the east, it is a county with many gifts to share.

The Chilterns, running like a spine through the county, are known for their incomparable beechwoods – all that remains of a vast forest that once covered the whole county.

In the very centre of the county lies the Vale of Aylesbury with the county town of Aylesbury at its heart. This is rich, flat farmland with occasional sudden heights such as Brill Hill, The Clump at Quainton and Lodge Hill at Waddesdon to add drama to the landscape.

The Vale is one of the most picturesque parts of Buckinghamshire and richly studded with grand country houses. Indeed, Buckinghamshire has a generous share of historic houses for visitors to see, including several of the great homes of the Rothschild family, the most glorious of which must surely be Waddesdon Manor.

The northern part of the county is dominated by the new city of Milton Keynes, created around several towns and villages in 1967. The area's waterways – the Ouse, its tributary the Ouzel and the Grand Union Canal – provide many opportunities for riverside walks, watersports and angling.

Here too are some fine old towns, like Buckingham and Olney. Along the county's southern boundary the River Thames flows through some fine scenery. This is mainly residential, green-belt land, crossed by country roads and lanes with pretty villages, parks, heaths and woods. One of the most famous, Burnham Beeches near Stoke Poges, was a favourite haunt of the poet Thomas Gray.

Oxfordshire

The colourful history and satisfying scenery of Oxfordshire are closely linked in today's landscape. Prehistoric man, Romans, Saxons and Normans had all left their imprint by the time the medieval wool merchants endowed magnificent churches with the profits of their trade, and for at least seven centuries scholars have explored and extended the boundaries of knowledge at Oxford. This extraordinary city combines the bustle of the marketplace with the hush of a monastery; the crackle of the new with the quiet confidence of the well-established; and the cutting edge of research with the patient knowledge of centuries.

Many of the county's other towns and villages have a claim to fame as well: Wantage was the birthplace of King Alfred; Banbury is famous as the home of its cakes, cattle and the cross of the 'Ride a cock horse' nursery rhyme; and Winston Churchill was born at Blenheim Palace and lies buried at Bladon near Woodstock. As if this weren't enough, there is also an estate-sized wildlife park near Burford, an intriguing steam railway centre at Didcot and at Witney, a farm museum where the clock is always turned back to the hard work and country pleasures of Edwardian times.

Finally, there is the steady River Thames, wending its way through lush countryside and delightful waterside towns, gathering momentum on its journey towards London. Every summer Henley-on-Thames hosts England's best-known regatta and graceful punts ply Oxford's waterways. Despite its distance from the sea, Oxfordshire, with its many lovely rivers and the Oxford Canal, provides ample opportunities for relaxation afloat.

Congestion in the City Centre

Many of the buildings and streets at the centre of the city were constructed long before the appearance of motor traffic. Throughout the 1960s and 1970s traffic in the centre became increasingly congested, particularly in the summer months. As a result, a number of streets have been closed to traffic altogether. Others permit access to buses and cyclists only. Some roads have been designated **through routes**. At four points on the outskirts of the city there are free car parks with frequent bus services available into the city centre. Coaches are not allowed to wait on the city centre streets at any time, and they are prohibited from entering some areas altogether. However, since it is not the intention to discourage visitors completely, a number of agreed set-down and pick-up points have been established, as has a large coach and lorry park which empty coaches must use. Signs on the city ring road indicate which four roads may be used by coaches intending to enter Oxford.

Key Terms

quadrangles – courtyards or open spaces enclosed by buildings, usually on four sides.

through routes – road routes on which no stopping is allowed.

◇ *Exercise* ◇

Use the information below and the map opposite to plan a carefully-timed itinerary for a coach party wishing to visit the following places on a Wednesday in University term-time:

Pitt Rivers Museum, Christ Church Cathedral, The Botanic Garden, The Sheldonian Theatre, The Oxford Story.

PLACES OF WORSHIP

Times of regular services and meetings for worship are given.

3B **31 Blackfriars (RC),** 64 St. Giles: Sun 8am, 9.30am, 11.15am (Polish Mass), 6.15pm; weekdays 6.15pm; Holy Days 12.15pm, 6.15pm.

7D **32 Central Oxford Mosque,** 10 Bath Street, Tel: 245547.

4D **33 Christ Church Cathedral,** St. Aldate's: Sun 8am, 10am, 11.15am, 6pm; weekdays 7.15am, 7.30am, 6pm.

3A **34 First Church of Christ Scientist,** 36 St. Giles: Sun 11am; Wed 7.30pm. Reading Room Mon–Fri 12–3.

3B **35 Friends' Meeting House,** 43 St. Giles: Sun 9.30am, 11am; Wed 12.15pm.

MUSEUMS, GALLERIES AND LIBRARIES

3B **53 Ashmolean Museum,** Beaumont Street: Tue–Sat 10–4, Sun 2–4, B.H. Mon 2–5. Closed Good Fri, Easter, St. Giles' Fair in Sept. Free.

4D **54 Bate Collection of Historical Instruments,** Faculty of Music, St. Aldate's: Mon–Fri 2–5. Free.

4C **55 Bodleian Library,** Broad Street: **Divinity School and Exhibition Room:** Mon–Fri 9–5, Sat 9–12.30. Free. Guided tours of the **Divinity School, Convocation House** and **Duke Humfrey's Library:** Mar–end Oct, Mon–Fri at 10.30, 11.30, 2 and 3; Sat 10.30, 11.30, £2. Please note no children under 14 are admitted.

4E **56 British Telecom Museum,** 35 Speedwell Street: by appointment. Tel: 246601. Free.

4D **57 Christ Church Picture Gallery** (own entrance from Oriel Square): Mon–Sat 10.30–1, 2–5.30; Sun 2–5.30 (Oct–Mar closes at 4.30 and closed for Christmas and Easter). £0.40.

4C **58 Museum of the History of Science,** Broad Street: Mon–Fri 10.30–1, 2.30–4. Free.

3D **59 Museum of Modern Art,** 30 Pembroke Street: Tue–Sat 10–6, Sun 2–6. Adults £1, children £0.50. Good wheelchair access.

4D **60 Museum of Oxford,** St. Aldate's: Tue–Sat 10–5. Free.

4A **61 Pitt Rivers Museum** (entrance through University Museum), Parks Road: Mon–Sat 1–4.30. *Balfour Building* (music gallery), beside 60 Banbury Road: Mon–Sat 1–4.30. Free.

OTHER PLACES OF INTEREST

3C **64 Apollo Theatre,** George Street: Box Office Tel: 244544.

6D **65 Botanic Garden,** High Street: daily 9–5 (closes 4.30 in winter). Glasshouses daily 2–4 (closed Good Friday and Christmas).

4C **66 Carfax Tower,** late Mar–late Oct, Mon–Sat 10–6, Sun 2–6; late Oct–late Nov closes at 4. Adults £0.60, accompanied children under 16, £0.25.

4C **67 Covered Market,** Market Street and High Street: Mon–Sat 8–5.30.

2D **68 Ice Rink,** Oxpens Road: daily. Tel: 247676.

3C **69 Open Market,** The Gallery, Gloucester Green: Wed.

4C **70 The Oxford Story,** Broad Street: daily, Nov–Mar 10–4, Apr–Oct 9.30–5. Last admission ½ hour before closing. Closed Christmas Day.

4B **71 Rhodes House,** South Parks Road: Mon–Fri 2–5. Free.

4C **72 Sheldonian Theatre,** Broad Street: Mon–Sat 10–12.45, 2–4.45. Closes at 3.45 Nov–Feb. Please check in advance, Tel: 277299. Adults £0.30, children £0.15.

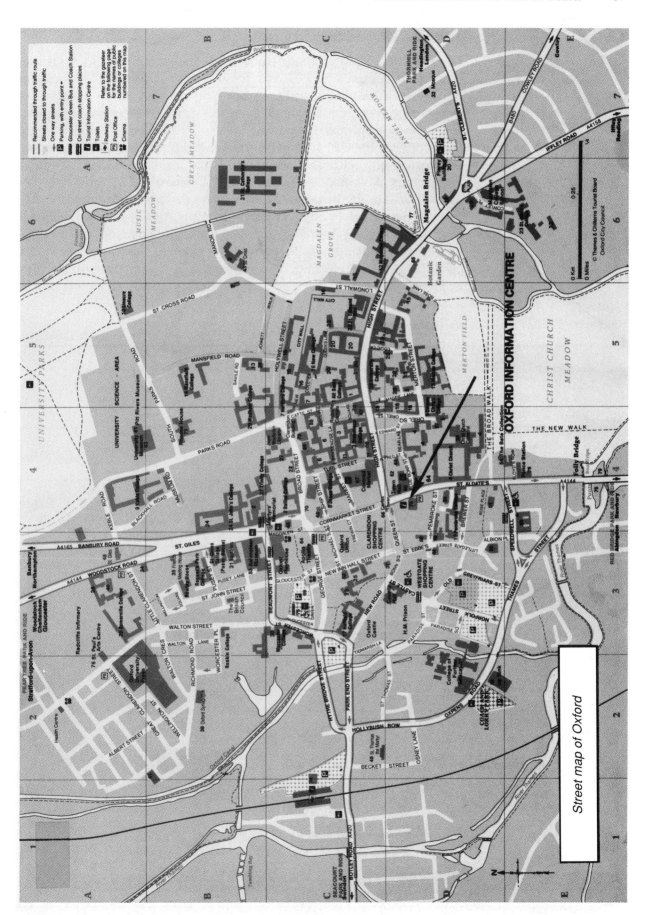

Street map of Oxford

The Position of the City Council

Though the Regional Board may wish to encourage more visitors, Oxford City Council may understandably wish to control the number of incoming visitors. With well over a million people visiting the city each year, the Council may decide that control of visitors is the major priority. In the hope of establishing what the best future policy might be, the Board offered the City Council a grant of £7,500 during 1988–9 as a one-third contribution towards a fresh study of tourism in the city, provided that the sum was matched from the City Council and the private sector. The study actually began in July 1990 and ran for twelve months. The overall cost, which had risen by this stage to £30,000, was split between the Thames and Chilterns Tourist Board and the English Tourist Board, the City Council and the **Chamber of Commerce**. The study was carried out by Oxford Polytechnic. It comprised exit and city centre surveys, residents' surveys, surveys of local businesses, and an economic impact appraisal.

Key Term

chamber of commerce – a group of business people working together to promote local trade.

◇ *Exercise* ◇

The Thames and Chilterns Tourist Board published in its Annual Report for 1988–9 the following figures relating to visitors to three attractions in Oxford:

Table 2 Number of Tourists at Key Attractions in Oxford

	Museum of Oxford	Carfax Tower	Bodleian Library
1980	41,758	49,054	175,338
1981	34,579	47,777	159,445
1982	32,261	52,601	173,594
1983	33,750	53,418	216,291
1984	29,182	51,435	250,199
1985	43,738	55,567	183,773
1986	56,770	52,717	188,352
1987	52,532	54,974	199,211
1988	47,357	51,429	217,262

a) What conclusions can you draw from these figures?
b) Transfer the figures onto a line or bar graph and then write a short report detailing the fortunes of tourism in Oxford during the period 1980–8.

The Future for Regional Tourist Boards

The regional tourist boards will continue to be responsible for providing a public information service and for raising non-government funds to further their marketing and development activities.

The 1989 Review of Tourism

The government's long-awaited *Review of Tourism*, published in July 1989, has resulted in additional funds being made available to the regional boards. Much of the previously centralised activity of the English Tourist Board has now been devolved to the regions. However, most of this funding is contractual, which means a set amount of money will be provided by the ETB for particular projects. The regional boards will have to carry out a number of tasks, including co-ordinating the work of Tourist Information Centres, maintaining accommodation grading and classification schemes, developing employment training schemes, offering business advice and monitoring progress on developments which received grants from the now-abandoned section four grants scheme.

The following extract gives an idea of the aims of the Thames and Chilterns Tourist Board in the period following the 1989 review:

... we must carefully and unobtrusively manage our visitors. They must be spread more equally throughout the region and throughout the year. Our overall target must be to improve the value, not simply the volume of visitors – whether they are here for one day or several weeks. The Board will also need to develop a Regional Management Strategy to link promotion with development, thus taking into account environmental consciousness and securing from the tourism industry and those who live locally, a commitment to finding a common ground.

As already stated, overseas visitors play an important role in the value of tourism to the region. The coming of the Single European Market in 1992, followed by the Channel Tunnel, opens up a tremendous opportunity for the region – and the potential for embarrass-ment. Are we ready for the European 'invasion'? Can we provide the types of accommodation required? Do we have the quality camp sites and caravan parks that are commonplace in Europe? We want the Europeans to stay in our five counties, but will they return if the infra-structure is under-developed? The Board is planning to mount an intensive marketing campaign in Europe in 1991 to ensure that we capture our share of this promising market. This needs to be linked to a development strategy that encourages the construction of the kinds of accommodation that will persuade our new visitors to stay in the region.

John Bethell, Managing Director, TCTB
(from the Thames and Chilterns Tourist Board Annual Report, 1990)

Performance Targets

The government will set targets for each of the contracts a regional tourist board undertakes. The success of the Thames and Chilterns Tourist Board in meeting their targets will certainly affect its short-term future. Performance will be monitored through a system of reports, and failure to meet prescribed targets will result in financial penalties.

Business Partnerships

The regional tourist boards may also develop projects in collaboration with trading companies. Private publishers might well find the idea of adopting some of the tourist boards' publications attractive. Another idea which some see as potentially profitable is the establishment of English holiday shops. These would be sited in high streets and their purpose would be to expand the market for domestic holidays, as well as providing an information service.

◇ *Exercise* ◇

Study the details provided below about the Millwaters Hotel in Newbury, Berkshire.

MILLWATERS

London Road, **Newbury** RG13 2BY.
Tel: (0635) 528838
Telex: 83343
Fax: (0635) 523406

👑👑👑👑👑

Hotel Group/Consortium: Consort/
Thames Valley Hotels

Millwaters is a delightful Georgian country house set in an exceptional environment and has an attractive Summer House with terraces and a patio overlooking the lake. Two famous rivers, the Lambourn and the Kennet, flow through the eight acres of grounds, and by night the water and the trees are romantically floodlit. There are 32 luxurious bedrooms each with private bathroom, radio, television and tea/coffee making facilities. The resident proprietors offer a friendly, personal service, and the restaurant has a selection of high quality food and wine at reasonable prices. Car parking is available for 50 cars.

Prices
Twin Room: From £87.00 including VAT

Single Room: From £70.00 including VAT

Weekend Rate: £39.75 (inclusive of £13.00 towards dinner). Single room supplement £10.00

Group Rates
Minimum Group size: 12

Maximum Group size: 36

Per person sharing twin room including breakfast £40.00 midweek.

Per person sharing single room including breakfast £48.50 midweek.

Conference Facilities: Include the Summer House which is comfortably furnished and well equipped with its own bar and dining facilities, and the Barn, a spacious attachment to the main building, also equipped with a bar. Both offer a choice of theatre, classroom or boardroom layouts, with a capacity of up to 72 people. Facilities include flipcharts, screens, projectors, blackboards, lectern and a photocopying service.

Prices
Day Rate: From £28.00 per person

24 Hour Rate: From £93.00 per person

Special Interest Breaks: Details on requests. Cover Music, Painting, Needlecrafts, Horseracing, Horseriding and Fishing.

Access and facilites for the disabled.

Devise a programme for an inspection of the hotel to make sure that the hotel is meeting its Crown classification requirements. The inspection is to be carried out by a representative of a private company. You should explain how the inspection would be done and how long it would take.

List all the expenses of the inspection and estimate the size of fee which a private company might ask for carrying it out.

Local Community Needs

Some services, such as providing information, contributing to regional planning, and offering advice free from commercial interest, would appear too important not to be available to communities in all regions.

It is also important to do research into people's travel and accommodation preferences and habits. This should enable practical strategies for dispersing tourists around the regions to be developed. Financial and professional advice to small businesses will help them to develop quality products. The regional boards can play their part in planning developments by ensuring there is liaison between planning authorities and developers.

It remains to be seen how much of the cost of these services, as well as the cost of creating information databases and staff training programmes, can be met from the boards' expanding marketing activities.

◊ *Discussion points* ◊

1 Why do you think the Crown classification scheme is voluntary?

2 What qualities would you look for in the kind of hotel which you would personally describe as 'perfect'?

3 What do you think commercial companies who contribute funds to regional tourist boards believe they are getting out of it?

4 How do you think the choice was made over which parish churches could be included in the 'Churches of the Thames and Chilterns' brochure?

5 Can you think of any other ways in which the number of visitors to Oxford could be controlled?

4 Thorpe Park – A Leisure Park

Introduction

It is a warm bank holiday and you and your friends or family decide you want a good day out with lots to do and see. You might choose to visit a leisure park. The majority of leisure parks charge admission for entry to a variety of attractions, including rides and opportunities for physical activity, as well as shows and live entertainment. Charging a standard entrance fee reduces the security risk and simplifies the role of many staff employed around the sites. But some parks offer free admission and charge for individual activities. They all aim to entertain visitors for at least two-thirds of a day, long enough for them to spend money on food and souvenirs and have a good time. Although themed entertainments may offer information of an educational nature, the emphasis is more likely to be on having a light-hearted, enjoyable day out. One of the best known and most popular activities at Thorpe Park is the giant roller-coaster.

Although leisure parks may make use of the existing geography of the site, as in the case of the water-filled gravel pits at Thorpe Park, the environment of most parks is constructed specifically for the purpose of entertainment.

Thorpe Park – A British leisure park

Theme Parks

The term 'theme park' is often used to describe modern amusement parks. The best-known theme park, Disneyland, was opened in 1955 and many of the activities it offered featured characters or scenes from Walt Disney's cartoon films. However, it is more accurate to describe many similar recent developments as leisure parks, because many of the activities they offer do not share a common theme.

Where are Leisure Parks Constructed?

Leisure parks are not necessarily constructed in traditional holiday areas. A lot of their visitors will be on day trips, hence the need to be easily accessible from major population areas. The importance of leisure parks to the tourist industry can be judged from the fact that in 1988 they attracted 11 per cent of all the visitors to tourist attractions. The increasing popularity of leisure parks has coincided with the declining numbers of day visitors to traditional seaside resorts. Towns such as Blackpool, Margate and Southport have tried to reverse this trend by developing seaside leisure parks, each capable of attracting more than three-quarters of a million visitors annually.

◇ *Exercise* ◇

1 Find the leisure parks listed below on a map of Britain. Consider the location of each one. Is it near to major population centres and accessible by road and rail? How do you think people get to it?

Major Leisure Parks in England

Alton Towers, Staffs	Heights of Abraham, Derbyshire
American Adventure Theme Park, Ilkeston	Lands End, Cornwall
Beamish Open Air Museum	Lightwater Valley Action Park, Ripon
Bembon Brothers Theme Park, Margate	Littlecote, Berks
Beaulieu, Hants	Needles Pleasure Park, Isle of Wight
Blackgang Chine, Isle of Wight	Paultons Park, Hants
Blackpool Pleasure Beach	Pleasureland, Southport
Camelot Theme Park, Lancs	Pleasurewood Hills American Theme
Chessington World of Adventures, Surrey	Park, Lowestoft
Drayton Manor Park, Staffs	Thorpe Park, Surrey
Flambards, Helston	West Midland Safari Park
Flamingoland Zoo, North Yorks	Windsor Safari Park
Frontierland, Morecambe	Woburn Abbey and Park, Beds

2 Now identify four sites in Britain which you think would make good locations for new leisure parks.

The Economics of Running a Leisure Park

Construction Costs

A major problem in developing a leisure park is that the initial costs of construction are very high. Many of the costs have to be met at a time when the park is not producing any revenue. Major items of expenditure are likely to include car-parking facilities, internal roadways, sewage pipelines and pumps, bridges and perimeter fencing. Electricity, water, gas and telephone lines all have to be installed. Depending on the contours of the land and the use of the site being developed, major landscaping may be required both to improve appearance and limit disturbance from noise.

Running Costs

Staffing is a major cost in the open season. The range of activities on the site require thorough supervision, while catering, maintenance and cleaning have to be kept to a constant, efficient level.

Pricing Policy

If a single admission charge is made it has to be set at a level which will not deter visitors. Research can indicate the amount visitors are willing to spend during a day visit and the park owners must assess what proportion of this sum will go on food and souvenirs. Since repeat visits are essential for economic survival, people must be made to feel they have received value for money.

Retail Outlets

On-site catering and **retailing** are clearly major sources of income for leisure parks. These include all outlets selling food and drink, as well as those providing souvenirs. Some leisure parks also offer visitors the opportunity to hire such items as cameras and video equipment.

A retail outlet at Thorpe Park

Open Season

Most leisure parks are open to the elements, so they usually close during the coldest months of the year. This saves costs in that fewer staff have to be employed during the closed season. It also gives an opportunity for new developments and refurbishments to be completed.

Key term

retailing – selling direct to the public.

◇ *Exercise* ◇

You are to plan a new food outlet for Thorpe Park. Before you start, read the statements below, and the guidelines which follow.

'£50 is a reasonable amount to spend on a family day out.'

'If people only pay once at the gate and don't have to keep getting out more money for every ride or attraction, their resistance to spending money on food is lowered.'

'People want fast food when they are out enjoying themselves. The trouble is, fast food produces a huge amount of unsightly litter.'

'The only way you can build up attendances and encourage repeat visits is by investing in new rides, new attractions and even new food outlets.'

'Most people arrive at Thorpe Park in the morning and stay for six hours or so. It seems highly probable that children in the party will help to decide on the food eaten by families while they are on the site.'

Working in groups of three or four, discuss how the points raised in these statements will affect the planning of your food outlet.

You should also consider all of the following factors:

♦ location
♦ size and layout
♦ construction material and cost
♦ decor
♦ type of menu
♦ price range
♦ staffing
♦ type of service
♦ equipment
♦ how it would be marketed in a new brochure.

Advertising

Television advertising is an important means of raising regional awareness of attractions like Thorpe Park. It is more expensive than advertising in the local press but it reaches more people and, by choosing the times carefully, it can be targeted at particular age groups.

Agencies are often hired to do this work because they are able to negotiate better rates. The theme park will provide a **brief** for the advertisement, explaining the market it is intended to reach. Some agreement about the length of the advertisement will be needed. This may depend on the purpose of the advertisement or on how often it will be shown. The sum of money budgeted by the company for the production of the advertisement will be a major factor in deciding its length. Some advertisers think they can get their message across on television in ten seconds; others use up three or four times that amount of viewing time. A longer advertisement can be used to attract viewers' attention, followed by a number of shorter ones to act as reminders. Once these things have been agreed the agency will go away and prepare a storyboard. This looks rather like a comic strip and is usually a series of drawings showing the proposed sequence of camera shots. It may also indicate the content of the soundtrack. When both parties are happy with the storyboard, the filming can begin.

Child (in plaintive voice): "Can't we do something more exciting tomorrow?"

Shot in sunlight.

Family flash past on Flying Fish. Voice over: "Your whole family can enjoy a fun day out at Thorpe Park."

Still frame. Voice over: "Phone 0932 569393 for details."

A student's storyboard for a Thorpe Park advertisement

Key terms

agencies – organisations which carry out a particular job on behalf of others.

brief – a short statement describing in general terms what is required.

◇ *Exercise* ◇

Prepare a storyboard for a ten-second advertisement for Thorpe Park featuring some of the following attractions:

'The Flying Fish' – A roller-coaster for all the family.
The Flying Fish is an exciting new family ride themed on the antics of a flying fish. The brightly coloured blue and green monster fish dives, twists and turns, carrying over 1,500 visitors an hour, at speeds of up to 30 mph, riding over waterfalls, tumbling streams and rock pools.

A Drive in the Country – Thorpe Park goes green.
A 1930s car ride will take the family on an old-time drive through the countryside in scaled-down vintage reproduction cars. Typical country scenes with a 'green' theme will educate children to preserve our countryside and animals in their natural habitat. There'll be a few surprises too, just as there used to be 60 years ago. Perhaps you might catch sight of rabbits playing or sleeping ducks.

'Carousel Kingdom' – New under-cover family entertainment area.
There's plenty to occupy the family in Thorpe Park's brand new 'Carousel Kingdom', themed on an attractive medieval town square and castle. The centrepiece of this vast under-cover play area features the first 'double decker' carousel in the UK. This beautifully hand-painted, traditional merry-go-round is an exact replica of the old steam-powered carousels from the early 1900s. Children ride on the brightly coloured galloping horses, flying elephants, cockerels and spinning balloons suspended from the upper deck and dancing to the old-time piped organ music.

Origin and Brief History of Thorpe Park

There have been travelling fairgrounds all over Britain and America since the 1930s. They traditionally featured a mixture of booths and stalls offering fortune-telling, air-rifle shooting and games of chance, as well as an increasing number of roundabouts and exciting mechanical rides. Modern leisure parks are a development of this idea, except that they occupy permanent sites. In other parts of Europe leisure parks have been developed on sites which were the traditional winter quarters for travelling shows, fairs and circuses.

As long ago as 1941 excavation of gravel began on the site on which Thorpe Park now stands. The area was part of the River Thames flood plain and gravel deposits were present to a depth of about four metres. A company called the Ready Mixed Concrete (RMC) Group took over the land when they purchased the Hall and Ham River Company in 1968. RMC owned a number of similar sites where the level of the water table meant that gravel excavation had left behind extensive lakes. These were used in a limited way for fishing and sailing, but the company wished to develop their use further. They wanted to make them profitable operations but also to show that exhausted gravel pits could be landscaped and put to valuable recreational use. The company had to decide which of the sites they owned offered the greatest potential for development. It would require:

- proximity to major population centres
- easy access by road
- ability to handle a high volume of local traffic
- parking facilities on a large scale.

Advantages of the Thorpe Park Site

The surroundings of the new park and its approaches needed to be attractive, both because this would appeal to visitors and because it would place the development proposal in a more favourable light. The 500 acres which became Thorpe Park were sited just 21 miles from London, and approximately half the surface area consisted of lakes.

Securing Approval for Development

In 1970 there were a number of planning regulations relating to Thorpe Park, most of which set a time limit by which the excavations had to be refilled and returned to agricultural use. Permission had to be obtained from the County Council to waive the original agreements and allow the lakes to remain so that the site could be developed for leisure use. The Council agreed, as long as there were no local objections. Public meetings were organised, and the company used these to explain their proposals and to look at alternative plans for industrial development. It took a further eight years to obtain all the necessary permissions and to overcome local reservations about the development.

Landscaping

Changing the physical shape of the landscape was also a major task at the outset, costing some half a million pounds. All the banks had to be **contoured** and a number of mounds were built to break up the otherwise flat landscape. In areas where activities such as water skiing might create backwash the gradient of the banks was made shallower to reduce this effect. Areas of banking were also built up to provide terraced viewing facilities and a measure of sound-proofing. Once the new land surfaces had been constructed some 40,000 trees and shrubs were planted.

Coping with Extra Traffic

The County Council traffic engineer expressed concern about the potential strain on the local road system. The company decided to contribute over £200,000 towards the building of a new roundabout intended to ease the flow of traffic. They also decided that car parking would be free, thus avoiding long queues of motorists waiting to pay at the entrance.

The cable ski tow

Admission Charges

Thorpe Park opened in 1978, charging a single price on admission. Once inside, visitors would have free access to most attractions, with the exception of the hire of roller skates, tuition in water sports and coin-operated amusements. By 1985 the admission price had been set at £4.50 for adults and £4.00 for children under 14 and senior citizens. Parking was free and there were reductions for parties, the disabled and schools. By 1991 the high season charge for adults was £9.75, for children £8.25 and for senior citizens £8.25. Registered disabled people paid £6.00. Roller skate hire and coin-operated amusements are still the only additional charges for attractions inside. There are reductions of almost £1.00 per person for coach parties of more than 20 and if such **party bookings** are made at least seven days in advance, a further reduction of 50p per person is available.

Shortly after its opening, in 1979, Thorpe Park was presented with the British Tourist Authority's 'Come to Britain' trophy for the best new tourist attraction in the United Kingdom. Since 1983 more than a million people have visited the park each year.

Key terms

contoured – shaped.

party bookings – advanced purchase of tickets for groups, usually at a lower price.

◇ *Exercise* ◇

You are going to plan your own theme park based on the Thorpe Park site. Divide into groups of three or four and study the outline map on the following page, showing the configuration of land and water as it was on the Thorpe Park site during its initial development. Now study the following list of specific developments, each of which has been allocated an approximate cost:

Major rides: £2 million each
Cinema/theatre: £2 million
Restaurants: £250,000 each
Main car park: £200,000
Roller-skating rink: £200,000
Children's rides: £100,000 each
Overflow car park: £100,000
Fast food outlet: £75,000 each
Information centre: £50,000
Rowing boats: £50,000
Conservation area: £25,000
Lost property centre: £20,000
Picnic site: £20,000

Water rides: £2 million each
Ballroom: £2 million
Scenic railway: £250,000
Farm: £250,000
Waterbus: £100,000
Shops: £100,000 each
Toilet block: £100,000
Cafeteria: £75,000
Craft centre: £75,000
Crazy golf: £25,000
Amusement arcade: £20,000
First aid centre: £20,000
Water skiing: £20,000

Roads: £40,000 per inch on the map
Bridges: £20,000 each

MAINTENANCE: 20% of cost for high standard; 10% of cost for moderate standard

UPGRADING FACILITIES: 30% of cost

Year One:
You have a budget of £10 million. Decide what you will develop from the list above and mark *in red* the position on the map where you intend to site each development. You will need to remember the cost of roads and bridges.

Year Two:
You have a budget of £11 million. Decide what additional developments you will sanction and mark these *in blue* on the map. Include the cost of roads, bridges, upgrading, and maintenance.

Year Three:
You have a budget of £12 million. Decide on your new developments for the year and mark these on the map *in black*. Include the cost of roads, bridges, upgrading and maintenance.

Year Four:
Assess the developments your group has planned so far and discuss what your next priorities are. Draw up a budget which includes a convincing explanation of why the company should invest the sum you suggest.

Now compare the proposals of each group. Which was the best development plan?

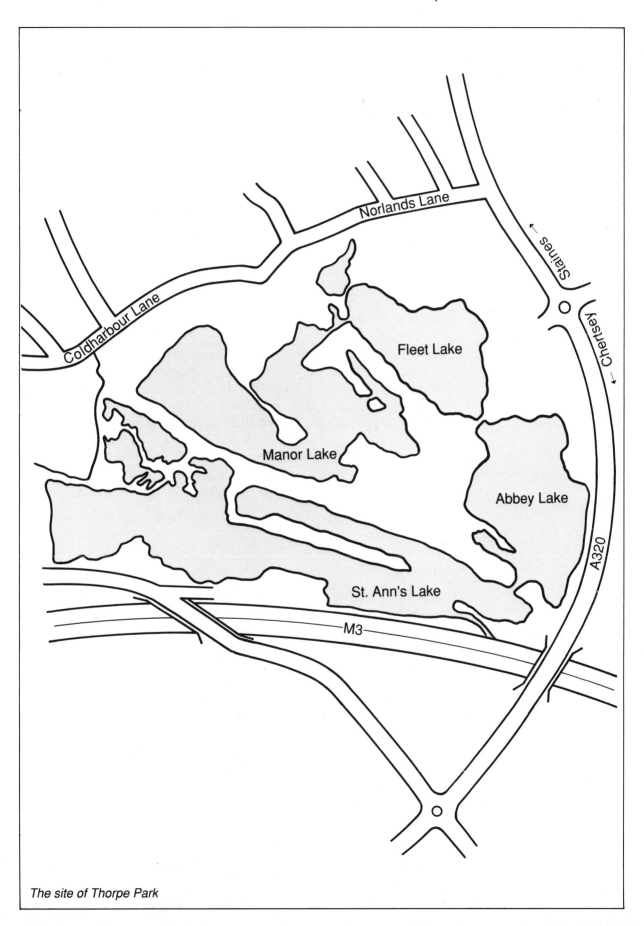

The site of Thorpe Park

Facilities and Attractions

Thorpe Park Farm

Eighty per cent of the visitors to Thorpe Park spend an average of three-quarters of an hour on the farm. Thorpe Park Farm is a working farm carefully designed to accommodate visitors without seriously disrupting daily activity. The use of double gates and flexible fencing which does not obscure vision means that animals can be moved easily without affecting the freedom of movement of visitors. Activities such as sheep dipping, sheep shearing and lambing can be conducted in pens with public access on all sides.

The farm can be considered an educational attraction, particularly for children. There are 15 breeds of sheep, most of which are rare breeds. Children can touch the sheep and judge the differences in the quality of the wool. They can help to weigh the lambs and establish the differences in physique between breeds developed for different purposes. They can see evidence of historical change through explanations about the medieval woollen trade and the more recent breeding of sheep for meat. If an animal is sick it may be isolated in a separate pen with a notice explaining what is wrong and what treatment the animal is receiving.

A collection of old farm machinery has been established in one of the farm's outbuildings. It includes milking machines showing how milk is obtained, cooled, filtered and bottled. The older harvesting machinery must be handled with great care, and two staff are always on hand whenever it is being demonstrated, one to operate the machinery and one to ensure that no-one encroaches beyond the surrounding barrier.

Nature Area

Close to the farm a nature area has been developed through carefully-planned planting of reeds and positioning of nesting boxes. Small islands offer sheltered nesting areas for a variety of ducks, geese and other wildfowl. Boards placed at strategic points around the area enable visitors to identify the birds and find out about the designs of the nesting boxes and the feeding habits of the different species. This area requires careful management. The bird population must be monitored, and sufficient nesting areas provided. Reed beds have been established and the waterside growth of trees and shrubs is controlled to enable suitable viewing points. On a mound of land rising above the area a viewing platform has been constructed, complete with a powerful set of coin-operated binoculars.

Conservation Area

A conservation area was constructed around the edge of one of the lakes. Many areas of marshland in Britain have been drained, significantly reducing the **habitat** of species of birds and animals which favour wetlands. This area introduces children to a waterside habitat and shows them a glimpse of underwater life. There are a number of workbooks available to enable younger children to identify what they see and find out more information about it.

Key term

habitat – usual living place or surroundings.

◇ *Exercise* ◇

The plan to develop the farm as an activity centre is in its early stages. The intention is to offer children an opportunity to participate in activities involving practical skills.

a) List a range of suitable activities. For each activity discuss the following issues:

- whether skilled demonstrators could be acquired easily
- what resources and materials would be needed
- how much space would be needed
- how frequently demonstrations could be provided
- how many participants could be involved at any one time
- what cost implications there would be in employing demonstrators
- what safety precautions would be needed
- whether protective clothing would be needed and could be available in a range of sizes.

b) Draw up a timetable for a week's activities.

Model World

Model World consists of a collection of famous buildings, all constructed on a scale of 1:36. Twenty-two of these models occupy a one-acre site and they include well-known buildings such as the Taj Mahal and the Leaning Tower of Pisa. Model World puts the scale of these constructions into an interesting perspective. Given that the height of most observers of these models would be under two inches if they were reduced to the same scale, the model of Toronto's CN Tower, standing at over 50 feet, seems very imposing.

Entertainments

Exciting rides remain the most obvious attractions for crowds in many leisure parks. Those at Thorpe Park include a log flume ride, a family roller-coaster, a train ride, waterbus trips and a number of themed rides intended to offer thrills and excitement. A similar intention lies behind Cinema 180, a domed building containing a 180-degree screen. The audience stand, almost surrounded by the visual images which feature American roller-coaster rides, car chases and panoramic mountain scenery.

Activities on the Water

Each of the five main lakes at Thorpe Park is allocated to a particular sporting or public boating activity. Water skiing is available in the remotest of the water areas, lessening the likelihood of the noise becoming a nuisance. An electrically-driven cable system, installed in 1983, increased water-ski use through its ability to carry up to eight skiers at a time. However, the space and equipment required means that many water sports are still not very profitable and so, with the exception of some wind-surfing, water sport activities have now been **franchised** out to a company who pay rent for the use of the water and the facilities.

The Thunder River ride at Thorpe Park

Retail Outlets

Income is also derived from the sale of souvenirs, some of them relating to Thorpe Park in general and others relating to particular areas of the Park, such as the farm. This has two retail centres, a shop and a craft centre. The craft centre houses facilities for a number of people to demonstrate pottery, spinning, basket-making, macramé, wood-carving, and doll-making.

There are eleven major food outlets within the Park, including a riverboat restaurant, a pizza bar, a burger restaurant, a pub and a French café. They include both waitress service and self-service operations, so that visitors can choose quick snacks or more leisurely meals.

New Attractions

Each year new attractions are introduced. 1990 saw the appearance of a new ride, the Flying Fish roller-coaster. A new under-cover family entertainment area, complete with a double-decker illuminated carousel ride, was completed and a new show for younger visitors, featuring animal characters from Thorpe Park's television commercials, was developed.

The Flying Fish roller-coaster

Key term

to franchise – to give sole rights to a company to sell goods or services in a particular place.

◇ *Exercise* ◇

In addition to its permanent attractions, Thorpe Park has in the past promoted a number of special events. These were felt to be necessary to increase the visitors' sense of value for money when there were fewer attractions than there are now. They included:

♦ a sea-plane taking off
♦ a jousting competition
♦ show-jumping events
♦ the mock staging of Roman gladiators in combat
♦ an antiques fair
♦ an airship display

♦ an open-air drama production
♦ water-ski championships
♦ a marching band performance.

Choose a special event which you think would fit in well with the site and the themes now featured at Thorpe Park. List the details which would have to be planned in advance of the event.

Plan the outline of a single-page leaflet to be distributed in major shopping centres in London and the South-East, drawing attention to your special event.

Staff and Training

All new staff at Thorpe Park work under a supervisor. They are each given a booklet to read, introducing them to their role within the Park. The booklet emphasises the four things expected of each employee – safety, courtesy, efficiency and a smart appearance.

Safety

Safety has to be a high priority in a leisure park. Each employee receives a copy of a *Terms and Conditions of Employment* manual, which includes a safety policy. This policy stresses both safe working conditions for employees and the safety of visitors. Care over the use and maintenance of all machinery is regarded as vital. Individual workers are encouraged to keep themselves and their own work areas clean, tidy and free of hazards. Staff at most points of the Thorpe Park site are in radio contact with Security, so can draw their attention swiftly to any fire alert or first aid emergency. There are well-defined procedures in case of fire or bomb alerts.

A member of the Thorpe Park staff using two-way radio

Security

Thorpe Park is a large site attracting many visitors and so all staff have to be made aware of security issues. This may simply be a matter of knowing where to report such things as theft or damage or being responsible for lost property until it has been handed in at the official Information Point. While on duty staff must always carry a security pass which enables them to obtain such things as uniforms and locker keys.

Courtesy

Staff receive training in visitor service before they actually start work. The emphasis is on courtesy, especially in situations where the visitors may have been kept waiting or where they may have a complaint. The open nature of a leisure park's site means that most staff activity is very visible. Employees are encouraged to help visitors with any problems and, in particular, to be aware of those who may need special help such as young children and older or disabled visitors.

◇ Exercise ◇

The following letter has been received by the Customer Relations Department at Thorpe Park. Write what you consider to be a tactful reply.

> 3 Acacia Drive
> Swindon
>
> 27th June
>
> Dear Sir/Madam,
>
> My wife and I and our two young children spent a day at Thorpe Park on Wednesday June 20th.
>
> Though we had a very pleasant morning, the afternoon was ruined by the fact that my wife's handbag was stolen while we had lunch in the burger restaurant. We didn't discover it was gone until we'd finished eating. A member of staff in the restaurant sent us to the Lost Property place, but of course they hadn't seen it. We left our name and address.
>
> I am writing this because I think there would be less chance of this sort of thing happening if you had more uniformed security guards all round the park, so that people could see them frequently. You could also have some large notices put up warning people about thieves and pickpockets. This would put the thieves off and make people feel more safe.
>
> I would like to hear from you about what kind of action you intend to take on this matter.
>
> Yours faithfully,
>
> Ian Davis

Efficiency

As Thorpe Park may receive up to 18,000 visitors a day, efficiency is crucial if people are going to enjoy themselves. The Park is open seven days a week in the summer, which means that all staff can expect to work on some weekends and bank holidays. Employees are responsible for checking the hours they are due to work each week. Successful communication between staff is necessary in fostering a good atmosphere and maintaining efficiency. A fortnightly paper, *Thorpe Park People*, provides news, information, gossip and details of social events. Notice boards are also used to give announcements about safety and working conditions.

Staff structure at Thorpe Park

DIRECTOR/GENERAL MANAGER

HEAD OF ADMINISTRATION	HEAD OF SALES AND MARKETING	HEAD OF OPERATIONS
● *Training/Personnel – Manager*	● *Corporate Sales*	● *Engineering – Manager*
● *Nursery*	● *Public Relations*	● *Rides and Attractions*
● *Bookings and Enquiries/Admissions*	● *Advertising*	● *Maintenance/Cleaning*
● *Turnstiles/Information Points*	● *Promotional Activities*	● *Retail – Manager*
● *Accounts and Office Management*	● *Research and Surveys*	● *Shops*
● *Wardrobe*		● *Restaurants*
● *Security*		● *Landscape – Manager*
● *Audit*		● *Entertainments – Manager*
● *Bank*		● *Farm – Manager*

Appearance

Appearance is also regarded as important and advice is offered to new recruits about being smart, appropriate hairstyles, the wearing of jewellery, and personal cleanliness. The rules about clothing and appearance are quite detailed because it is felt that the visitors attach great importance to this.

Qualifications and Career Prospects

Thorpe Park has a workforce of almost 1,000, a high proportion of whom are young people. In order to make a career in leisure seem more attractive to young people, Thorpe Park has joined with Lackham College in Wiltshire to offer a new course in Leisure Attraction Management, involving a wide range of studies including administration, catering, retailing, maintenance, conservation and visitor care.

◇ *Exercise* ◇

Five students made the following comments while being shown around Lackham College before an interview for admission to the course in Leisure Attraction Management.

'I went to work in a library when I left school. I like reading but I found the job rather uninteresting. It was repetitive and I didn't learn any new skills. I'd like to do something which is more lively, but where I feel I can also personally achieve something. Though you met a lot of people coming into the library, you didn't get much chance to chat to them.'

Helen Tanner, 18

'I did well at school but I didn't really know what I wanted to do. I worked in a travel agency but they moved and it was a bit far to travel. I've since had a job with the local authority, an office job. I organise all the social activities, like outings and parties, and I've done some voluntary work in the middle school where my mum works, including organising a Christmas pantomime for the local community centre.'

Pervez Shah, 20

'I want to work in the open air. I like working on cars and other kinds of machinery. I thought about working in a garage but I went to one on work experience and I didn't like it much. My dad thinks I ought to get a good qualification before I decide what to do.'

Daniel Cross, 16

'I'm mad about sport, especially swimming and tennis. I've represented the county at swimming and I think, if I practised hard, I could just get into the national squad in the coming year. I'm good at maths and thought about being an accountant, but really I'd like to do something that's connected with my sporting interests.'

Martine Verney, 16

'Now that my children are old enough to look after themselves I feel it's time to decide how I want to spend the rest of my life. I worked in a shop when I was young but that's not enough. I did do some 'O' levels at evening class but that was more for fun than because I knew what I wanted to do. The newspapers keep saying tourism and leisure are the major employers of the future so it seemed sensible to look for a qualification in those areas. I think that the more experienced you are in life, the better you are at dealing with other people and their problems.'

Rosa McMichael, 40

You are now going to interview these people. Devise ten different questions (two for each applicant) which you will ask.

Divide into groups of three or four, each group representing a panel with the task of deciding which applicants to admit to the course. Role-play the interview.

Which two of the five candidates would you be mostly likely to accept?

The Future of Leisure Parks

Thorpe Park, like most attractions within easy reach of London, faces growing competition. Chessington World of Adventures is only a short journey away, round the M25. Originally a zoo, its owners, the Tussauds group, invested more than £10 million to improve existing attractions and to add new rides and better catering and retail facilities. Competition also comes from further afield as many families wanting a day out opt to spend a day at the seaside, at a historic country house or at a museum. As the competition for visitors grows, so marketing becomes more competitive and absorbs a higher percentage of income. Many leisure parks now spend between 7 and 15 per cent of their annual **turnover** on marketing.

Indoor Entertainment

The weather is a major factor affecting attendance at leisure parks. A high proportion of attractions are in the open air, which creates obvious difficulties on wet days. Leisure holiday centres such as Center Parcs have shown that technology can be used to overcome this problem, but there is a high investment cost involved. Attractions like the Jorvik Centre in York and The Tales of Sherwood Forest use models and an array of sound and visual technology to provide indoor entertainment which leisure parks may seek to imitate. The Cinema 180 at Thorpe Park is an example of an indoor entertainment which simulates some of the excitement of **'white knuckle' rides**, and such simulation techniques will no doubt grow in sophistication.

Cinema 180

Investment Priorities

If leisure parks are to maintain their current popularity they will have to decide whether their priority is to maintain a high standard of service within the scope of their existing attractions or whether they should pursue a policy which enables regular changes and additions to available attractions. Success will depend on getting the balance right.

Site Limitations

Whether leisure parks are able to change rapidly may in part depend on the nature and size of the sites they occupy. There is a physical limit to the number of visitors who can be admitted, and if queues form for the most popular attractions, visitors may become dissatisfied and less inclined to make return visits.

New Theme Parks

For any new park to be successful it would need a mixture of attractions. It would have to be located within two hours' drive of several major areas of population and be easily accessible from motorways or major trunk roads. Advertising on regional television or through direct mail would be important in areas where there are close major competitors. A variety of databases would be used to provide the addresses of likely visitors. It would also be vital to establish the right identity for a new park. Finally, the site would have to be in an area which could supply enthusiastic and committed staff.

Key terms

turnover – total incoming money (obtained from admission charges and retailing activities).

'white knuckle' rides – rides involving frightening changes of height, speed and direction.

◇ *Exercise* ◇

Information about visitors to Thorpe Park is very useful in planning for the future. However, many visitors do not wish to interrupt their day in order to fill in lengthy surveys and, of course, once they have returned home the likelihood of them responding to questionnaires lessens.

The management of the Park have asked you to devise a way of acquiring and storing useful information from visitors without the process becoming an irritation to them. Technological hardware will be available if necessary.

You will need to take into account the type of information which would be most useful and decide whether to record opinions as well as fact. The method of storing this information will have to be determined by whether the information needs analysing, and how rapidly it needs to be accessed.

You decide to write a brief report to the management with your conclusions.

◇ *Discussion points* ◇

1 What do you consider to be a reasonable sum to spend on a day out, and what proportion of this might you spend on food and souvenirs?

2 What elements in a television advertisement would be most likely to encourage *you* to visit a tourist attraction?

3 Do fairgrounds and theme parks spoil the surrounding landscape?

4 Should nature areas such as the one at Thorpe Park be managed and cultivated, or left to grow wild?

5 Do you think souvenirs serve a genuinely useful purpose?

6 Why do you think 'white knuckle' rides are so popular?

5 Ironbridge – An Industrial Heritage Site

Introduction

Many manufacturing industries in Britain have declined during the twentieth century. As factories and mills closed, so buildings and **artefacts** remained as reminders of a former way of life. Local authorities in areas once dependent on single industries, such as coal mining, saw the opportunity of using an apparent nostalgia for a disappearing world to attract visitors. Former dockyard offices, factories and warehouses have been converted to museums concentrating on the industrial past. These are called industrial heritage sites or museums.

Traditional methods of exhibiting items of interest, in display cases, have been used alongside other methods bringing the past back to life. Models, films and video technology are sometimes used. Some museums employ people, sometimes dressed in period costume, to give demonstrations of former industrial processes.

Open-air sites have proved popular because they enable the larger, more spectacular engines and methods of transport to be exhibited in working order. Sometimes old buildings are dismantled and moved to the site in order to enhance the sense of the period.

Britain's Industrial Past

Britain was the first industrial nation in the world. For two centuries its society and landscape have been affected by industrial activities. The nature of industries such as cotton and wool led to the construction of mills, often on a very large scale. Factories and mines required increasingly powerful machinery. Transport systems of all kinds were essential for the supply of resources and the delivery of manufactured products.

The Industrial Revolution brought many changes to Britain in the latter part of the eighteenth century and the early part of the nineteenth century. The use of new power to drive the machines which were already speeding up spinning and weaving processes created a large demand for coal and iron. Wooden machines, operated by hand or by animals, and later by water power, were replaced by steam-driven machinery. Coal became important both because it was needed to generate steam power and also because it was used in the **smelting** of iron.

The Pennines and Derbyshire attracted the early **textile** industry because of the fast-running streams which could be used to power machinery by means of mill wheels. However, the arrival of steam power meant that many of the mills moved closer to the coalfields. Steam power had been used to pump water from the mines and in 1782 James Watt invented a steam engine with a **rotary** movement which meant that it could be used for a much wider range of industrial purposes.

The Importance of the Ironbridge Area

Iron was worked at Coalbrookdale in the early sixteenth century and it had been made in small quantities for many centuries before that. However, it was Abraham Darby's use of coke rather than the traditional charcoal to smelt iron which radically changed the scale of iron production and the variety of its uses. A network of canals was constructed in the north of England to bring together the major sources of coal and iron. The speed of change in this period is evidenced by the fact that the output of iron rose from 250,000 tons in 1800 to four times that amount in 1835. Likewise, the production of coal quadrupled between 1770 and 1830. The consumers of all this coal and iron included the textile industry, the manufacturers of pottery and hardware, and, of course, bridge builders.

The Iron Bridge

Key terms

artefacts – objects which people make, often by hand.

smelting – melting so that the iron is separated from the ore.

textile – woven fabric and products from it.

rotary – turning like a wheel.

◇ *Exercise* ◇

A small woollen mill in North Wales has been manufacturing woollen products for about 150 years. Read the information below from a leaflet about the mill and describe what it suggests would be the main benefits of visiting the mill.

The mill is set in the heart of the countryside between the entrances to two beautiful valleys, **Cwm Cynog**, wild and unspoilt, and **Cwm Beris** with its reservoir, the source of the river **Clydd** which has provided water to turn the mill wheel for centuries.

The mill was originally a corn mill and about 150 years ago was converted to woollen manufacture by ancestors of the present owners. Since then it has been in continuous production and in recent times much modernised and enlarged. The water wheel can still be seen turning although its power is no longer utilised. The available water is now used to generate electricity by means of a turbine and altenator and this is supplemented by mains electricity.

While at the mill visitors can view at their leisure the complicated machinery used viz: Tenterhook Willey, Carders, Spinning Mules, Doubling and Hanking Machines, Cheese and Bobbin Winder, Warping Mill and the Looms on which the fabrics are woven, and then browse in the spacious shop to appreciate the finished products of which we are justly proud.

If you are looking for something genuine to take home as a gift or a souvenir of Wales, the mill shop is the ideal place to buy. All the woollen products on sale here have been carded, spun and woven on the premises from Pure New Wool. You will be pleasantly surprised by the wide variety of items on sale - probably the largest selection of Welsh woollens in the whole of Wales.

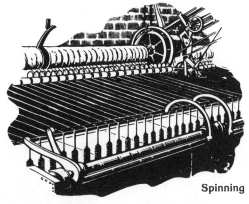

Spinning

Here is an opportunity you should not miss to see for yourself the fascinating processes involved in the making of our exclusive woollens.

Weaving

The Economics of Running a Site or Museum

Museums as popular as Ironbridge, which attracts over 350,000 visitors a year, require a large number of staff. Wages and salaries are always a major cost in a labour-intensive operation. In a situation where annually both receipts from ticket sales and the wages and salaries bill are likely to exceed £1 million, a high degree of financial expertise is needed.

Many museums are **subsidised**, sometimes by local authorities and sometimes by local companies. Other funds may be raised by social events, by business membership schemes, and by **covenanted** gifts which provide an annual income for the museum. Industrial heritage sites are increasingly exploiting their distinctive environments to attract conferences, meetings, dinners and other income-generating events.

Income and Expenditure

Most museums charge for admission, and so they must employ people to collect, count and bank the money. Retail and catering facilities also provide income in most museums. Acquiring, cleaning and preparing exhibits for display will involve employing highly-skilled people, often for an extended period of time.

New Projects

In order to remain attractive both to new and repeat visitors, most museums aim to complete new projects each year. These will require capital expenditure. An idea of the level of investment which may be involved can be drawn from the list below, which shows the major capital projects at Ironbridge in 1989:

Blists Hill Victorian School	£25,000
Blists Hill Estate Office	£35,000
Blists Hill Ironworks	£25,000
Spry (river vessel)	£20,000
Jackfield Tile Museum	£15,000
Quaker Houses	£30,000
Museum of the River	£155,000
Other exhibits	£30,000
Demountable Classrooms	£30,000
New Stores	£10,000
New Tourist Information Centre	£15,000

The Jackfield Tile Museum

Key terms

subsidised – receiving a grant of money to support the organisation or one of its activities.

covenant – an agreement to make a regular payment, often to a charitable organisation.

◇ *Exercise* ◇

Look carefully at the ticket information below:

TICKET INFORMATION
Effective from 1 January 1991. All information is subject to change without notice.

PASSPORT TICKETS
Passport tickets offer excellent value for money. They give admission to all of the Museum sites. You can visit the sites in any order and at any time in the future until you have visited them all once:

Adult	**£6.95**
Child/Student	**£4.50**
Family	**£20.00**
(2 adults and up to 5 children)	
Senior Citizen	**£5.95**

SINGLE SITE TICKETS
Single site tickets are also available, but it is always cheaper to buy a passport if you are visiting other sites now or at any time in the future.

	Adult	**Child/ Student**	**O.A.P.**
Blists Hill Open Air Museum	£5.00	£3.30	£4.25
Coalport China Museum	£2.75	£1.65	£2.20
Museum of Iron	£2.75	£1.65	£2.20
Jackfield Tile Museum	£2.75	£1.65	£2.20
Rosehill House	£1.75	£1.45	£1.75
Museum of the River	£1.75	£1.45	£1.75
Tar Tunnel	£0.75	£0.50	£0.75

Group discounts for parties of 20 or more. Group discounts are only available on party tickets. Non-student party discounts:

> 30% Winter discount .... 1 Jan to 29 March
> 20% Spring discount .... 30 March to 30 April
> 10% Summer discount .... 1 May to 31 August
> 20% Autumn discount .... 1 Sept to 31 Oct

1 How much would each of the following visits cost altogether:

a) a couple from overseas wishing to make a single visit to the Jackfield Tile Museum and the Museum of the River only?

b) a party of two adults and 20 children wishing to visit all the sites in high season?

c) two families and a senior citizen requiring passport tickets?

d) a coach party of 45 senior citizens wishing to visit Blists Hill Open Air Museum in low season?

2 In what way do the prices encourage party visits to be spread throughout the year?

Marketing and Public Relations

Museums which are frequently in the public eye are more likely to attract funding. A museum like Ironbridge has the advantage of appealing to photographers and film makers, because of its authentic and dramatic setting. This means that in addition to direct coverage of events and developments at the museum's various sites, there may be photographic features in newspapers and magazines, and fictional television dramas. Press coverage may also come indirectly through advertising campaigns for products such as cars, where unusual visual backgrounds are popular.

Patronage

A patron is someone who agrees to represent the interests of an organisation on public occasions. If a museum can secure a famous person as its patron, this will generate greater publicity. The fact that the Prince of Wales is the patron of the Ironbridge Museum ensures local and national coverage on occasions such as his visit to the Museum of the River when he gave it its official opening.

Visitor Surveys

A museum might try to assess its relationship with the public by carrying out visitor surveys. These may help to establish the popularity of particular exhibits or whether visitors are satisfied with services such as transport or catering. The results may help future planning, particularly in determining how much to invest in new developments, and what is needed to sustain and improve existing attractions and services. They may also indicate how to promote the most successful sections of the museum.

Special Events

Visits and special events form an important part of many museums' public relations operations. Politicians, journalists, professional groups and tour operators from home and overseas may be invited to visit. Events such as lectures, conferences and dinners may also help to raise the public profile of a museum.

◊ *Exercise* ◊

Look at the two pie diagrams below.

Where visitors to Ironbridge come from

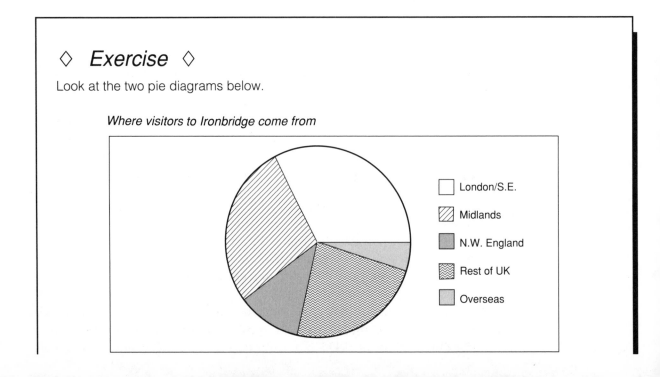

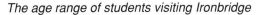

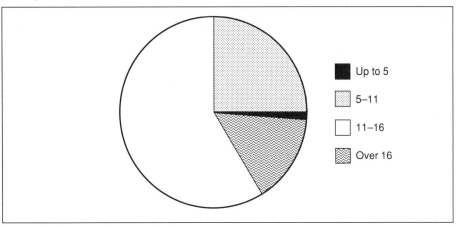

1 What reasons can you find for:

a) the proportion of visitors arriving from the different regions?

b) the proportion of students in each age group visiting the museum?

2 a) If the Marketing Department decided that these pie charts showed that Ironbridge was not very well known in the North-West, particularly among 5 to 11 year-olds, what suggestions might they come up with to counter this trend?

b) Which of these suggestions do you think would make the most impact, and can you think of reasons why some would be more practical than others?

Historical Research

Giving an accurate picture of what life was like in the past needs careful research. People can be trained to deliver a memorised talk about Victorian times and can be dressed in Victorian clothing, but they should also be able to answer the questions visitors are bound to ask.

Heritage sites also rely on research to improve their ability to conserve and manage monuments and collections of artefacts, and to record relevant historical information. Effective research is not only dependent on the skills of the researcher, but also requires a broad range of resources, including books, trade catalogues, photographs, paintings, plans and drawings.

In 1978 the Ironbridge Institute was founded to organise research and courses on industrial history and archaeology. This was a joint venture between the museum and Birmingham University.

Heritage Management Skills

A heritage site needs expert staff to advise on how the site and site buildings and exhibits are to be preserved. This is not always an easy task in a museum which receives thousands of visitors each year.

Consideration must also be given to the most interesting ways of recording and interpreting surviving remains. Useful skills include the ability to draw and **survey** buildings, and to interpret old maps and documents.

Key term

to survey – examine the structure of buildings.

◇ *Exercise* ◇

Imagine the house or flat in which you live is excavated 200 years in the future. As it is one of the few surviving examples of twentieth-century domestic architecture, it is decided to turn it into a visitor attraction showing how twentieth-century technology affected life in the home.

The developers decide that visitors would be most interested in twentieth-century methods of transmitting information and images.

Prepare a series of notes and sketches showing how the visitors' experience might be organised in any single room. You will need to consider the following:
- which aspects of technology are to be included
- what basic principles need explanation
- what means of presentation are to be used
- how visitors to the site are to be managed.

Origin and Brief History of the Ironbridge Gorge Museum

Long before the existence of the museum, the Iron Bridge drew visitors from far beyond the immediate locality. It was the best-known feature of the Coalbrookdale area. As the world's first iron bridge, it also became a symbol of the Industrial Revolution.

By the 1950s the furnace where the iron for the bridge had been made was buried under the debris of more than 130 years of disuse. However, in 1959, Allied Ironfounders Limited, the owners of the site at that time, decided to uncover the furnace in order to mark the 250th anniversary of Abraham Darby's discovery of coke smelting. A small collection of Coalbrookdale products was displayed in a nearby building, acting as a forerunner to the Museum of Iron, which opened in 1979. In 1982 a roof covering was built and the enclosed furnace was further developed as a visitor attraction by the addition of a taped commentary and sound and light effects.

Today's Range of Attractions

Today the Ironbridge Gorge Museum is a collective title for an area which encompasses a collection of museums and sites of interest.

The Furnace and the Museum of Iron

The Coalbrookdale Furnace and the Museum of Iron are important because they illustrate the beginnings of a process which completely changed our technology and our way of life, namely the use of coke in iron smelting.

The Museum of Iron occupies the Great Warehouse, once used for the storage of **castings** to be despatched to the Severn Warehouse and then transported down the river. The museum contains exhibits made at Coalbrookdale including pots, art castings and a small saddle-tank steam locomotive. The history of iron-making from the Iron Age to the mid-nineteenth century is brought to life with illustrations of the techniques used.

An exhibit from the Museum of Iron

In addition to a sound and light programme in the Old Furnace, there are displays, exhibits and models. There is a full-sized replica of an Iron Age furnace known as a 'bloomery' and a reconstruction of a blacksmith's shop. A range of books, guides and leaflets give detailed background information about the site and its history.

Key term

castings – shapes made by pouring molten iron into moulds.

◇ *Exercise* ◇

Prepare a short introductory talk to be given by a guide accompanying a coach party of American tourists as they are approaching Ironbridge. You will find reference books giving information about the development of iron production in Coalbrookdale useful.

Blists Hill Open Air Museum

Blists Hill Open Air Museum is the largest of the sites of interest at Ironbridge, covering 50 acres. It was opened in 1973 and contains the only wrought ironworks in the western world, as well as carefully rebuilt and restored examples of Victorian shops, offices and houses.

Blists Hill itself was originally the site of several coal mines established in the late eighteenth century. Between 1791 and 1793 the Shropshire Canal was constructed along the edge of the hill and the Hay Inclined Plane was built to link the canal with the River Severn via the Coalport Canal. Blast furnaces were built between 1830 and 1840 and a brick and tile works was added in 1851. Much of the industrial activity was over by the beginning of the First World War, by which time both the blast furnaces and the canal had been closed.

Among the many examples of the region's industrial past, the engine house of the Blists Hill mine is striking. A working steam engine winds a cage up and down a shaft while the driver explains to visitors both the workings of the steam engine and also the safety procedures which were essential. In the foundry visitors can watch iron being melted and poured into sand moulds to make castings. The ironworks show the technique of puddling, a method of forging wrought iron developed in the late eighteenth century. It was a vital process since the structure of wrought iron enabled it to be hammered, stretched or rolled while at the same time retaining much of its strength.

The High Street at Blists Hill

Other Victorian buildings have been brought to Blists Hill and reassembled to recreate town life at the end of the last century. The High Street contains a printing shop, a cobbler's, an inn, a candle factory, a butcher's shop, a chemist, a locksmith's, a blacksmith's forge, a bank and a sawmill. The experience is reinforced by the Victorian dress of the staff working in this part of the museum and by the regular demonstrations of the crafts in common use a hundred years ago. In the

The chemist's shop,
Blists Hill

candle factory, for example, the process and the machinery is as it was in 1850. The candles, used in huge quantities in the mines, were made from tallow rendered down from animal fat obtained from butchers. The chemist's shop shows how people who could not afford doctors' fees would seek advice and medicines elsewhere. There was a great variety of ready-made, or patent medicines available, while special mixtures could be made up from ingredients stored in the shop. Sometimes the chemist also acted as a dentist and optician.

Transport Links

The site is covered by a network of plateways, primitive railways along which wagons could be hauled. Before the advent of the railways, the Shropshire Canal provided the main means of moving goods. Wooden tub boats, measuring about 20 feet by 6 feet, were pulled by horses. The Hay Inclined Plane enabled a pair of boats loaded to a weight of five or six tons to move up or down the 207-foot incline separating the canal at Blists Hill from the Coalport Canal which ran parallel to the River Severn. This only took about three and a half minutes.

◇ *Exercise* ◇

Look carefully at the diagram of the Hay Inclined Plane. Although it is not marked on the diagram, a steam engine could be used to turn the winding drum.

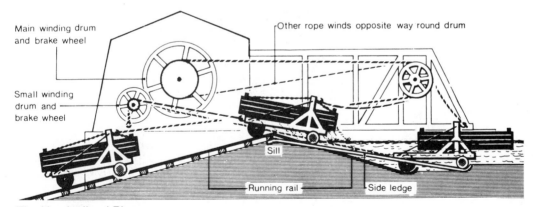

The Hay Inclined Plane

Write an explanation of how the Inclined Plane worked which you think could be understood by a 7 year-old visitor to Ironbridge.

The Jackfield Tile Museum

This museum occupies the original premises of the Craven Dunnill tile works which were founded in 1871. The area around Ironbridge was rich in high-quality clays essential for tile-making. Coal for firing the kilns was also available locally, and the industry expanded rapidly as decorative tiles became fashionable. They were used for floors, shop counters, the front of public buildings and as decorative backgrounds to washstands. The museum shows the processes involved in making tiles.

Originally the tiles were made in buff and red clay and modelled on medieval designs. Later up to six colours were used and the designs became more complex. Glazed tiles were commonly hand-painted and used to decorate fireplaces. The museum contains many colourful examples of tiles, including large patterns made up from many different individually-numbered single tiles. These were popular as floor designs in large public buildings.

◇ *Exercise* ◇

Look at the pattern on the four decorative tiles below:

a) Are the four tiles identical?

b) How many ways can you find of dividing the whole four-tile panel into identical sections?

c) The tiles are numbered. If they were reassembled differently, which of the following arrangements would give an alternative pattern?

2	3
4	1

4	2
3	1

3	4
2	1

d) Use squared paper to sketch a tile design in which four identical tiles would create a single repeatable pattern.

The Iron Bridge

The Iron Bridge itself has attracted visitors since it was first opened to traffic in 1781. Before its construction heavy goods such as limestone and iron ore had to be ferried across the river or taken to bridges some distance away.

The construction of the bridge presented a number of technical problems. The steeply-rising sides of the gorge and the volume of barge traffic on the River Severn meant that a single span construction was essential. The success of the final design was due as much to the practical skills of the iron-founders as it was to the bridge's designer, Thomas Pritchard. The cost of erecting the bridge amounted to over £2,700.

The original users of the bridge had to pay a toll which varied from one halfpenny for each foot passenger to two shillings for a coach large enough to require six horses to pull it. The tollhouse displays the original table of tolls and houses a display about the building of the bridge.

The Coalport China Museum

China and porcelain were manufactured in Coalport from the 1770s until the company manufacturing them moved to Stoke-on-Trent in 1926. Coal and clay were readily available locally, though porcelain required the importing of Cornish china clay by river. A number of innovations originated from Coalport, including the use of feldspar rather than lead, which was a serious health hazard, in the glazing process. The products of Coalport achieved an international reputation, winning a gold medal at the Great Exhibition of 1851 and commissions from European royal households.

*The Coalport China
Museum*

The Coalport Museum exhibits a variety of china and features kilns and workshops. On the wall an illustrated dictionary explains the terminology used in the processes of porcelain production. An audio-visual programme describes the life of the china works at the beginning of the century. The history of ceramics in the Severn Gorge is illustrated by a chart which shows the parallel chronological history of the Coalport Company, of other clay industries in the Gorge, and of events in other parts of the world.

The Museum of the River

This is the most recent museum to be opened, in 1989. Here a 12-metre model of the Severn Gorge as it was in 1796 shows in detail where the greatest concentrations of industrial activity were, and how the various transport networks connected them. The River Severn was navigable for some 160 miles from the sea to Pool Quay near Welshpool. Below Gloucester the river became tidal and so larger craft were needed for shipments beyond. A variety of wooden vessels was used and an example of one of the larger vessels, known as a trow, is currently being restored at Blists Hill.

◇ *Exercise* ◇

The Spry, the last known Severn trow which is in a restorable condition, is being rebuilt to as near her original sailing condition as possible by the Upper Severn Navigation Trust, which is part of the museum.

Once the Spry has been fully restored, it will be moved from Blists Hill to a situation in or alongside the River Severn.

Draw up a list of ideas which you think would enable the Trust to use The Spry most effectively to fulfil their aim of showing the historical significance of Severn navigation.

Other Places of Interest in the Area

Rosehill House, built in the eighteenth century and lived in by the youngest son of the builder of the Iron Bridge, illustrates how the Quaker ironmasters lived during the early part of the nineteenth century. In the Long Warehouse there is an art gallery and a library, while along the river in the direction of Coalport is a tunnel from which natural bitumen was extracted between 1786 and 1843. The bitumen was boiled to make pitch and used in the same way as tar.

Awards

The Ironbridge Gorge Museum was the winner of the first Museum of the Year Award in 1977 and followed this with the first European Museum of the Year Award the year after. Awards sponsored by the AA, by *Which?* magazine, and by *The Times*/Shell plc have been won in recent years. In 1987 UNESCO designated the whole of the Ironbridge Gorge a World Heritage Site, thus recognising its importance in tracing the development of European social and economic history.

The Museum Trust

The Museum Trust was established in 1967, with the task of restoring, preserving and interpreting the monuments at Ironbridge. Aid came from the Telford Development Corporation, set up to implement the establishment of neighbouring Telford as a new town. As an educational charity the Trust has sought and achieved industrial sponsorship through its Development Trust, set up in 1971. It also receives donations and grants from other charitable and educational trusts, all of which enable new development to continue. Some companies who support the museum offer funds to enable specific projects to be completed, often relating to the company's own activities. Thus GKN, a major iron and steel producer, and National Vulcan, boiler makers, have both supported a scheme to build a replica of the first steam railway locomotive, 'The Trevithick'.

◇ *Exercise* ◇

Study the map of the Ironbridge area on the following page.

The museum sites are open from 10 a.m. to 5 p.m. in the summer, during which time a museum bus service is provided.

Divide into groups of three or four and discuss what evidence you would need and how you could collect it in order to make the following decisions:

a) whether it would be better to use 50-seater coaches, smaller 25-seater buses, 13-seater minibuses or a combination of these

b) which places would be the most suitable starting points for a park and ride service and what facilities would be needed there

c) what routes the buses should follow

d) how frequently services would be needed

e) where, at peak times, the densest traffic would occur and whether there were any ways of avoiding this.

The Future for the Ironbridge Gorge Museum

Government economic and environmental policies are certain to affect the future of industrial heritage sites. Maintaining public interest may well depend on the capacity of individual sites to continue to fund new developments. Many of Ironbridge's **administrative**, repair and maintenance costs have been met in the past by government money paid through Telford Development Corporation. This support is to continue via a one-off Department of the Environment endowment.

Telford Town Centre M54 & M6

Shifnal Wolverhampton (A464 T)

Coppice Farm roundabout

A4169

Halesfield roundabout

Brockton roundabout

A442

A442 Bridgnorth Kidderminster

Sutton Hill roundabout

Camping Site

Cuckoo Oak roundabout

Madeley roundabout

Wellington B4373

Woodside roundabout

Lees Farm roundabout

Castlefields roundabout

A4169

Wellington A4169

St. Michael's Church

Entrance

Blists Hill Open Air Museum

Hay Inclined Plane

Tar Tunnel

Coalport China Museum

Coalport Bridge

River Severn

Camping Site

Jackfield Footbridge

Jackfield Tile Museum

B4373

Broseley

Bedlam Furnaces

The Free Bridge

Quaker Burial Ground

Rosehill House
Old Furnace
Museum of Iron

Carpenters Row

Long Warehouse (Elton Gallery)

Educational Resources Centre

Ironbridge Gorge Youth Hostel & Walker Study Centre

Rose Cottages
Greenwood Trust

Museum Visitor Centre

Limekilns

Shop in the Square

Museum Offices

The Iron Bridge & Tollhouse

Information Centre

Shrewsbury B4380

Ironbridge Power Station

River Severn

Scale

0   0.5   1

Miles

Map of the Ironbridge area

Government schemes to support job training may affect the number of new employees which a heritage site can afford to take on.

Renovation

The nature of industrial heritage sites means that the buildings, equipment and workings are often in need of considerable renovation. In areas where there has been a lot of mining there is the additional problem that the ground may be unstable. Blists Hill suffered a landslip in 1988 and a number of buildings had to be dismantled and relocated, while one was lost completely.

Adding new Attractions

Industrial heritage sites benefit from added features of interest. A replica of the 1802 Trevithick Steam Locomotive was recently built for the Ironbridge Gorge Museum. Yet such new developments are of limited value if the **infrastructure** to support additional visitors is not developed at the same time. This means considering car parking facilities, catering services, and those with particular needs such as families with small babies and visitors in wheelchairs. In the case of the locomotive it is important to assess the most effective way of explaining how it works, both in terms of presentation and of cost.

Changes in Visitor Patterns

Changes in the economic situation may lead to more people taking domestic holidays, especially short breaks. Traffic jams and airport delays may encourage more people to think of taking out-of-season holidays. If the weather is bad, they will seek interesting places to visit. These factors will help to determine how long places like Ironbridge close down in the winter. A longer season may well bring more visitors, but it also raises staffing costs and may increase other costs such as cleaning, heating and path maintenance.

Skilled Labour

The heritage movement in general has often depended on volunteers. Heritage sites need to be able to recruit skilled people to research the industrial skills and techniques employed in the past and to develop interesting and appropriate methods of presenting this information.

The Local Community

The extent of individual heritage development will also be dependent on maintaining a good relationship with the local community. The economic benefits they receive may be offset by traffic congestion, crowds, and inflated shop prices. This may be a particular problem for industrial heritage developments, especially those in densely-populated urban areas.

Key terms

administrative – relating to the management of an operation, especially its office and clerical requirements.

infrastructure – the system of communications and services which support a commercial operation, e.g. roads, postal services.

◇ *Exercise* ◇

The following products have all been manufactured in Britain:

- textiles
- ships
- cars
- shoes
- cutlery
- railway engines
- aeroplane engines
- detergents
- lace
- furniture
- jewellery
- electrical appliances.

In each case suggest an appropriate place for a museum to commemorate the history of the processes by which these products have been made.

Choose one example and research the major changes which this industry has undergone over the years. How could a museum stimulate interest in the industry? Write a list of proposals for such a museum.

◇ *Discussion points* ◇

1 Which areas of Britain still contain noticeable evidence of their part in the Industrial Revolution?

2 Why do you think famous people agree to act as patrons for museums like Ironbridge?

3 What characteristics of a modern high street would you include if you were planning to construct a model or replica for the benefit of future generations?

6 The Cheltenham International Festival of Music

Introduction

In past times feasts were often held to mark important occasions, either seasonal points like harvest-time or days on which significant events such as military victories, treaties, births, deaths, publications or discoveries originally occurred. Entertainments generally followed the food and drink and in some places these became permanently linked to a specific time of year. Today festivals are based on a variety of themes, and a lot of activities will develop around these themes.

Festivals often attract visitors from outside the locality because they offer entertainment, but they may also widen people's horizons, making them more aware of their historical, religious, cultural, industrial and political **heritage**. In this respect they are vital to the local community as well as to visitors.

Festivals frequently act as a stimulus to tourism. People travel to Oberammergau specifically for the passion play and to Munich for the Beer Festival, and the towns derive economic benefit from this. Sometimes festivals give rise to events which become separate attractions in their own right. For example, the Tetbury Woolsack Races hark back to the days when porters would race to the market with loads of wool because the first lots to be sold at auction generally fetched higher prices. The races were revived as part of the Tetbury Summer Festival but proved so popular that they became a separate event held on the spring bank holiday.

Successful festivals will probably need the support of both the local authority and the regional tourist board. Most festivals are organised and marketed by a committee, probably containing representatives from the local authority, the local community and perhaps local arts or historical societies. Funding will have to be arranged, either through sponsorship, the local authority, tourist boards, regional arts associations or a combination of several of these.

The size and length of a festival will largely be determined by the size of the host town and its capacity to cope with a significant influx of visitors. The adequacy of transport, accommodation and venues for events are all limiting factors. The timing of the festival is also important. A small town may cope with festival visitors more successfully on a bank holiday or in the spring or autumn than it might at the height of summer or on a busy working day.

Key term

heritage – the ideas and products of previous generations which are thought to be valuable and worth preserving.

◇ *Exercise* ◇

Discuss which of the following you think would be good ideas for festivals:

♦ The Age of the Victorians 1837–1901
♦ A 'Trivial Pursuits' Festival
♦ A Hundred Years of Zip Fasteners 1893–1993
♦ A Century of Moving Pictures 1891–1991
♦ A Madonna Festival
♦ A Magna Carta Festival
♦ Fifty Years of Aerosols 1941–91
♦ A National Anti-Litter Festival.

Add some suggestions of your own, stating when it would be appropriate for these festivals to take place and where they might be held. Then draw up a brief outline of a suitable programme of events for each one.

Organising the Cheltenham Music Festival

Most festivals rely on a management committee which advises on artistic and financial policy. Cheltenham Arts Festivals Limited, a charitable company set up to administer the Festival, also pays for a programme director who, together with his or her administrators, shares the responsibility for the smooth organisation and successful promotion of the Festival. They are responsible to the management committee. The Festival administrators come from within Cheltenham Borough Council's Department of Festivals, Entertainments and Tourism. The programme director will produce the musical ideas and the Festival administrators then check on the availability of artists and **venues** and make all the necessary arrangements for their engagement. More recently a development committee has also been established with the aim of broadening the fund-raising activities supporting the Festival, and in particular increasing the number of business **sponsors**.

Planning the Musical Programme

The planning for a major music festival begins up to three years in advance. The first task for the programme director is to decide on the theme of the musical programme, and also which composers are to be commissioned to write new works. There will be a range of proposals because some of the artists and composers may have prior commitments. The Festival administrators then assess these proposals in terms of their cost, the availability of the artists, and how practical it would be to perform the works suggested. In the case of Cheltenham, the Festival administrators aim to carry out the artistic wishes of the programme director and the programme director aims to produce a programme which will be sufficiently interesting to a range of audiences, while at the same time achieving a balance between **classical** and **contemporary** music.

First Performances

If new works are to be included, advanced planning is essential. Longer works take time to complete and it is sometimes difficult to predict precisely how long they will take to create. It is equally difficult to tell how successful a new work will be – some music is never heard again in public after its first performance. The importance of first performances to a festival is that they attract publicity. It is more likely that they will be reviewed in the press or broadcast on the radio than works which have been performed already.

The 1991 Festival programme boasted a number of world premieres

---

Premieres... and beyond

Sat 6th **Bliss** *Hymn to Apollo* revised version:
26th Anniversary of Cheltenham Festival premiere

Sun 7th, Fri 12th, Sun 14th, Mon 15th, Fri 19th
Haydn *Symphonies No 93–96:* 200th anniversaries

Mon 8th **Maxwell Davies** *Mishkenot:*
FIRST PUBLIC PERFORMANCE

Tue 9th **Whettam** *Violin Sonata No.3:* WORLD PREMIERE

Tue 9th–Sat 13th
Romeo and Juliet: new 1991 production

Wed 10th **Camilleri** *Clarinet Quintet:* WORLD PREMIERE
Commissioned by David Campbell with funds from
South West Arts

Fri 12th **Maxwell Davies** *Ballet Suite 'Caroline Mathilde':*
WORLD PREMIERE
Maxwell Davies *St Thomas Wake Foxtrot:*
22nd Anniversary of Cheltenham Festival British premiere

Sat 13th **Nyman** *Where the Bee Dances:* WORLD PREMIERE
Commissioned by the Bournemouth Sinfonietta with
funds from the Arts Council

Mon 15th **Maxwell Davies** *Ojai Festival Overture:*
BRITISH PREMIERE

Tue 16th **Bennett** *The Four Seasons:* WORLD PREMIERE
Commissioned by Cheltenham Festival
with funds from the Arts Council
Maxwell Davies *St Michael Sonata for 17 winds:*
32nd Anniversary of Cheltenham Festival premiere

Wed 17th, Thu 18th
Requiem: BRITISH PREMIERE
There is a Time: World Premiere of Company production

Wed 17th **Maxwell Davies** *Dangerous Errand:* ENGLISH PREMIERE

Fri 19th **Maxwell Davies** *Jimmack the Postie:* ENGLISH PREMIERE

Fri 19th, Sat 20th
Rubies: British Premiere of Company production
Apollon Musagète: British Premiere of Company
production
Cobras au Clair de Lune: BRITISH PREMIERE

Sat 20th **Goehr** *Two Bertolt Brecht songs:* WORLD PREMIERE
Birtwistle *Paul Celan Songs:* WORLD PREMIERE

Contracts and Agreements

Once the programme is agreed contracts are sent out to artists. These are based on agreed programmes of music and agreed dates and fees. Larger organisations, such as opera and ballet companies, require strict contracts because their costs are extremely high. A star performer failing to appear or cancelling at short notice would cause considerable disruption, but this happens infrequently. Performers with a reputation for cancelling engagements at short notice usually find it more difficult to gain invitations to major events.

Key terms

venues – places where events take place.

sponsors – those who provide money to support an event or activity.

classical music – music played on instruments of the orchestra, especially used of music written in traditional forms like the symphony and the concerto.

contemporary music – music written in the style of the present time.

◇ *Exercise* ◇

The following events formed part of the 1990 Festival programme:

● **Leicestershire Schools
Symphony Orchestra**
with **Cheltenham Bach Choir
Stuart Johnson**, **Neil Page**,
conductors
Janáček
Taras Bulba
Dvořák
In Nature's realm, Op.63
Symphony No.7 in d minor
Tippett
The Shires Suite

Twenty years ago the Festival gave the premiere of an important new work for young players. Tonight the orchestra that gave the premiere returns, in honour of our Composer-in-Residence, to perform the work prior to a tour of France. We are pleased to again involve a local choir in the Festival in this exciting programme.

● **Sounds for Silents**
James Dower, flute
David Fuest, clarinet
John & Kathryn Lenehan, piano
The Crazy Twenties

A lost art revived: the marriage of short silent films and music from the golden era of the '20s, with chamber works for flute, clarinet and piano duet by composers of the period, including **Gershwin**, **Satie**, **Martinů** and **Milhaud**.

● **Anner Bylsma**,
baroque cello
JS Bach
Cello Suite No.2 in d minor
Cello Suite No.4 in E flat
Cello Suite No.5 in c minor

Three of Bach's glorious cello suites played by Dutch cello virtuoso Anner Bylsma, famous for his recordings which have shown baroque music in a totally fresh light

● **British Youth
Festival Opera**

Mozart
Così fan tutte, K588

This company of young professional singers gives its first appearance at a festival, in its 1989 production of Mozart's satirical story of faithful love teased by weary cynicism. Sung in English, it makes the perfect opera for young and old alike — each drawing different conclusions on the constancy of love! Further performances on Thursday and Saturday.

● **Nicola Hall**, guitar
Praetorius
Three Dances from Terpsichore
JS Bach transcr Hall
Partita No.2 in d minor
Dodgson
Partita No.4 (World Premiere)
Ponce
Sonatina meridianal
Rachmaninov transcr Hall
Preludes Op.23 No.4 in D,
No.5 in g minor
Mertz
Hungarian Fantasy, Op.65 No.1
Brouwer
Elogio de la danza
Paganini transcr Hall
Caprice in a minor, Op.1 No.24

The winner of the 1989 Royal Over-Seas League Gold Medal is already acknowledged as one of the most exciting talents to emerge for many years, and makes her solo record debut in several days' time. She gives the premiere of Dodgson's Fourth Partita, 27 years after his First Partita received its premiere here in the hands of her teacher, John Williams.

● **Benko Dixieland Band**

Hungary's most dynamic trad jazz band will receive a warm welcome from all lovers of great jazz — and great entertainment. Its first UK tour last summer led to immediate return bookings — catch it here!

● **Cambrian Brass
Quintet**
Lord Berners arr Lane
March and Fanfare
M Berkeley
Music from Chaucer
Eben
Chorale Variations
Simpson
Prelude, Fugue and Scherzo
(World Premiere)
McCabe
Rounds
Oliver
Ricercare No. 5

A major premiere by Robert Simpson is the centrepiece of a wide-ranging programme by this young brass quintet.

● **Georgian State
Dance Company**

Another Festival coup ... we have secured the only UK festival appearance this summer, for one night only, of the world-famous Georgian State Dance Company. Superlatives are unavoidable in any description of this troupe — 'electrifying', 'stunning', 'breathtaking' and 'exhilarating' hardly seem adequate. An unforgettable evening is promised!
We are grateful to the sponsor for making available its headquarters at Arle Court to site the Big Top for this event.

● **Union Dance Company
Steve Williamson
Quintet**

Steve Williamson

A new collaboration of jazz and dance, with saxophonist Steve Williamson (from last year's Indo-Jazz Fusions) leading his quintet and inspiring astounding rhythm and movement from the dynamically-charged Union Dance Company. Its multi-cultural influences have already led to award-winning choreography, and tonight's project, their only joint appearance in England this summer, promises to be very special.

● **BBC Symphony
Orchestra**
Andrew Davis, conductor
Copland
Music for the Theatre
Tippett
'New Year' Suite
(European Premiere)
Dvořák
Symphony No.9 in e minor, Op.95
('From the New World')

A very special occasion — the BBC Symphony Orchestra with its new Chief Conductor present a programme of transatlantic connections: Copland, celebrating his 90th birthday this year; Tippett's work, based on the opera for Houston Grand Opera; and Dvořák's ever-popular symphony, written from America with memories of his homeland.

● **Northern Ballet
Theatre**

Giselle/Northern Ballet Theatre

Giselle

We welcome back Northern Ballet Theatre in its only visit to any festival this year. Sell-out notices in 1987 and 1988 encourage a high interest in this new production of the classic tragic ballet, not seen for over thirty years in Cheltenham. Nightly until Saturday (mats. Thursday and Saturday).

Which three events would you select to take place on the same day? You will need to consider the following:

◆ the size of venue needed
◆ the type of audience each event might attract
◆ the overall aims of the Festival, particularly with regard to encouraging new works and varied programmes.

The Cheltenham Fringe

Many of the residents of Cheltenham do not think of a Festival consisting mainly of classical music as being for them. Festival fringe events usually represent an attempt to involve the local community in a range of activities intended to appeal to a wide age range as well as catering for a mixture of tastes. The Cheltenham Fringe has included brass bands, folk music, films, plays, cabaret, fireworks, children's events, jazz, parades, workshops, and rock music.

Cheltenham Fringe performers

Free Events

One way in which a fringe can enhance a festival is by introducing a number of free events on the opening day of the festival. On the first day of the 1990 Cheltenham Festival a traditional jazz band played at two different open air venues. A colourful open air show, featuring themes from the circus, was mounted in the afternoon. If this was calculated to appeal to the young, the open air ceilidh which followed was aimed at those fond of folk music and dancing. The same evening saw a torchlight procession move from the centre of the town to a public park where a firework display set to music was timed to take place at 10.15 p.m.

Timing of Fringe Events

The timing of Fringe events has to be carefully planned. Though Fringe events will inevitably overlap with some events in the main Festival, the organisers have to decide when people might want to combine events from the Festival and the Fringe. For this reason the torchlight procession was planned to pass the Town Hall just as the concert there was ending so that the audience had a chance to join in. Clearly events which are aimed at a young audience tend to be earlier, while the popularity of late-night film shows means that films are scheduled to begin at 11 p.m. on the Saturdays during the Festival.

Experimental Fringe Events

Fringe programmes often include more experimental styles of entertainment, particularly in the fields of comedy and drama. Fringes also give an opportunity to local individuals and societies to demonstrate the strengths of the performing arts in the region. The 1990 Cheltenham Fringe featured the Gloucestershire Youth Jazz Orchestra, as well as local comedians and musical solo artists. However, the Fringe is far from being just a local event. In 1990 it featured a large community choir from Canada and the Quimantu band from Chile.

Comedy

Comedy events have rapidly become established as traditional fringe material. They range from alternative to traditional comedy and from evenings which feature several performers each doing a slot to shows featuring a single artist. Some performers use comedy to criticise the political scene or to challenge popular social values and practices. Others appeal to particular age groups by dwelling on nostalgic themes, and some simply rely on the art of being able to tell good stories.

Other Art Forms

Dance often features in the fringe programmes, whether it be morris dancing, ballet, ballroom or modern. The music in a fringe may include rock bands, jazz and folk music. The visual arts, such as painting, photography and pottery may also be represented. Local artists may be

The Cheltenham Fringe ball

invited to display their work in open air exhibitions, while other shows may feature crafts such as patchwork, quilting and appliqué.

Workshops

One important feature of recent Fringes at Cheltenham has been the workshops. These give children and young people, recognised as the performers and audiences of the future, the chance to participate in activities as varied as juggling, sword dancing, playing musical instruments and mime.

◇ *Exercise* ◇

Read the description of the 1990 Cheltenham Fringe in the Festival guide:

FRINGE '90 —

THE TOTAL EXPERIENCE

Just when you thought the Festival covered it all, the 1990 FRINGE promises yet more. Blow your mind with the hip-hopping, heart-stopping, foot-tapping, free-wheeling Fringe frolic. Whatever takes your fancy, the Fringe has it, from Hank Wangford for those tongue-in-cheek Country 'n Western fans, to the Jiving Lindy Hoppers for all you swinging jazz dance groovers. And of course we haven't forgotten the unforgettable . . . comedy. There's hilarious female theatre with Spare Tyre and Lip Service. Ken Campbell will be yarning a hysterical tale in 'Recollections of a Furtive Nudist' and

from the alternative comedy circuit, Pillar Talk guests will have you reeling home to bed. The many music acts include Eduardo and Antonio for dudes into the serious sounds of jazz fusion, Live-Jive, the cream of local bands, the Gloucestershire Youth Jazz Orchestra and the multi-national flavour of the Grand Union Orchestra. There's dance, rock, folk, mime, jazz, street theatre and even an open air Ceilidh. So make sure you don't miss out on the best Fringe yet!

a) Who do you think the account is intended to appeal to? Which words and phrases show this?
b) You have been asked to write a press release about the Fringe, intended for the local press. (A press release is an official account of a news item which will be circulated to the press.) Rewrite the paragraph above in an appropriate style. Try including three or four events not mentioned in the original paragraph, but which you think might have been interesting additions.

Origin and Brief History of the Festival

Cheltenham first began to attract visitors in large numbers in the eighteenth century. Interest in the spa waters, popularised further by a visit from George III in 1788, led to the development of its many **Regency** buildings. It attracted those who felt that 'taking the waters' would be good for their health. Music concerts were provided to entertain visitors, but these were often small in scope and did not form part of an organised programme. Though Cheltenham's popularity declined to an extent in Victoria's reign, its parks and formal gardens, and the hosting of social events such as flower shows, balls and horse-racing, helped to maintain a steady stream of visitors. Then, as a result of improved health care and changing fashions, spa towns ceased to attract as many visitors as in their heyday. The proposal for a musical festival was an attempt to revive interest in the town.

Cheltenham before the
First World War

The First Cheltenham Festival

In 1944 Cheltenham's Entertainments and Publicity Manager, Mr George Wilkinson, made the initial proposal for a Music Festival. The intention was to feature contemporary English music, and in particular to enable the performance of a new work each year.

The first Festival took place in June 1945, just five weeks after the end of the Second World War. The London Philharmonic Orchestra played works by Benjamin Britten, William Walton and Arthur Bliss. It was not easy for composers to get new works played in those days and so no compositions had to be specially **commissioned**. The composers were simply asked if they had any new works they wished to be performed, and two pieces by Britten were selected. There were no grants to support the initial Festival and George Wilkinson reported that overall the event lost £258.

The Founding of Cheltenham Arts Festivals Limited

Cheltenham Corporation met the costs of the first two festivals. However, in 1947 the Arts Council, then a relatively new organisation, provided a grant of £100. As the law prevented the Arts Council from giving this money to local authorities it became necessary to set up a company to administer the Festival. The company, now known as Cheltenham Arts Festivals Limited, still performs that task today.

The Choice of Music

In 1946 the Festival became known as the Cheltenham Festival of British Contemporary Music. The Festival featured music by Britten, Bliss, Rubbra, Tippett, Delius and Elgar. The introduction of so much new music meant that the orchestra required additional rehearsals. This not only increased the cost to the organisers but also led in subsequent years to a move from the London Philharmonic Orchestra to the Halle Orchestra, then conducted by Sir John Barbirolli. This association lasted for the next 15 years.

Opera and Ballet

Opera was introduced in 1948 but did not become a regular feature until the 1980s, partly because of cost and partly because of the difficulty of finding suitable venues. As the Festival grew, so did the number of **subsidiary** events. Ballets were staged for the first time in 1950.

The Festival Expands

In 1959 a fresh policy statement declared that in future the Festival would include important British music written during the previous fifty years, twentieth-century masterpieces which need not necessarily be British, and one concert in which more progressive works would be featured. By 1961 the difficulty of finding sufficient new works which were considered of high quality led to a review of the way future festivals were to be planned. It was decided to base the programme on a theme, or themes. In 1962 it was a celebration of Stravinsky's 80th birthday. Nineteen sixty-three saw the celebration of Britten's 50th birthday, while the following year featured Richard Strauss's centenary. This idea of themes has continued up to the present day with 1991 featuring music in celebration of the 200th anniversary of the birth of Mozart, and the Arthur Bliss Centenary. Although there were criticisms of the increase in the works of foreign composers, attendances rose significantly. By 1974 the word 'International' was included in the Festival title, which had dropped the reference to 'British Contemporary' in 1963.

Recent Developments

During the 1970s the Cheltenham Opera House was renovated and renamed the Everyman Theatre. It now provided a more suitable venue for both opera and ballet. In 1973 master classes were introduced, in which internationally-known musicians gave public lessons to talented young singers and instrumentalists. More recent developments include the appointment of a Composer-in-Residence, initiated in 1986, and the more formal planning of the variety of events which constitute the Fringe. Other festivals, such as Almeida and Huddersfield, have come to be more closely associated with experimental and electronic music. Cheltenham has continued to promote classical music played on traditional instruments, while at the same time encouraging new composers who work within that framework.

The Everyman Theatre

Key terms

Regency – relating to the years 1810–20, when the Prince of Wales (later George IV) was Prince Regent.

commissioned – arranging for a specific composition to be written in return for payment.

subsidiary – connected but regarded as less important.

◇ *Exercise* ◇

The following figures represent the income and expenditure of the very first Cheltenham Festival in 1945:

Cheltenham Festival of British Contemporary Music, June 12th–15th 1945

Expenditure	£ s d	Income	£ s d
London Philharmonic Orchestra	852.10. 0	Receipts from talks	34. 5.0
Mr Basil Cameron	4. 0. 0	Receipts from June 13th concert	286. 8.6
Miss Valda Aveling	12.12. 0	Receipts from June 14th concert	288. 5.0
Composer/Conductors	89. 5. 0	Receipts from June 15th concert	274.16.6
Speakers	70. 5. 0	Programme Sales	55.14.0
Advertising/Printing/Programmes	69.10.10		
Reception	6. 6. 4		
Staff	3. 0. 0		939.9.0
		Excess of expenditure over income	248. 0.2
	£1187.9.2		£1187.9.2

The organisers were keen for the Festival to continue and they could have taken any of the following courses of action in an attempt to balance the books in the following year:

♦ engaged a cheaper orchestra
♦ cut the Festival to two days
♦ raised admission charges
♦ invited more internationally-known performers
♦ printed fewer programmes
♦ invited fewer speakers
♦ offered the concerts to BBC radio for a fee of £250
♦ declined to advertise the Festival.

a) Which of these methods would have created direct savings?

b) Which would have generated greater income?

c) Which would have had effects which were hard to predict?

d) Which would have been contrary to the aim of the Festival, namely the encouragement of contemporary British music?

The Music Shop Project

One of the five objectives of the Cheltenham Festival is to enable 'the education of audiences towards a better understanding and enjoyment of music.' One of the priorities of Cheltenham Arts Festivals Limited is to promote events in schools, including open rehearsals and music workshops. In 1989 sponsorship enabled the company to develop a practical project, called the Music Shop Project.

The main aim of the project was to take examples of good new music out to schools in an attempt to stimulate interest. The activity was intended to encourage an understanding of musical forms and to highlight creative ability and skills of self-expression. Composers and groups of musicians were sent out to secondary schools. Students were encouraged to accompany the instrumentalists, as well as experimenting with **improvisation** and composition. The musicians who took part had skills in contemporary music, including electronic music and modern jazz. Musicians who would support experimentation and exploration were chosen.

Local Groups Participate

A number of local organisations, such as the Cheltenham Music Society, were approached with a view to putting on concerts, preceded by workshops in participating schools. Existing young amateur performing groups, such as the Gloucestershire Youth Orchestra, were given the opportunity to take part in workshops alongside composers and professional ensembles, with the idea of playing in a concert at the end of the scheme.

Key term

improvisation – making up music as it is being played rather than preparing it beforehand.

◇ *Exercise* ◇

The following composers and musicians have agreed to spend a day at your school or college:

♦ a string quartet specialising in works by Mozart
♦ the writer of the lyrics of three successful West End musicals and a number of Broadway hits
♦ a trumpet player in a local jazz band
♦ a composer of keyboard music used largely for television theme tunes and incidental music
♦ a local four-member steel band.

The objectives of the visit are as follows:

a) musicians should have time during the day to work with individuals and small groups
b) the day should involve at least some students who do not already have proven musical ability
c) there should be some performance opportunities for the visitors during the day
d) the day should be organised so that both visitors and participating students can evaluate what they got out of it and what implications it might have for similar future activities.

Suggest a programme for the day. You do not have to invite all the musicians who have agreed to come. Give reasons for your plan.

The Financial Basis of the Festival

Cheltenham Arts Festivals Limited is a company, registered as a charity, set up to administer the annual Music and Literature Festivals held in the town. Although company status means that records and accounts have to be produced and independently checked, there are advantages. Because the company is a charity it can receive covenanted donations which will not be liable to income tax. This means that the amount donated is increased by the amount of tax which would normally be paid on it.

Expenditure

Expenditure on the Festival has more than doubled since 1985, reaching a sum of around £330,000 by 1989–90. The major part of this sum goes on artists' fees, which account for about two-thirds of the total cost. Marketing accounts for about 18 per cent of total expenditure and includes the cost of printing and distributing leaflets and handbooks. Administrative costs, such as administrative staff salaries, postage, telephone bills, and stationery, have to be met. There are also a number of miscellaneous expenses such as piano tuning, performing rights, travel and accommodation expenses, ticket production, and floral decorations, which have to be set against income.

Table 1 Annual Expenditure of the Festival

	1987 Actual £	1988 Actual £	1989 Actual £	1990 Draft 6.11.89 £	1990 Revised 1.2.90 £	1991 Actual £	1992 Projected £
Artists fees	142,140	186,800	189,800	175,000	193,300	200,000	230,000
Hire of music and PRS*	150	100	150	200	200	250	2,300
Piano hire/Tuning	1,880	1,450	1,800	1,500	1,500	1,600	1,800
Advertising, distribution	12,950	12,000	13,350	14,400	14,400	15,000	16,000
Printing	13,610	11,650	10,600	12,200	12,200	13,000	14,000
Handbook	9,210	13,000	10,550	12,000	12,000	12,500	13,000
Travel, subsistence, hospitality	7,660	10,000	7,000	7,500	7,500	8,000	8,500
Fund-raising	8,510	14,950	16,200	17,000	17,000	18,500	20,000
Stationery	1,530	1,350	500	600	600	750	800
Hall hire	12,870	14,200	20,000	17,000	17,000	18,500	20,000
Postage, staff, telephones, miscellaneous	16,400	23,850	24,000	21,000	21,000	22,000	23,500
Director's fee	6,500	7,500	8,500	9,000	9,000	9,500	10,000
Floral decorations	1,150	1,350	1,050	1,150	1,150	1,250	1,500
British Arts Festivals Association	500	650	500	500	500	550	600
SURPLUS	7,300	13,650	–	–	10,000	10,000	–
	£242,360	£313,000	£304,000	£289,050	£317,350	£331,400	£362,000

*PRS stands for Performing Rights Society, and includes some copyright payments.

Reserve Funds

As a limited company, Cheltenham Arts Festivals Limited has to present accounts each year. These will indicate expenditure, broken down into such items as artists' fees and hire of halls, and income, detailing the various sources from which this comes. If a loss is sustained in any particular year it will be covered by reserve funds but will have to be balanced by the programming of a less expensive Festival the following year. The reserve fund fluctuates but the company's aim is to keep it between $7\frac{1}{2}$ and 10 per cent of overall income.

Sponsorship and Patronage

In recent years sponsorship has become the major source of Festival income, rising from 19 per cent in 1984 to 42 per cent in 1991. Sponsors may be local companies or branch offices of major national companies. Each year the company sets a target for sponsorship income. The figure proposed for 1990–1 is £120,000. This may be made up from donations to sponsor a single concert or larger sums for a series. A patronage scheme also allows individuals to give up to £1,000 annually.

Sponsors like to feel they are putting something back into the local community. It is in their interests for the Festival to do well, since this increases the chance that outsiders will have a favourable view both of Cheltenham as a whole and of the sponsor. The press, radio and television will give the sponsor favourable publicity. Leaflets advertising the Festival are widely distributed and carry the sponsors'

Table 2 Annual Income of the Festival

| | 1987 Actual | 1988 Actual | 1989 Actual | 1990 Draft 6.11.89 | 1990 Revised 1.2.90 | 1991 Actual | 1992 Projected |
	£	£	£	£	£	£	£
Ticket sales	84,580	109,900	96,700	101,480	99,780	107,400	114,000
Handbook	12,770	14,300	16,500[†]	16,000	16,000	17,000	18,000
Management fees	2,400	2,400	1,500	1,600	1,600	2,000	3,000
Sponsorship	68,700	114,900	93,000	90,000	120,000	120,000	125,000
Investment income	3,150	6,000	10,500	8,000	8,000	8,000	9,000
Arts Council of Great Britain	37,600	38,500	38,500	40,470	40,470	42,500	45,000
Cheltenham Borough Council	23,740	25,000	29,500	24,000	24,000	26,000	28,000
Gloucestershire County Council	1,390	2,000	2,000	2,500	2,500	2,500	3,000
Patronage	N/A	N/A	–	5,000	5,000	6,000	7,000
AFAA Direct Grant*	8,030	N/A	N/A	N/A	–	–	–
DEFICIT	–	–	15,800	–	–	–	10,000
	£242,360	£313,000	£304,000	£289,050	£317,350	£331,400	£362,000

*From French government   †Including VAT refunds backdated

names to a wide audience. If new works are successful, the sponsor will gain prestige as they can be credited with enabling the performance. Finally, the sponsors may receive complimentary tickets to performances and receptions.

Retailing Activities

Direct merchandising, such as the selling of mugs, T-shirts and key rings was tried on a limited scale in 1989. Some retailing activities are offered to other companies as special concessions during the Festival. Thus a company called Goodmusic sold music and records at Festival venues in 1989 and Watercolour Facsimiles sold prints of Cheltenham in aid of the Festival.

Box Office Takings

The proportion of the Festival's income which comes from takings at the box office has remained fairly constant in recent years, standing at around 35 per cent of the total income. Ticket prices will depend on a number of factors, such as the reputation of the performers, the expected popularity of the programme, the size of the venue and the type of audience expected. For example, if Fringe events are to attract a high proportion of local residents they must not be priced more highly than other comparable local entertainments.

Public Funding

Public funding of the Festival has been provided by Cheltenham Borough Council since 1945, and by the Arts Council since 1947. These sources now provide a much smaller proportion of the Festival's total income than they did in the past. Their contributions have decreased in value from 38 per cent in 1984 to 17 per cent in 1991. Though Cheltenham is still funded directly by the Arts Council, there are proposals to make more arts funding regional in the future.

The Council provides other kinds of support which have financial implications. They are able to make venues like the Town Hall available for hire on flexible terms. They also pay for the salaries of some, though not all, of the administrators.

◇ *Exercise* ◇

Major international competitions exist for many instruments but, at present, no such competition exists for the guitar. The organisers of the Cheltenham Festival feel that an international competition would enhance its reputation and that they have the necessary expertise and administrative structure.

The competition would have to be self-financing, largely through sponsorship, but some funding would be necessary at the outset to get it established.

a) Draw up a draft letter about the proposed competition to be sent to potential sponsors.

b) Write two lists, one giving the main areas of cost of putting on such a competition and the other giving the main income to be derived from it.

c) Draw up a plan outlining the preparation required before the competition and the way in which the event itself might be organised.

Marketing the Festival

The perception of the Cheltenham Festival has as much to do with its setting and location as with the music itself. The Festival is not marketed in conjunction with the Cotswold area but there is no doubt that people are attracted by the surrounding attractive countryside and picturesque villages, not to mention the appearance of the town itself. Cheltenham has long been associated with Regency architecture and interiors and the style, elegance and sophisticated leisure habits characteristic of that period. However, Cheltenham is still not widely thought of as a holiday centre, except perhaps for weekend breaks, and over half the visitors to the festival either live in Cheltenham itself or within a 30-mile radius.

Target Markets

Each year a specific market may be targeted. In 1988 the town of Cheltenham celebrated its bicentenary and the Festival staged an open-air pageant and promenade concert aimed largely at a local audience. Workshops and open rehearsals in school venues may be used to create interest among young people. Each Festival has a number of sub-themes and some of these, such as Indian music or contemporary jazz, may need to be targeted at specialist groups. In 1988 the Music Festival published a version of its programme in Braille.

Chinese opera being performed at the Cheltenham Festival

Radio and Television Coverage

Coverage on television and radio makes it far more likely that international performers will be persuaded to take part. Radio coverage is generally good, with Radio 3 regularly broadcasting concerts and recording others for future transmission. Although the Festival has featured in television programmes previewing and reviewing the arts, no complete concert has yet been shown.

Printed Publicity

Various kinds of publicity relating to the Festival are printed each year. In 1988 75,000 postcards, 100,000 broadsheets and 2,500 handbooks were printed. The postcards and the broadsheet (which outlines the main programme of the Festival) are distributed in advance of the Festival to addresses on a previously-compiled mailing list and to Tourist Information Centres and hotels thought to be within reasonable travelling distance. The handbooks provide much more detail about the artists and the works to be performed, and are on sale to the public before and during the Festival. Posters are also available for display in shop windows, arts centres and on billboards.

The Press

Press releases are sent to journalists, and these often result in articles previewing Festival events. Invitations to journalists to attend specific events may lead to reviews in the local and national press. The local press is also used to advertise events, particularly where the box office computer suggests that sales for a particular event are progressing slowly.

Symphony
Chamber
Solo
Dance
Mime
Jazz
Film
Fringe

47th Cheltenham International Festival of Music

6-21 JULY 1991

TICKETS AND FULL BROCHURE FROM
FESTIVAL BOX OFFICE (0242) 523690/521621
TOWN HALL, IMPERIAL SQUARE, CHELTENHAM GL50 1QA

Arts Council Funded

A poster advertising the Festival

◇ *Exercise* ◇

Study the bar graphs below giving 1986 Cheltenham Festival survey results, based on a random sample of 1,000 concert attenders.

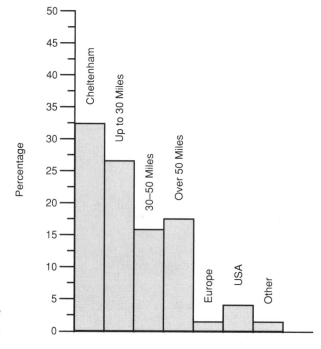

Where the Festival audience come from

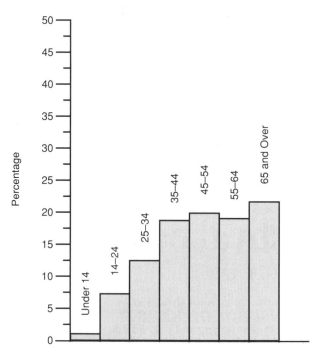

The age range of the Festival audience

What implications would these graphs have for those planning a marketing strategy for the following year?

The Future of the Music Festival

The Cheltenham Music Festival has secured a reputation for artistic integrity and innovation which should guarantee its continued existence. Artists and audiences alike commonly express the view that the Festival offers an interesting programme in an attractive environment and a pleasant atmosphere.

The priorities for the future development of the Music Festival fall into five distinct areas – promoting and commissioning new music, attracting artists of international repute, developing community projects, promoting events in schools, and developing theatre work.

New music will remain a major focus of future Festivals, and its preparation and rehearsal will demand the investment of fresh resources. Michael Berkeley has been commissioned to write a new full-length opera which will receive its first performance at a future Festival. The importance of continuing to attract international stars is crucial in attracting good audiences and increasing box office income, media coverage and sponsorship.

Although the size of the Everyman Theatre restricts the scale of theatrical events, dance and opera are thought to have an important part to play in future Festivals. The Festival can also be linked with other art forms, particularly the visual arts. Films and exhibitions of painting, sculpture and photography could be used to develop themes planned for the Music Festival.

Finance

The main concern over the future of the Festival is a financial one. Politicians do not agree about how much money should be put into the arts, and legislation giving more local funding powers to regional arts associations may affect the funds available for international festivals such as Cheltenham. Government schemes providing grants to match the investment of sponsors have been reduced, and such funds are in any case soon exhausted. Business funding of the arts is likely to be reduced when the national economy enters a difficult period in which company profits fall.

Collaboration with other organisations working in the arts, such as record companies and publishers, would provide another possible source of income. The only potential drawback to this is that the Festival would be unlikely to remain artistically independent. The organisers would not wish to think that programmes were being dictated by the wishes of record companies.

Market Research

It was agreed that in 1990 funds should be provided for research to establish more information about the audiences who attended individual events. The box office computer was used to store some information about those purchasing tickets, while a survey was taken to establish the impact of sponsorship on the audiences and their reaction to the use of a large marquee as a venue.

◇ *Exercise* ◇

Suppose that a future Cheltenham Festival is planned to celebrate a particularly significant date in history. For example, 1992 might be identified as the 500th anniversary of Christopher Columbus' discovery of the New World, America.

Choose an example of your own and suggest a programme of visual arts – exhibitions featuring paintings, sculpture, photography and films – which might be put together in support of a Music Festival illustrating this theme.

◇ *Discussion points* ◇

1 How might the musical programme for a future festival be designed to appeal particularly to a younger audience?

2 Is it possible to tell whether a particular piece of experimental music will be well-liked ten years after its first performance?

3 Do you think opera and ballet are minority interests?

4 Should composers receive a fee every time a piece of music they have written is performed?

7 *Air Europe*

Introduction

An airline is a company which organises flights for passengers or cargo. This involves negotiating routes, securing all the permissions needed to operate, obtaining aircraft, making sure that all the necessary supplies and services are available, and advertising and selling the seats on the flights. Airlines will need reliable sources of fuel and spare parts, as well as good maintenance and repair services. Passengers will also expect ground services such as reception and baggage handling to be efficiently organised.

How did Airlines Develop?

It was widely recognised in the early 1930s that there was much profit to be made from transporting passengers by air. However, the majority of those who travelled abroad went by road, rail and sea. The Second World War prompted both a wider interest in foreign places and an improvement in aircraft technology. For the first time there was an abundance of aircraft and trained pilots. The growth of commercial aviation was further stimulated by the development of jet engines and, in 1958, the appearance of the Boeing 707, able to carry greater numbers of passengers than before, heralded the arrival of mass air travel.

In the 1950s the practice of **chartering** aircraft to fly to specific holiday destinations enabled tour operators to fill all seats on aircraft and so reduce the cost of individual tickets. By the early 1960s air **package tours** were widespread and led to the rapid development of Mediterranean holiday destinations, in particular those along the Spanish coast.

Popularity of Air Travel

Airlines are now the most important means of long distance travel. The development of wide-bodied jets such as the Boeing 747 'jumbo' jet has helped to increase the number of air passengers, while at the same time reducing the cost of flights. The time required to travel long distances has also been dramatically reduced.

Key Terms

chartering – hiring out aircraft for specific flights.

package tours – holidays which include transport and accommodation in the price.

◇ *Exercise* ◇

Read the following extract from a newspaper article:

> ... the introduction of the single European market in 1992 will remove many of the restrictions currently applying to particular air routes.
>
> If more airlines compete for the same routes, then fares are likely to come down. Though in Britain Heathrow and Gatwick will still carry the most passengers, there will be increased opportunities for provincial airports. Business travellers especially will want to save time, and the smaller airports may well be able to move passengers through more quickly.
>
> There would also seem to be a future for small airports nearer city centres, like the London City Airport, which are able to accommodate smaller, less noisy aircraft which don't require such long runways. However, their development may be hindered by the difficulty of obtaining further planning permissions in view of current concerns about noise and fuel pollution, security and general safety.
>
> Regional airports in Britain are already increasing their passenger numbers significantly. Half a million passengers used Southampton Airport in 1989, while a quarter of a million pass through Exeter Airport each year. Apart from services to the Channel Islands, these two airports serve major cities such as Paris, Munich and Amsterdam. Yet if regional airports in Britain are looking to extend their services, surely they should be looking carefully at regional airports abroad such as Le Touquet and Caen?

You will need a blank map of Europe. Find the United Kingdom and mark as many United Kingdom regional airports as you can, excluding those close to major cities such as London, Manchester, Glasgow and Birmingham.

Identify at least three routes from any of these airports to regional airports in Europe which you think might be capable of carrying sufficient passengers to support a scheduled (regular) service.

Choose the route you think would be the most popular and prepare a short report outlining the kind of service you think could be offered. You should mention what kind of customers you would be targeting, the size and number of aircraft needed, the frequency of the service and any difficulties which you foresee.

Operating an Airline

Before an airline can operate at all it must have obtained a number of approvals issued through the **Civil Aviation Authority** (CAA).

An Air Operator's Certificate

Acquisition of an Air Operator's Certificate is dependent on a number of individual approvals. The airline must prove that it has been allocated slots at the airport from which its flights are to depart. To obtain these the airline must apply to the CAA and negotiate specific times at which they will fly from the nominated airport to particular destinations. At the end of each year these slots may be renegotiated, taking into account changes in the quantity and type of each airline's business.

Airlines must also be in possession of route licences enabling them to operate on specific routes. A separate licence is required for each different route. Although these are issued by the CAA, liaison with overseas governments and airport authorities is also required in order to obtain permits to fly into foreign airports and to establish the prices which can be charged for scheduled flights. If an airline wishes to operate its own aircraft maintenance scheme or its own pilot training school, it must also first obtain CAA approval.

Equipment

Once an airline has all the necessary approvals, it can begin to plan the range of equipment, support and services it will need at the airport. Aircraft are very expensive items and new companies may choose to **lease** planes from another airline or from a leasing company.

Engineering Services

In order to keep the aircraft operating smoothly, well-qualified engineering staff must be available 24 hours a day. The technology of modern aircraft is sufficiently complicated to require engineers to gain separate certificates qualifying them to service individual aircraft types. The engineers cannot work effectively without support from the team which purchases, controls and stores materials and spare parts.

In-flight Catering

In-flight catering will need to be supplied to all airports the airline intends to use. The kind of meal served on a flight will depend on the time of day and the length of the flight. On shorter flights this may be a matter of offering breakfast or lunch. A **long-haul flight** will require several meals to be available. The airline will also have to plan the most appropriate times to serve meals on flights where a number of **time zones** are crossed. Flights carrying more than one class of passenger will need different menus, in addition to allowing for special requirements such as vegetarian meals.

A meal being served on an Air Europe flight

Key Terms

The Civil Aviation Authority – the organisation which controls all regulations relating to commercial airlines and their operation.

lease – make a payment in order to use equipment owned by another company.

long-haul flight – a long flight, usually in excess of eight hours.

time zones – divisions of the globe within which regions share the same standard time.

◇ *Exercise* ◇

A new airline operating between Birmingham and Berlin decides to offer cheaper seats on flights offering no in-flight catering.

Discuss what problems you think they might encounter.

How do you think they might set about marketing these flights?

Would you suggest that the airline should plan other ways of keeping passengers occupied and, if so, what activities do you think would be suitable?

Ground Services

Fuel is perhaps the most important of the ground services needed. Fuel prices have to be negotiated in advance with suppliers to ensure that the best price is obtained. The airline must then make sure that the fuel is stored and handled safely. Any airport facilities which the airline has to use, such as check-in facilities and baggage handling, will involve the airline both in payment and in conforming to local and international regulations. If an airport is used extensively the airline may employ staff as representatives, with the responsibility of assisting and advising the airline's passengers.

Baggage handling

Staff

The final essential requirement before the airline can begin to function is the staff who operate the aircraft and attend to the passengers. The staff will include airline pilots, cabin staff and reservations staff.

Pilots are required to possess a British Commercial Pilot's Licence with an Instrument Rating Performance of 'A'. They must have 1,500 hours' flying experience, at least 500 hours of which must have been in a jet or heavy turboprop aeroplane. Generally speaking, they are also required to be under 55 years of age. Pilots receive regular refresher training courses, often using **flight simulators**. These courses include all aspects of safety.

An attractive appearance and a bright personality are seen as essential qualities in cabin staff. Knowledge of a foreign language and experience in first aid are also valued by airlines recruiting cabin staff. Training normally covers safety and methods of survival in the event of an accident, cabin services, first aid, Her Majesty's **Customs and Excise** regulations, and bar service and sales.

Reservations staff make bookings through computerised reservations systems, and offer advice and information to clients about their travel arrangements. They need a bright, confident telephone manner, good keyboard skills, and an ability to work under pressure.

Key Terms

flight simulator – a machine which creates the same conditions a pilot would encounter in flying an aeroplane.

Customs and Excise – the body responsible for checking regulations and payments relating to imports and exports, as well as monitoring the actual movement of the goods.

◇ *Exercise* ◇

The following qualities have been identified as important attributes for all applicants to the travel and tourism industries:

- an interest in working with people, answering their questions and solving their problems
- a feeling that public service is important
- a high regard for a neat and smart personal appearance
- a desire to be thorough and organised
- a belief that clear and accurate speech is important
- a belief in the importance of good manners and courtesy
- a strong sense of honesty, particularly if dealing with money
- an ability to remain patient under pressure
- a willingness to work flexible hours
- an ability to concentrate despite distractions.

Discuss which of these you think are most important. One way of doing this would be to work in small groups and attempt to place them in order of importance.

Now discuss whether you think the order would be the same for an applicant for each of the following jobs:

a) a reservations sales agent
b) an airline pilot
c) a member of an aircraft's cabin staff
d) a computer software designer.

A check-in desk

Operations Staff

Airlines may have a number of departments which are run by operations staff. Their responsibilities may include the recruitment, training and well-being of the flight deck crews, and ensuring that all CAA regulations are observed, particularly those relating to flight safety. They will provide up-to-date information about navigation and route planning changes caused by alterations in military **air space**. They need to ensure that time spent in the air by pilots and cabin attendants does not exceed the limits set by the CAA. The position of every aircraft belonging to the airline has to be constantly monitored, necessitating close liaison with **air traffic control** centres. Larger airlines will also need staff responsible for a host of other duties, such as negotiating the cost of flights, organising in-flight duty-free sales, supplying uniforms, issuing security passes, arranging overseas bookings, organising staff travel, and planning and updating all communications and computer systems.

Scheduled and Charter Services

Most airlines run scheduled services and charter operations. Scheduled services run to a fixed timetable and serve destinations in regular demand. Though scheduled flight seats are sometimes used by tour operators to form part of holiday packages, the majority are purchased direct by customers either through the airline's reservations team or through a travel agent.

Charter services are usually arranged with tour operators, generally on a seasonal basis, and run most frequently to popular holiday resorts. On a charter flight the airline sells blocks of seats or an entire aircraft capacity to tour operators who use them as part of package holidays. It is not possible for customers to buy seats on charter flights direct from the airline.

Key Terms

air space – the area above a particular state or country.

air traffic control – a system of regional centres which control the routes and altitudes of aircraft.

◇ *Exercise* ◇

You work for a local newspaper somewhere in the vicinity of Gatwick Airport.

The Editor decides to run a feature article which gives a picture of how an airline operates. You have been asked to research and write the article but, just as you are about to begin, you receive this note from the Editor:

```
AIRLINE OPERATION ARTICLE

Please bear in mind the following points:
- not too long - our readers can't cope with more than 500 words
- make sure they can relate what you write to their own
  experience of flying
- remember our three promises, 'Light, Entertaining, Local'
- try to find a bit of 'human interest'

- DEADLINE: 09.30 TOMORROW
```

Now write the article!

The Economics of Running an Airline

The current cost of a larger aeroplane, like the McDonnell Douglas MD11, is somewhere in the region of £120 million. Other major costs involved in operating an airline include fixed operating costs (aircraft **depreciation**, aircraft and passenger insurance, rental payments), handling charges (baggage handling, check-in facilities), landing and take-off charges made by airports, fuel bills, engineering and maintenance costs, catering, commission paid to travel agents for booking seats, passenger taxes, and payments to the air traffic control of each country whose air space is crossed. The two pie charts overleaf show the relative contributions which each of these items makes towards the cost of a seat in Air Europe's Business Class and a seat in Economy Class.

Variations in the Price of Oil

Oil prices, a major cost for airlines, are not always easy to predict. Political crises in the Middle East can cause sudden increases in the cost of aircraft fuel, which generally have to be passed on to the passengers in the form of **surcharges** or increased fares. Charter seats are often negotiated 18 months in advance and so there is a necessity to build into the cost the possibility of increases in fuel costs.

Income

The main revenue of an airline comes from selling scheduled and charter seats on flights. However, income is also generated by carrying

Pie charts showing how the cost of a flight in (a) Business Class and (b) Economy Class can be broken down.

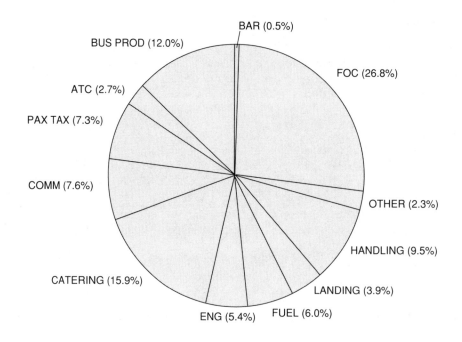

(a)

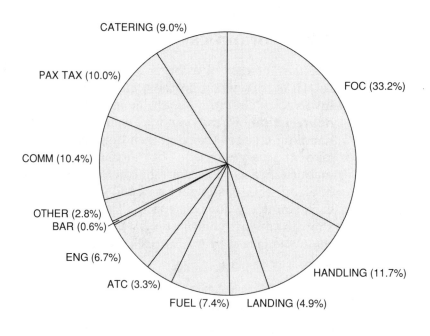

(b)

Key
ATC: air traffic control fees
BAR: commission paid for duty free sales
BUS PROD: business product extras
CATERING: in-flight food costs
COMM: travel agents' commission
ENG: aircraft engineering
FOC: fixed operating costs
FUEL: fuel costs
HANDLING: handling agent's fee
LANDING: airport landing fees
PAX TAX: airport passenger tax

freight and cargo. At some times of year particular aircraft may be sub-leased to another company. This means that an airline which has leased an aircraft proceeds to lease the same aircraft out to another business. Sometimes aircraft can be chartered or sub-chartered to other companies for the period of time when they are not in use. Air Europe Express sub-chartered whole aircraft to the Royal Mail for the night-time carriage of parcels and post to the continent.

Ticket Pricing

Working out the price of a ticket is an important part of an airline's economic formula. The airline will first work out the cost of each Business and Economy Class seat. They will then calculate the load factor, which is the number of seats which would need to be filled in each class in order for the airline to break even. The Civil Aviation Authority monitors the process to see that both classes are independently profitable and that one is not subsidising the other. Some comparisons will then be drawn between this calculation and the prices being charged by competing airlines on similar routes. This may result in some price adjustment if there are significant differences. **International exchange rates** may also affect ticket prices because airlines have to buy the use of services and facilities abroad in foreign currencies.

Effects of the Economic Climate on Profitability

Domestic economic events, such as a **recession**, can reduce the number of passengers and so cause a marked decrease in income for an airline. The airline could respond by using smaller aircraft on existing routes. This would reduce handling charges at airports as well as fuel costs. If it is thought that the situation is long-term, the airline may withdraw services on a route altogether. Once they hold a licence to fly a particular route, they can always resume that service at a later date. However, it is costly to close a route as this may involve staff redundancies and the necessity of closing down offices. Discounted fares may sometimes be used where demand for a particular route is variable according to the season or the time of day.

Costs of Long-haul Flights

Costs for air traffic control, catering and cabin crew are higher on long-haul flights. Air traffic control is more expensive because the aircraft will cross more air traffic control sectors and will have to pay a fee to each one. Air crew have to be paid for extra hours on duty, as well as receiving an allowance for being away from home. They will also require hotel accommodation, transport and meals, as their hours of consecutive flying duty are restricted by law. However, as take-off and landing burns up more fuel than cruising at a high altitude, long-haul flights are more efficient per mile than short-haul flights. However, fewer passengers can be carried on long-haul flights because people require a greater degree of comfort on longer flights. Thus, although the overall price of a long-haul ticket is higher, a short-haul journey is more expensive per mile.

Key Terms

depreciation – the fall in value of goods as they age.

surcharges – extra charges added on to the original price.

freight – bulk goods loaded onto transport such as aircraft.

international exchange rates – the values of particular currencies when exchanging them for others.

recession – a period when trading activity is reduced.

◇ Exercise ◇

The cost of overheads for short-haul flight A are the same as those for long-haul flight B. Other costs are estimated as follows:

Short-haul flight A (500 miles)	**Long-haul flight B** (5000 miles)
To cross one air traffic control sector £530	To cross five air traffic control sectors £1,000
To provide 200 meals @ £4 a head £800	To provide 180 meals three times @£4.50 a head £2,430
	To provide overnight meals, accommodation and transport for cabin staff £4,000
Fuel costs £725	Fuel costs £3,000

a) Work out the total cost of each flight, excluding the overheads the airline will have to pay.
b) Which flight is cheaper per mile?
c) Bearing in mind that flight A can carry 200 passengers and flight B can carry only 180, which flight is cheaper per passenger/mile?

(Answers are on page 153.)

Customer Relations

Most people who have flown have had experience at some time of flight delays, lack of information or loss of luggage. It is hardly surprising, given the number of passengers now using airports like Gatwick and Heathrow, that such things happen. Airlines must respond to complaints about these problems if they are to continue to attract passengers.

Flight Delays

Flight delays are most frequently caused by difficulties with air traffic control. Industrial action by air traffic controllers can significantly disrupt **flight schedules**. Any staff shortages or industrial action affecting engineering work or baggage handling are also likely to cause delays. Other reasons for late departures may be technical faults or bad weather conditions.

Baggage Handling

Baggage handling at most modern airports is fully automatic. The baggage handling system at Heathrow Airport's Terminal 3 is intended to cope with up to 5,250 bags an hour. All charter passengers are legally required to be insured against any permanent loss of luggage, but users of scheduled flights have to be compensated by the airline. An international agreement requires the airline to pay compensation for lost luggage, up to a maximum of £13.62 per kilo.

Passengers queuing to check in for a flight

Response to Complaints

Most airlines will respond to complaints by letter initially. The time taken to reach a decision on what action will be taken will generally depend both on how major the complaint is and on whether it is necessary to contact overseas representatives for information. Compensation may be agreed on where it is thought to be appropriate, although this often takes some form other than cash. It may be in the form of gifts such as clocks, Filofaxes, games or perfume. In cases where substantial disruption has occurred free or discounted tickets may seem the right kind of recompense.

Key Term

flight schedule – the timetable for arrivals and departures.

◇ *Exercise* ◇

Any airline will receive a mixture of complaints. They will have to decide how much they are legally responsible and how much they are morally responsible for what has occurred. They may decide to take no action beyond a written response. They may offer gifts, discounted tickets, or a cash sum.

Discuss whether you think an airline should be held liable for each of the four complaints listed below, and what sort of compensation, if any, you think would be appropriate. Then write what you consider to be polite and appropriate responses to each of the complainants.

a) Ambrose Bayliss of 12 Old Street, Guildford, Surrey has written complaining bitterly that, during a turbulent flight from London to Paris, the passenger in the seat next to him spilled red wine down his light-coloured trousers. Dry cleaning has cost £5 and failed to remove the stain.

b) Alexander Kirton of 43 Govan Road, Middlesbrough, Cleveland has written to complain about damage to his luggage during a flight returning from Crete to Gatwick. His suitcase, which was three years old, had split open, some of the clothing inside had got dirty and a shirt had been ripped, and finally, what irritated him most, two Greek vases which he had wrapped inside the clothing had been smashed.

c) Owen Prothero of The Red House, Aberaeron, Powys wrote to complain that his return flight from Palma had been ruined by the rowdy behaviour of other returning holiday-makers. He stated that there had been almost non-stop singing, some of which was held to be offensive as well as loud. Attempts to ask for quiet had resulted in abusive comments, loudly directed at Mr Prothero and other passengers throughout the flight.

d) Janice Gabriel of 6 Shirelands Road, Hanwell, London W7 wrote to say that her flight to Paris had been delayed by six hours. As a result she had missed a connection to Guadeloupe where she had been due to deliver legal documents finalising a major leisure development. Her company had subsequently been forced to pay a £25,000 penalty for failing to meet an agreed deadline.

Origin and Brief History of Air Europe

In April 1973 the first passengers to have booked holidays through the tour operator Intasun left Gatwick. After Intasun had completed five years of successful holiday package tours a decision was taken to form a new airline company to be known as Air Europe. This enabled the International Leisure Group (ILG) who owned Intasun to acquire its own aircraft. By the end of 1979 they were in possession of three Boeing 737-200s, costing £30 million and purchased through the financial backing of Japanese bankers.

Air Europe's first commercial flight took off from Gatwick on 4 May, 1979, bound for Palma, Majorca. By November of the same year the airline was also operating flights out of Manchester. In that first year a quarter of a million passengers were carried to 29 different destinations.

Coping with Recession

Two years later a recession resulted in financial difficulties for a number of airlines. Air Europe managed to emerge successfully from this period

A Boeing 737–200

by using leasing arrangements. They leased extra jet airliners during the busy summer months and lent out their own aircraft to other airlines during the quieter months. Aircraft leasing became an important part of the company's business.

Changes in Airline Agreements

In the early 1980s it was becoming clear that changes in the airline agreements between European countries were due. Since 1984 many of the air service agreements between the United Kingdom and other European countries have been renegotiated. These agreements cover a range of issues including the rights of stopping and picking up passengers, schedules, capacities, specific destinations and **tariffs**. Air Europe, like any new airline, had to compete strongly for licences to operate new routes, for good time slots for their aircraft to depart in, and for the right to offer some fare reductions on Business and Economy Class flights.

Table 1 Who Operates European Air Routes*

From	Number of routes	Operated by more than one airline	Operated by airline from outside country of origin or destination
France	153	2	11
Greece	39	0	6
Italy	99	1	9
Spain	108	2	5
Belgium	45	1	4
Denmark	37	0	7
Germany	173	7	17
Ireland	43	2	3
Luxembourg	15	0	2
Netherlands	65	7	9
Portugal	33	2	1
United Kingdom	178	24	14

*The table gives data on return journeys for community air services during the summer of 1987.

Links with Other European Airlines

The relaxation of airline agreements which began in 1984 encouraged Air Europe to develop strong links with other European airlines. Air Europa, a Spanish charter airline, was launched in 1986, the first of a number of sister airlines in Europe established to work in partnership with Air Europe. They were independent commercially but used Air Europe's logo, uniforms and orange and red **livery**. The other airlines to join the partnership were Norway Airlines, Nurnberger Flugdienst from West Germany and Air Europe SpA from Italy.

The cabin staff of Air Europe in their uniforms. The aeroplane displays the orange and red stripes of the airline's livery.

Development of Scheduled Services

Air Europe operated solely as a charter airline for six years, but in 1985 its first scheduled services, to Palma and Gibraltar, were introduced. These had already proved their worth as successful charter destinations and so a twice-weekly scheduled service was introduced. During 1988 Air Europe launched its Business Class and extended its scheduled services, taking over some of the British Caledonian routes when that company merged with British Airways.

Expansion

By 1990 over 20 per cent of all the flights in and out of Gatwick were accounted for by Air Europe's schedule and charter operations. The scheduled destinations had increased from the original two to 15 from Gatwick and six from Manchester, and included such cities as Brussels, Copenhagen, Rotterdam and Stockholm. The company had expanded into the charter long-haul market using extended range Boeing 757s to fly to Orlando, Mexico, Goa, Bangkok and the Maldive Islands. The purchase of Connectair and Guernsey Airlines enabled the formation of Air Europe Express, a network of European commuter routes using a mixture of jets and smaller aircraft. A freight service between the United Kingdom and Europe, and lounge and check-in facilities at Gatwick for the sole use of Air Europe passengers were both developed in the late 1980s.

Key Terms

tariff – an agreed set of charges.

livery – the distinctive colours, uniforms and logo displayed by the staff and goods of a particular airline.

◇ *Exercise* ◇

Study the following explanation of how to use a timetable of scheduled air services, including the various symbols which are used:

How to use this timetable

An example timetable is shown below. Notes to explain each item of information are listed underneath. All times are local as applicable to country of arrival or departure.
Connections information is shown after the direct flight schedules.

Brussels   1

London Gatwick to Brussels **2**   **11**   *air europe*

Date	Frequency	Dep	Arr	Flight No.	Aircraft	Class of Travel	Meal Serv.
25 Mar-27 Oct	1,2,3,4,5 - 7	**0730**	0930a	AE026	100/737	C, Y	⍾⍾
31 Mar-27 Oct	- - - - - 6 -	**0920**	1120a	AE026	100	C, Y	⍾⍾
26 Mar-26 Oct	1,2,3,4,5 - -	**1130**	1330a	AE028	100	C, Y	⊘
26 Mar-26 Oct	1,2,3,4,5 - -	**1415**	1615a	AE030	100	C, Y	⊘
25 Mar-27 Oct	1,2,3,4,5 - 7	**1800**	2000a	AE032	100	C, Y	⊗ ♀·
25 Mar-27 Oct	1,2,3,4,5 - 7	**1945**	2145a	AE034	100/737	C, Y	⊗ ♀·

a – 1 hour earlier from 30 Sep

3   **4**   **5**   **6**   **7**   **8**   **9**   **10**

Brussels to London Gatwick

Date	Frequency	Dep	Arr	Flight No.	Aircraft	Class of Travel	Meal Serv.
26 Mar-27 Oct	1,2,3,4,5,6 -	**0725a**	0725	AE025	100/737	C, Y	⍾⍾
25 Mar-27 Oct	1,2,3,4,5 - 7	**1030a**	1030	AE027	100/737	C, Y	⍾⍾
31 Mar-27 Oct	- - - - - 6 -	**1205a**	1205	AE027	100	C, Y	⊘
26 Mar-26 Oct	1,2,3,4,5 - -	**1415a**	1415	AE029	100	C, Y	⊗ ♀·
26 Mar-26 Oct	1,2,3,4,5 - -	**1700a**	1700	AE031	100	C, Y	⊘
25 Mar-27 Oct	1,2,3,4,5 - 7	**2045a**	2045	AE033	100	C, Y	⊗ ♀·

a – 1 hour earlier from 30 Sep
·⊗ – Business Class/♀ – Economy Class

1 Destination City
2 Flight routing
3 Period of operation
4 Days of operation
5 Departure time (local time)
6 Arrival time (local time)
7 Flight number
8 Aircraft type
9 Class of Travel (C – Business, Y – Economy)
10 Meal Service
11 Member airline operating these flights

Explanation of symbols used in this timetable

Days of Operations:
1 Monday; 2 Tuesday; 3 Wednesday;
4 Thursday; 5 Friday; 6 Saturday; 7 Sunday.

Airline Codes:
AE–Air Europe/Air Europe Express	*DA–Dan-Air*
BA–British Airways	*NS–N.F.D.*
BC–Brymon Airways	*SN–Sabena*
BU–Braathens S.A.F.E.	*TE–Air New Zealand*
BZ–Capital Airlines	*UK–Air UK*
CO–Continental Airlines	*VS–Virgin Atlantic Airways*
CX–Cathay Pacific Airways	

Meal Services:

⍾⍾	*Hot Breakfast*
⍀○⍀	*Hot Lunch or Dinner*
⊗	*Cold Lunch or Dinner*
⊘	*Continental Breakfast Light refreshment or afternoon tea*
♀	*Bar Service*
☕	*Hot Beverage Service*

Complimentary bar service is available on all flights, except services to/from Channel Islands where a pay bar is available. Where two meal codes appear together, adjacent to a flight, the first symbol refers to the business class cabin, and the second to the economy cabin.

Aircraft Symbols:
ATR Aerospatiale ATR-42	*100 Fokker 100*
BAT British Aerospace ATP	*146 British Aerospace 146*
B11 BAC 1-11	*73S Boeing 737-200 series*
DHT Twin Otter	*733 Boeing 737-3/400 series*
D10 McDonnell Douglas DC10	*747 Boeing 747*
SH6 Shorts 360	*757 Boeing 757-200 series*
	EQV Equipment Varies

Now look at the timetable of scheduled services between London and Paris for the period of March to October, and answer the questions which follow it.

London Gatwick to Paris

air europe

Date	Frequency	Dep	Arr	Flight No.	Aircraft	Class of Travel	Meal Serv.
26 Mar-27 Oct	1,2,3,4,5,6 –	**0715**	0915a	**AE036**	737/100	C, Y	↿↾
25 Mar-26 Oct	1,2,3,4,5 – 7	**0825**	1025a	**AE038**	100	C, Y	↿↾
26 Mar-26 Oct	1,2,3,4,5 – –	**0930**	1130a	**AE040**	100	C, Y	↿↾
26 Mar-26 Oct	1,2,3,4,5 – 7	**1240**	1440a	**AE042**	100	C, Y	⊗ ⊤ *
25 Mar-21 Oct	– – – – – – 7	**1500**	1700a	**AE044**	757	Y	⊘
26 Mar-26 Oct	1,2,3,4,5 – –	**1515**	1715a	**AE044**	100	C, Y	⊘
1 Jul-21 Oct	– – – – – – 7	**1630**	1830a	**AE046**	737	C, Y	⊗ ⊤ *
26 Mar-26 Oct	1,2,3,4,5 – –	**1715**	1915a	**AE048**	737	C, Y	⊗ ⊤ *
25 Mar-21 Oct	– – – – – – 7	**1900**	2100a	**AE048**	757	Y	⊤
25 Mar-27 Oct	1,2,3,4,5 – 7	**1900**	2055a	**AE050**	737/100	C, Y	⊗ ⊤ *
31 Mar-27 Oct	– – – – – 6 –	**1930**	2130a	**AE048**	100	C, Y	⊗ ⊤ *
31 Mar-27 Oct	– – – – – 6 –	**1745**	1945a	**AE046**	100	C, Y	⊗ ⊤ *

a – 1 hour earlier from 30 Sep

Paris to London Gatwick

Date	Frequency	Dep	Arr	Flight No.	Aircraft	Class of Travel	Meal Serv.
26 Mar-27 Oct	1,2,3,4,5,6 –	**0745a**	0750	**AE035**	737/100	C, Y	↿↾
26 Mar-27 Oct	1,2,3,4,5,6 –	**1000a**	1000	**AE037**	737/100	C, Y	↿↾
25 Mar-27 Oct	1,2,3,4,5 – 7	**1130a**	1130	**AE039**	100	C, Y	⊘
26 Mar-26 Oct	1,2,3,4,5 – –	**1215a**	1215	**AE041**	100	C, Y	⊘
25 Mar-27 Oct	1,2,3,4,5 – 7	**1540a**	1540	**AE043**	100	C, Y	⊘
25 Mar-21 Oct	– – – – – – 7	**1800a**	1800	**AE045**	757	Y	⊤
26 Mar-25 Oct	1,2,3,4,5 – –	**1800a**	1800	**AE045**	100	C, Y	⊗ ⊤ *
1 Jul-21 Oct	– – – – – – 7	**1930a**	1930	**AE047**	737	C, Y	⊗ ⊤ *
26 Mar-26 Oct	1,2,3,4,5 – –	**2000a**	2000	**AE049**	737	C, Y	⊗ ⊤ *
25 Mar-21 Oct	– – – – – – 7	**2145a**	2145	**AE049**	757	Y	⊤
31 Mar-27 Oct	– – – – – 6 –	**2215a**	2215	**AE049**	100	C, Y	⊗ ⊤ *
31 Mar-27 Oct	– – – – – 6 –	**2030a**	2030	**AE047**	100	C, Y	⊗ ⊤ *

a – 1 hour earlier from 30 Sep
Note: All Air Europe flights depart and arrive from Charles de Gaulle Airport Terminal 1
⊗ – Business Class/⊤ – Economy Class

1 What time does the last Sunday flight leave Paris?

2 What refreshment is available on the 1715 Gatwick to Paris flight?

3 Which flights from Gatwick to Paris do not offer Business Class?

4 How much information could you give about flight AE043?

5 Why do some of the flight numbers appear more than once?

(Answers are on page 153.)

Selling and Marketing Air Europe

Air Europe began as an airline specialising in charter flights. The increase in its scheduled operations, amounting to over 300 flights a week by the end of 1990, needed to be communicated to the public. As many of the scheduled flights were to European cities commonly visited by business travellers, it was important to make the business market aware of the service. The cost of Business Class flights was reduced by the use of smaller aircraft which operated with fewer empty seats.

The major Air Europe advertising campaign during 1989–90 was aimed at the business traveller. The main purpose of the campaign was to get across the message that the airline was a high quality, low cost, scheduled airline. A series of advertisements was designed and these were placed in national newspapers, colour supplement magazines and business magazines. These publications were chosen on the grounds that they were believed to have a high proportion of business readers. At the same time a poster campaign was mounted, mainly in the South-East, with the intention of emphasising the size of Air Europe's scheduled network.

The advertising campaign was prepared by an agency, which produced an advertising **specification** outlining the evolution of Air Europe's scheduled services and describing what the campaign should achieve. The main needs of business travellers were assessed as being frequent and punctual flights, comprehensive schedules, and quality service. The advertising campaign sought to establish Air Europe as a scheduled carrier in the minds of business travellers and to demonstrate that its Business Class had a style distinctly different from its competitors. A top photographer was engaged to take photographs in Air Europe destinations which emphasised the fact that the airline had a European, rather than a British, outlook and that the range of its scheduled services was wide.

Key Term

specification – a detailed description of requirements.

◇ *Exercise* ◇

Look at the Air Europe advertisement on the following page before answering the following questions.

1 Headlines are intended to catch people's attention. What impressions did the advertisers want you to gain from 'The Time, The Place, The Airline'?

2 What conclusions are we meant to draw from the appearance and pose of the man in the photograph?

3 How many connections can you find between the text of the advertisement and the photograph?

4 How many of the claims made by the advertisement are verifiable facts?

5 List the other claims made on behalf of the airline and suggest ways in which their accuracy is likely to be tested.

6 What is the connecting idea between the first and last paragraph of the advertisement?

7 Although the advertisement concentrates on Air Europe rather than its competitors, what does it suggest about the competition?

Direct Marketing

Direct marketing involved contacting individual clients, companies or travel agents who had used Air Europe in the past. A database listing some 60,000 contact names was held on a computer and could be easily divided into different interest groups.

The Time, The Place, The Airline.

Times are changing.

Today's successful businessman, or woman, is just as likely to be catching the next plane to Paris as the next train to Waterloo.

But doing business in another city, in another country, presents its own problems.

Not least of which is being in the right place at the right time or better still, with time to spare.

That's why an increasing number of business travellers are choosing to take off with Air Europe.

Currently we have over 280 scheduled flights from Gatwick each week, bound for a total of 18 European cities.

And we're still growing. Faster in fact than any other UK airline serving Europe.

But helping you arrive at your destination on time is only part of what makes Air Europe tick. We also help you arrive at your best, beginning even before you fasten your safety belt.

At Gatwick, Business Class passengers

18·57. CAFE COSTES, PLACE DES INNOCENTS, PARIS.

can use one of our exclusive lounges.

Far from the crowds you can collect your thoughts, make that last minute call or just relax with a drink.

The same high standards of comfort extend to the flight – something you'd expect from an airline with one of the world's most modern fleets – and service in the air, as on the ground, is impeccable.

What's more, our value for money

policy means Air Europe fares are around 15% lower than our rivals. In short, it's a pleasure flying business with us.

For more information see your travel agent or contact us on 0345 444737.

Europe is on the verge of becoming one country. One airline is ready.

air europe

THE EUROPEAN AIRLINE

An advertisement used by Air Europe during the 1989–90 campaign.

Trade Shows

Air Europe was represented at a number of consumer and trade shows annually, the most important of which was the World Travel Market.

Incentive Schemes

They were also involved in two promotional schemes, one with Barclaycard and the other with American Express. Both schemes involved the collection of points by holders of **charge** and **credit cards** each time the cards were used. Seats on Air Europe flights were among the gifts which card holders could acquire.

Key Terms

charge card – a card which can be used in places which accept it instead of cash in order to pay for goods, leaving the card holder to make a monthly settlement with the card-issuing company.

credit card – a card similar to a charge card but leaving the card holder with the option of not settling the account fully and paying interest charges on the sum still owed.

◇ Exercise ◇

Sponsorship is commonly used by multinational companies as a means of promoting a positive image of their company. Under sponsorship schemes companies provide money in support of an organisation or activity. The sponsor's name will appear on any publicity produced, so it is a form of advertising. Although at one time Air Europe had been co-sponsors of the South of England show, eventually they decided not to place much emphasis on sponsorship.

Read the marketing profile of Air Europe described below:

What is Air Europe's Profile?

Air Europe is the second largest carrier into Europe after British Airways.

Air Europe is trying to project the image of a young, fresh and dynamic new European carrier, with very high quality at a lower cost. Through mostly direct marketing, they wish to show that Air Europe is good value for money, and build up a loyal base of clients who would use Air Europe again.

The most recent press advertising campaigns have all used images that evoke quality.

If the company had decided to investigate the possibility of new sponsorship agreements, what requirements would any event or activity have had to fulfil before it would have been regarded as suitable for sponsorship?

Name one example of an appropriate event or activity and describe briefly what arrangement might have been organised.

The Collapse of Air Europe

Some of the hazards likely to face European airlines in the future can be illustrated by the events leading up to the collapse of the International Leisure Group. Air Europe's determination to develop its scheduled services ultimately led to the company's failure. Acquiring a fleet of aircraft, largely with borrowed money, left the company with an annual interest bill of £17 million. With many other airlines competing for the same short-haul routes, there was an over-supply of seats on many flights. Short-haul scheduled flights have not proved particularly profitable for other airlines recently and national airlines, such as British Airways, probably have some advantages in negotiating preferred routes and slots.

The ILG lost £50 million in the three months leading to January 1991. Attempts to raise extra funds proved unsuccessful and city banks, through whom money had originally been borrowed, repossessed some of Air Europe's aircraft. They had come to doubt whether a company sustaining such losses would ever be able to repay what they had borrowed. Once the aircraft had been repossessed, Air Europe could no longer transport passengers and had to cease trading. Its assets were put up for sale in order to recover some of its debts and its staff were made redundant.

Factors Likely to Affect the Future of Other Airlines

Deregulation

Airline deregulation is likely to prove the most significant cause of change for European airlines in the 1990s. Along with telecommunications, the energy industries and banking, airlines have been selected by the European Community for major regulatory reform. Deregulation in America, which took place more than a decade ago, meant that airlines were suddenly allowed to fly to any destination within the United States without regulatory controls over routes, capacity or fares. This would be more difficult to achieve rapidly in Europe, largely because there are very few new airports with the scope for expansion and there is much environmental opposition to the building of new ones.

Deregulation in Europe would initially apply only to international scheduled flying within the European Community, representing only about 10 per cent of all passenger airline travel. By the end of 1992 it is hoped that airlines will be able to determine their own fare levels on scheduled flights, free from the influence of any other existing commercial agreement. The restriction on the number of passengers each airline can carry will be relaxed and there will be a greater opportunity to develop regional routes.

1 Terminal for scheduled and
  charter traffic
2 Central building with
  underground rapid transit
  rail station, restaurants,
  shops, travel agencies and
  car rental firms
3 Parking
4 Tower
5 Hotel
6 Car rental centre

*The new Munich Airport
– an artist's impression*

New Operators

The success of any new airline will depend on the airline's ability to
establish a competitive cost base, particularly in terms of their wage
costs. They will need a fleet of aircraft which effectively meet the needs
of their customers, which are capable of giving a highly economic
performance, and which can spend as much time in the air as possible.
The two major requirements for users of scheduled services are
probably as frequent a service as possible, departing and returning at
convenient times, and flights which run on time. Any worthwhile route
probably needs four flights a day if it is to meet peak morning and
evening demand at both ends of the route.

Congestion at British Airports

The Civil Aviation Authority has recognised the need for a new runway
in the South-East in the 1990s, but the government has so far refused to
give permission for such a development at Heathrow, Gatwick or
Stansted. There is a similar need to develop extra terminal space to ease
congestion within the airports.

Congestion over Europe

Airports such as those in Paris, Brussels and Amsterdam are likely to be
used by more airlines as **hubs**, with an increasing number of routes
from them serving regional airports. Congestion may also be eased by
the fact that it is now easier to fly from Scandinavia to the
Mediterranean across Eastern Europe, thus avoiding detours into West
European air space. The reduction of military bases in Germany and
Eastern Europe will mean that less air space is dedicated solely to
military use.

Aircraft Pollution

European aviation regulatory bodies have agreed that they should try to have all noisy and fuel-inefficient aircraft out of service by the end of the 1990s. Some airports will introduce surcharges for older aircraft and others may follow the example of Belfast City Airport and ban them altogether. Most airports limit the number of night flights which are permitted.

Purchase of Airline Tickets

There is a need to simplify the procedure for purchasing airline tickets. Tickets are obtained from a range of sources, and it is not always easy to compare the different prices on offer or the services available. The customer should be able to find out more easily what the benefits are of buying a ticket from one airline rather than another.

Key Term

hub – an important centre from which minor routes (sometimes referred to as 'spokes') spread.

◇ *Exercise* ◇

All of the following proposals have been suggested as possible future means of improving the problems of airport congestion:

♦ easing the night-time curfews at airports for quieter jets
♦ increasing the tax on aviation fuel
♦ placing the clearing of flight paths and the allocation of slots on a centralised European computer system
♦ developing more routes from smaller airports
♦ reducing the permissable noise levels for all aircraft landing and taking off
♦ purchasing the same air traffic control systems for all member countries from a specially-established European Community fund.

Write a paragraph commenting on the suggestions from the point of view of:

a) someone living close to a major European airport
b) a regular user of scheduled European flights
c) the managing director of a developing European airline.

◇ *Discussion points* ◇

1 What factors will a new airline have to bear in mind in planning how to supply its in-flight catering to a particular airport?

2 How many pilots do you think should be on duty on each passenger flight?

3 Why don't airlines charge fares identical to those of other airlines offering the same routes?

4 Why do airlines regard time slots as a vital factor in how profitably they can operate scheduled services?

5 What measures can be taken to reduce the inconvenience suffered by those who live close to major airports?

Answers to the exercise on page 140 are:

a) Flight A costs, excluding overheads, amount to £2,055, Flight B costs to £10,430.

b) Flight B.

c) Flight B.

Answers to the exercise on page 146 are:

1 21.45.

2 Cold lunch or dinner, bar services.

3 AE044, AE048.

4 The flight is from Paris Charles de Gaulle Airport, Terminal 1. It operates between 25 March and 27 October, runs every day except Saturday, departs at 15.40 (local time), unless after 30 September, when it departs one hour earlier, arrives at 15.40 (local time). The airline is Air Europe/Air Europe Express, and the aircraft is a Fokker 100. It has both Business and Economy Class, and afternoon tea is served on board. There is a complimentary bar service.

5 Flight numbers are repeated when the service offered alters according to the day of the week.

8 American Express Travel Office

Introduction

A travel office is a place where travel tickets and holidays are sold. Customers may purchase package holidays, air or rail tickets and hotel accommodation. They may also buy services such as car hire or travel insurance. Travel offices will provide information and advice on travel. They may provide a currency exchange service. Recently some travel offices have developed reservation and advice systems for entertainments, such as plays, and visits to places of cultural or historical interest.

Some travel offices are run by companies which are also tour operators selling their own holidays, for example American Express. Their sales outlets are called travel offices, travel shops or retail travel centres. Travel agents are so-called because they act as agents for tour operators, selling other companies' products to the public.

Travel Information

Buying a holiday is a major expense and people choosing holidays want enough information to satisfy themselves that they have made the right choice. Usually, a travel agent provides information through a collection of travel brochures. However, travel companies are increasingly aware of the potential of videos, television programmes and **teletext** as means of providing information to the public.

Location of Travel Offices

Originally travel offices were generally located close to docks or railway stations. Nowadays they are most commonly found in main shopping streets, and as with a shop, ground floor premises are most sought-after. Window displays are used to attract people's attention. The exact location may depend on whether the agent intends to specialise in a particular type of travel. A company specialising in cheap, overland travel might favour an area frequented by young people, while a shop specialising in business travel might wish to be located fairly close to a number of large companies.

Travel Office Income and Expenditure

To set up a travel office, premises have to be purchased and staff employed and paid. Brochures are provided by the tour operators and there is no stock of goods to be purchased before selling to the public.

Travel agents earn their income by receiving commission from tour operators and airlines on all the tours and tickets they sell. Usually the commission is a percentage of the amount the customer has paid. Holiday travel is subject to considerable seasonal variation, which means that at quieter times of the year many companies have to develop a range of short breaks and special offers.

ABTA and IATA Membership

There are advantages for travel agents and travel shops in becoming members of the Association of British Travel Agents (ABTA). Members have to deposit a cash bond with the Association. This guarantees that customers will get their money refunded should their holiday arrangements be affected by the **bankruptcy** of the ABTA member. At least one member of staff working in a travel agency belonging to ABTA has to hold an appropriate professional qualification. Membership of the International Air Transport Association (IATA) is also important as it leads, through a licensing system, to rights to receive commission for selling international airline tickets.

Key Terms

teletext – written information, such as details of flights, which can be called up on a television screen.

bankruptcy – having insufficient funds to continue operating as a business.

◇ *Exercise* ◇

Faraway Places Ltd is a new travel agency in the high street of a medium-sized town. Its opening was shortly after Christmas and it has now been in operation for five months.

The agency is staffed by two full-timers, Mrs Davis and her nephew, Tristram. Mrs Davis has good professional qualifications in the travel agency and tourist information fields. Tristram worked in a garage for six months prior to joining his aunt. On Saturdays, Janice White, a student at the local sixth-form college, is employed for the day. Profits are not sufficient to enable any more staff to be taken on.

Faraway Places is open from 9 a.m. until 5 p.m. every day except Sundays and Mondays. Early to mid-morning is generally very quiet on weekdays, while Saturdays are so busy that customers often have to queue for attention or advice. Up until now most of the agency's business has been selling Mediterranean package tours, largely booked through nationally-known tour operators.

The main question mark hanging over the business' future seems to be the presence of a rival travel agency, at the opposite end of the high street, which belongs to a nationally recognised chain of travel agents.

In order to establish its own identity, Faraway Places Ltd decides to stress that it can offer a more personal service than a larger company would.

a) Note down ways in which Faraway Places Ltd might get across to potential customers the idea that it can offer a more personal service.

b) What kind of planning and resources would each of these methods require?

c) Outline what you think would be the most practical and appropriate overall plan.

Main Operations within a Travel Office

Retail Travel

The majority of customers buying holidays from a travel office will do so by talking directly to a **travel counsellor**, either over a counter or at a desk. Those more certain of their intentions may book by telephone. Computerised reservations systems enable availability to be checked and bookings to be made very rapidly. Each enquiry is likely to require discussion of issues such as dates, fares, type of accommodation required, facilities at the destination and attractions worth visiting. The time taken to meet each customer's needs may have no direct relationship to the amount of business generated. Travel counsellors rely on brochures, guides, videos, posters and on personal travel experience to help customers to choose.

The American Express Travel Office, Haymarket

Business Travel

Business travel differs from retail travel in that the destination is often not a matter of choice. Also, the booking is often made by someone other than the person actually travelling. Business travel is often booked at short notice and is more likely to be subject to last-minute changes of plan. Most offices specialising in business travel will treat companies rather than individuals as their clients. They will make all travel reservations requested by their clients, complete all the necessary paperwork and then despatch the tickets. Computerised client profiles mean that information about each company's travel policy and method of payment, as well as the individual preferences of their personnel, are easily available to the member of staff dealing with the account. Whereas payment is made in advance for retail travel, businesses settle their accounts after trips have been made. This can make it difficult for small travel companies to specialise in business travel because they may run into cash flow problems.

Traveller's Cheques

Travel agents and travel shops are usually able to offer customers a **traveller's cheque** service, though these are also obtainable from banks and building societies. Traveller's cheques can only be cashed by the person purchasing them, who has to sign the cheques in the presence of the cashier. This means they are less likely to be stolen than cash. It is possible to cash traveller's cheques in outlets throughout the world, in banks and often in hotels and shops. A small proportion of the face value of the traveller's cheque, often no more than 1 per cent, is split between the office or agency selling the cheques and the company which issued them. The company producing the cheques makes its profit by investing the payment they have received until they have to repay the foreign banks where the cheques were cashed. It is advisable to take traveller's cheques in the currency of the country being visited because it generally ensures a more favourable rate of exchange.

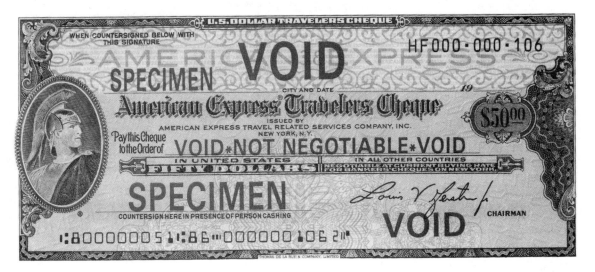

A traveller's cheque in US dollars

Foreign Currency Exchange

Customers going overseas usually take some foreign currency with them to pay for any expenses arising soon after their arrival, such as taxi fares. Travel companies with large numbers of offices are able to buy foreign currencies in bulk, and as a result get a better exchange rate than individuals would secure. Exchange rates depend on information gathered daily from business houses, banks and brokers. They vary as governments and large currency dealers buy and sell the stocks of currency which they hold.

Key Terms

travel counsellor – a person employed by a travel company to give travel advice and take bookings.

traveller's cheque – a cheque which is issued to an individual in one country which can be exchanged for local currency in another country.

◇ *Exercise* ◇

A major travel agency chain decides to open three new offices in the streets illustrated below:

(a)

(b)   **(c)**

(a) is in a county town in the West Midlands
(b) is in a well-to-do London suburb
(c) is in a large city in the North of England.

Discuss what different approaches you think each office might take in planning the window display for its opening. What common approaches do you think they should adopt?

The Development of Travel Offices

There have been travel agents in Britain for over a hundred years. Originally, railway and shipping companies sold tickets direct from offices in main city centres. Thomas Cook opened offices in London in 1865 to enable customers to arrange to join excursions and tours, as well as arranging accommodation. He also began to supply a number of guide books. Hotel coupons, banking and foreign currency exchange were services which his business subsequently provided.

The American Express Company in Europe

The original American Express Company was established for the purpose of carrying cash and parcels and promising their safe arrival. By 1890 there were over 300 company agents in Europe whose responsibilities involved both the receiving and forwarding of baggage, parcels and freight, and all the financial organisation required to complete these operations. Reliance on cash transactions was eventually replaced by postal money order services and it was an American Express employee, Marcellus Berry, who, in 1882, invented an unforgeable money order. Traveller's cheques followed in 1891, enabling people to travel across borders without constantly exchanging cash. Refunds were offered in the case of loss.

The first American Express office was opened in 1895. In addition to the services already described it provided reading and writing rooms and mail collection facilities. By the turn of the century there were offices in London, Southampton, Liverpool, Hamburg, Bremen, Antwerp, Rotterdam, Copenhagen, Naples and Genoa.

Early Tours

By 1902 the London office was authorised to sell steamship tickets, and two years later railways tickets were also on sale. By 1909 the office had been moved to the site of the modern American Express Travel Shop in the Haymarket and was organising tours within Great Britain. Before the First World War a 160-page booklet was available from the London office describing a complete range of tours by rail, motor coach and private car. The majority of tours were within Britain, but destinations such as Algeria were also featured.

Early Air Services

The First World War put a stop to much European travel. However, by 1919 daily air services were in operation between London and Paris and American Express were involved at the outset in booking both passengers and freight. One of the earliest aeroplane services the company offered its clients was the opportunity to hire private aeroplanes from the De Havilland Company at a rate of eight pence per passenger-mile.

Cruises

Sea cruises had the advantage of being more comfortable than air travel, and more passengers could be carried. American Express became agents for the Cunard company, and in 1919 organised the first escorted cruise from America to Europe, sailing in the *Mauritania*. In 1922 they chartered the cruise ship *Laconia* for a round the world cruise.

Further Developments

The increasing use of air travel and the growth of mass tourism after the Second World War left airlines with the difficulty of deciding how best to sell their services. Their main problem was that they operated from airports, and these were generally situated some distance away from where their potential customers lived. The obvious solution was to use

*An American Express
Travel Office in
Germany, circa 1940*

the existing network of outlets selling rail and shipping services, and so the modern travel agencies were born. By 1945 American Express had a network of offices covering most major European cities. The company was involved in tours to all parts of Europe, including pilgrimages to Rome, visits to the Olympic Games and tours to coincide with the coronation of Queen Elizabeth II. The company's financial services to travellers had also expanded significantly so that by 1955 American Express travellers cheques were available in US dollars, German marks, pounds sterling, French francs and Swiss francs. Since that time the financial services side of the company has expanded rapidly, but travel and the services related to it remain important elements in their future plans.

◇ *Exercise* ◇

1 Travel offices provide a wide range of travel-related services. You are a representative of a British or American travel company in a travel office in Yugoslavia. What would your initial response be to each of the following urgent telephone calls from British holiday-makers?

   a) '... I can't see a thing. I tripped on the hotel steps and my glasses fell off. They're supposed to be unbreakable but unfortunately they took the weight of my fall and now they're completely shattered ...'

   b) '... she's only 3 so I'm a bit worried. She was fine when she went to bed last night but this morning her face and neck are covered with a rash. The doctor in the village doesn't speak English ...'

c) '... he definitely cut in front of me before the accident but he swears I just drove into him. The local police seem to be claiming I was guilty of careless driving and I'm very concerned about what to do ...'

d) '... I left it on the table. Of course when I came back it had gone. I know it was stupid but I had all my cash and traveller's cheques, and a credit card, in the wallet. I have no funds left at all ...'

e) '... I'm sure I forgot to lock my back door before I came away and I know both my neighbours have already gone off on their own holidays ...'

f) '... I've lost my tablets. I'm supposed to take them every day. I have a heart condition and so I need to replace them fairly urgently ...'

g) '... Lou Shawhead his name was. It's a good camera and I'm sure he'll want it returned. I know he was touring around but he didn't say where he was going on to. Is there any way of contacting him?'

2 What other emergencies do you think such an office might have to deal with?

3 For the office to offer a reasonable range of services to British travellers they would need good contacts and reliable information. Make a list of the kind of information you think they would need.

The Haymarket Travel Office – Structure and Operations

The Haymarket Travel Office is a more complex business operation than most city centre travel agents. It not only sells holidays, but also deals with American Express traveller's cheque operations, foreign currency services, American Express cardholder enquiries, and money transfers by mail and by electronic mail.

Services requiring direct contact with the public, such as retail travel and currency and traveller's cheques, are provided in the Travel Office on the ground floor. This means that the Travel Office advertises its services to people walking past outside. There is also a business travel section in the Travel Office. Departments dealing with the administration of traveller's cheques, business travel, foreign currency, holiday sales and charge card services occupy offices on the floors above.

The Retail Travel Centre

The Retail Travel Centre is divided into four units – a retail counter, two telephone sales units and a holiday centre – all offering a wide range of products, including package holidays, hotel bookings, car rental, insurance, British and continental rail tickets, airline tickets and sightseeing trips. The retail counter deals with enquiries and bookings from people who walk in off the street. One telephone unit deals with enquiries about American Express holidays or general holiday enquiries from American Express cardholders. The other deals with calls from American Express offices worldwide. The holiday centre sells personal travel to employees of companies with significant business accounts with American Express.

Telephone Sales

Telephone sales units aim to take down all essential information in a single telephone call. A booking form is used to help travel counsellors to check that all vital information has been gathered. A computerised reservations system enables availability to be checked rapidly and bookings to be made quickly. The sales performance of the staff is important to maintain profit levels, but it is difficult to measure. Counsellors cannot choose the customers they respond to and cannot predict the time each enquiry will occupy or the value of the business it may generate. The company generally aims for a certain percentage growth each year.

Counter Sales

Although they perform much the same duties as telephone sales staff, counter staff have to develop slightly different skills. They must learn to be tactful in dealing with the many non-travel enquiries they receive. Some members of the public may simply ask for directions; others may not really be sure what they want. Some enquirers may have difficulty communicating in English. Travel counsellors in the Haymarket office are also trained to be aware of cultural differences which may mean that clients from overseas have strong views about methods of payment or about being served by female staff.

Design of the Retail Travel Centre

American Express has developed a concept known as the Model Office. In addition to good lighting and high standards of cleanliness and tidiness, this idea includes open-ended counters so that counsellors can greet customers as they enter, tour desks for discussion with customers making extensive travel arrangements, and standard designs for filing systems and interior and exterior **decor**. All the units at which travel office staff work are free-standing, and individual components can be linked to meet specific office requirements. Travel counter units are designed to encourage eye-to-eye contact with customers. Work stations for travel counsellors have travel caddies which hold brochures and travel folders in a way which makes them easily accessible. Filing and equipment units hold files, brochures, stationery, computer display terminals and self-contained lighting. Stands and wall units enable brochures, leaflets and transparencies to be displayed and stored in positions where they will be easily seen but will not obstruct movement.

Security

With so much foreign currency and so many traveller's cheques on the premises, security is essential. However, although security must be in evidence, it needs to be kept very much in the background so that it does not discourage customers by creating the impression of a hostile environment.

The Business Travel Centre

The Business Travel Centre is divided into three operational sections, one of which deals solely with the business of the single largest client, a business which has an annual expenditure of £4.5 million. Each client is assigned to an individual travel counsellor who will remain their regular point of contact with the company.

All incoming telephone calls to the Business Travel Centre go through an ACD (automatic call distribution) system. This enables the customer's call to be put through directly to the counsellor with responsibility for the account. The counsellor will then take details of the destination(s) required, the dates of travel and the length of stay. A computer reservations terminal called TRIPS gives travel counsellors direct access to approximately 250 airlines, 15 hotel chains and 10 car hire companies. Once the reservation has been made it can be put into a queue in the computer system. This means that it will be held until the day it needs to be processed into tickets, vouchers and documentation to be sent to the client.

Accommodation and Car Hire

The travel counsellor will also recommend accommodation. American Express has agreements with hotels worldwide. The company negotiates agreed rates with these hotels, having first sent someone to inspect them. The volume of business American Express generates enables the company to secure savings of between 10 and 40 per cent on the rates these hotels would normally charge. For the same reason American Express is also able to negotiate favourable rates with international car hire companies like Hertz and Avis.

Payment for Business Travel

Some companies pay for their business travel through an American Express corporate card arrangement, by which the client receives a detailed monthly statement of all business travel expenditure. Others prefer to be sent **invoices** with their tickets and monthly statements listing all the invoices raised. American Express in turn pays airlines on a fortnightly basis through a centralised accounting system.

Travel Management Services

AMERICAN EXPRESS

Business Travel Account - Statement

BILLING DATE 06/07/00
PAGE NUMBER 3

TRAVEL ACCOUNT
BARNETT PRESCOTT LTD.
PRESCOTT HOUSE,
BAILEY ROAD,
LONDON EC1B 4XX

ACCOUNT NUMBER 3742-942001-01004
FINANCE DEPARTMENT 12345

STATEMENT REFERENCE	INVOICE NUMBER	SUPPLIER/TICKET NO	DESTINATION	DEPART DATE	TRAVELLER	TRIP REQ'N	CUST REF *	AMOUNT
		CURRENT TRANSACTIONS						
153042400251	001836290	BA 125 3687 330129	RIO DE JANEIRO	17/06/00	NEWINGTON E.	026125	ABC	3,150.00
159060901126	001836295	DA 062 3687 330134	MANCHESTER	12/06/00	PRESTON S.	026115	BOY	140.00
159031500566	001836301	DA 062 3687 330140	GLASGOW	11/06/00	JAMISON J.	025999	POR	135.00
160060900121	001836302	AF 057 3687 330141	PARIS	13/06/00	NICHOLLS K.	026131	BAT 3	255.00 CR
153060904231	001836302	AF 057 3687 330141	PARIS	13/06/00	NICHOLLS K.	026131	BAT	255.00
151050302595	001836303	AF 057 3687 330142	PARIS	13/06/00	CLOUDSDALE D.	026132	REG	255.00
160059503256	001836312	BA 125 3687 330151	CHICAGO	17/06/00	HESKETH G.	026141	ABC	2,098.00
159060301126	001836341	BA 125 3687 330198	MADRID	21/06/00	RIEDLINGER S.	026188	POR	370.00
165069500613	001836357	BA 125 3687 330208	MANCHESTER	20/06/00	BRENT K.	026152	REG	140.00
166010100476	001836362	TW 015 3687 330213	NEW YORK	25/06/00	D'ARIENZO R.	026197	REG	1,980.00
166020501266	001836375	BA 125 3687 330225	ROME	25/06/00	COLLINS S.	026202	ABC	345.00
152060901266	010256323	AVIS CAR HIRE		22/06/00	CLOUDSDALE D.	026203	REG	52.48
160013200125	010256341	B.R. DOMESTIC	DARLINGTON	13/06/00	HUTSON C.	026166	HIT	42.00
158060900337	010256353	B.R. DOMESTIC	BIRMINGHAM	22/06/00	WATTS L.	026147	DAL	55.00
172060900775	010257041	B.R. DOMESTIC	DIEPPE	17/06/00	JAMISON J.	026148	POR	105.00
						TOTAL CURRENT TRANSACTIONS		8,867.48
						TOTAL ACCOUNT BALANCE		22,649.98

*1 = REMITTANCE   2 = ADJUSTMENT   3 = REFUND

An itemised statement of business travel expenditure

Passport and Visa Unit

The Business Travel Centre also provides a Passport and **Visa** Unit. This enables free and accurate information to be quickly available to clients travelling to countries where visas are required. Many of American Express's clients do not hold British passports, so there may be different regulations when they travel overseas and they will need to know what restrictions apply.

Key Terms

decor – decoration, usually including wall coverings, fabrics and furnishings.

invoices – documents giving details of goods or services which have been provided, including their price and quantity.

visa – a stamp or other addition to a passport giving the holder permission to enter a specific country.

◇ *Exercise* ◇

Sketch a design for a free-standing unit which would enable a member of staff in a retail travel centre to work quickly, efficiently and comfortably – both on the telephone and face to face with customers.

Traveller's Cheques

In the 1970s American Express sold traveller's cheques to over 400 travel agents. Then the relaxation of exchange control regulations allowed the company to sell cheques to banks and building societies, which quickly became a more important source of distribution.

Commission Rates

American Express gives a stock of traveller's cheques to a bank, travel agency or building society, which they hold in trust. They pay American Express as and when they sell this supply. Generally they charge the customer 1 per cent above the face value of the cheques. Of the 1 per cent profit a travel agent normally keeps two-thirds and pays American Express one third. However, large sellers would also be offered additional commission which would rise with every increasing sales target which was met. It is not just the actual sale of traveller's cheques which brings American Express the profit. All commission arrangements are based on banks or other institutions paying money received from the sale of cheques to American Express within seven days. American Express then invests the money. In the meantime the holiday-maker gradually spends the cheques. Each one has to go through the banking system of the country being visited. They are then forwarded to American Express's operations system in Salt Lake City, and they will repay the foreign banks. If this process takes, for example, 20 days to complete, American Express have made a profit by investing the money for this period.

Security of Traveller's Cheques

Traveller's cheques are generally stored in safes because until they are signed they can be cashed by anyone in possession of them. An Inspectors' Office based in the Haymarket Office will look into any suspected traveller's cheque fraud. Altered signatures on cheques usually arouse suspicion, and a number of security features aimed at preventing forgery are built into the design and printing process.

Marketing Traveller's Cheques

Marketing of American Express traveller's cheques is done in two main ways. Firstly, advertising campaigns are run on radio, television and in the national press. Secondly, leaflets are distributed through direct mailing and through branch travel offices, which may display related posters. Television has been a popular medium for American Express marketing. In 1985 the company began a TV advertising campaign aimed at 'raising product awareness' – making the public more aware of American Express traveller's cheques. The security of traveller's cheques was emphasised by contrasting what happened in cases of loss. Cash was generally not seen again, credit cards could be used by thieves and replacement would take time, but traveller's cheques offered the greatest likelihood of a full refund to cover any loss. Later advertising campaigns stressed quality. One way of doing this is to advertise new benefits or services which competing brands do not provide. For example, the Express Helpline service equips every purchaser of American Express traveller's cheques with a plastic card giving a Helpline telephone number. The service provides free travel information and help in emergencies.

◇ *Exercise* ◇

A high street building society, open six days a week, calculates that it sells £2,000 worth of American Express traveller's cheques each week.

a) If the building society makes a 1 per cent charge for this service to its customers, how much will be paid over the counter in one week by customers buying traveller's cheques?

b) If one third of the 1 per cent is returned to American Express along with the face value of the cheques, how much does the building society retain from these transactions each week?

c) If the time between receiving payment from the building society and paying the banks where the traveller's cheques were cashed averages 20 days, and American Express can earn 9 per cent a year by investing this money, work out a method of estimating the company's annual profit from the traveller's cheques sold in this particular building society.

Foreign Exchange Services

Despite the many ways of obtaining money overseas – for example traveller's cheques, credit cards, and Eurocheques – foreign currency business, based in the Haymarket, is very important to American Express. They provide both a retail and a wholesale supply. That is, they provide somewhere in the region of 70 currencies direct to customers travelling overseas and they also buy and sell foreign currencies in large quantities, profiting from changes in exchange rates.

American Express buys foreign currencies in bulk from dealers in the City. These dealers, who include companies such as Thomas Cook, will buy from large central banks abroad or in London. They will then sell American Express the number of, say, francs or pesetas they require, adding on a fraction of a per cent to the rate at which they themselves purchased them. Difficulties emerge when there are sudden changes in the values of particular currencies, often caused by events such as the British Government's announcement of its intention to join the European Monetary System.

Seasonal Demand for Currencies

Getting the balance right in terms of how much of each currency should be purchased at different times of year is very important. In April there should be sufficient stocks of European currencies to meet the demand from people intending to visit popular holiday destinations such as France, Spain, Greece and Italy. US dollars, on the other hand, are demanded at a similar, steady rate all year round.

The Foreign Currency Unit

The Foreign Currency Unit based in the Haymarket office buys and sells foreign currency daily to meet the needs of all American Express's regional travel offices. The distribution, security and insurance involved mean that keeping this supply of foreign currency going involves considerable cost. A security company is responsible for the passage of money from individual premises to the Post Office. The registered mail service is then used. The Post Office accept **liability** up to £2,000 for each piece of registered mail. Any sum above that is covered by an insurance policy.

Computer Control of Currency Transactions

Counter staff can check exchange rates through a computer monitor. They key in the sum to be exchanged, the date, and whether it is a currency or traveller's cheque transaction. The computer will calculate the exchange value, the commission and the total cost to the customer, as well as providing the customer with a receipt. The stock of individual currencies held can be checked by pressing a currency button on the computer keyboard.

Calculating Exchange Rates

Daily values for international currencies, based on banking and trade information, are used to calculate what is called a 'spot rate', which acts as an internationally-quoted exchange rate for a particular currency. If American Express buys or sells currency from a dealer, they will usually be quoted a rate of something like a tenth of a per cent above or below the 'spot rate'. However, dealers will vary these rates if they have a surplus of a particular currency or if a currency is in particular demand.

◇ *Exercise* ◇

There has been much discussion in the newspapers and on television about a common European currency, usually referred to as the European Currency Unit, or **ECU**.

1 a) Discuss the advantages of having a common currency in Europe.

  b) What reasons might some people have for opposing this idea?

2 Write a short speech proposing the idea of a World Currency Unit, perhaps to be known as a WORCU. You could mention the advantages of such a scheme, the difficulties of convincing world governments to adopt it, what problems might arise in implementing the scheme, and how some nations or individuals might try to take advantage of it.

Key Terms

liability – responsibility for providing money to cover any loss.

ECU – European Currency Unit – a single unit of money to be usable in all countries belonging to the European Community.

Consultancy Services Available from the Haymarket

Annual travel and entertainment costs for UK businesses are estimated to be in the region of £900 per employee, so there is clearly a need to manage travel and entertainment spending effectively. The consultancy service available from the Haymarket office offers advice about how companies can save money or get more for the amount they have allocated to travel and entertainment. Some companies lose money by reimbursing employees who have used credit cards for travel expenses before those employees are required to settle their credit card accounts. Short-term investment of the large sums involved would bring extra income.

Analysis of Company Travel Spending

An in-depth study of an individual company may reveal that the company is sending personnel from several different departments to a particular destination. American Express may then be able to negotiate a money-saving deal with a single airline on the basis of the number of journeys on this particular route. Sometimes reports produced by the consultancy service suggest that some of a company's practices are wasteful or that some expenses are unnecessary. They may recommend internal reorganisation, especially where travel arrangements have been left in the hands of individual employees. It may also be suggested that they conduct a regular review of the travel agent they use to check how competitive their rates are, what additional services they offer, and how efficient they have been.

Travel and Entertainment Policies

The consultancy service advises companies to produce written policies specifying the type of transport to be used for particular journeys, the class of transport appropriate for employees at different levels within the company, the length of stay acceptable before and after meetings and the maximum spending permissable for meals and entertainment. Such policies need to be regularly updated and to be distributed to all company employees who travel.

◇ *Exercise* ◇

Many companies predict that changes in Europe during the coming decade will lead to an increase in business travel. As one means of controlling this growth in expenditure, many companies are reviewing the kind of expense reports they ask for from their employees and also the means by which they check the accuracy of these.

a) Design a form which you think would enable a company sending employees overseas on business for the first time to receive accurate, up-to-date information about the travel and entertainment expenses of each of its staff.

b) What methods might be used to test the accuracy of this information? Suggest advantages and disadvantages of each of the methods you propose.

Training and Career Development at the Travel Office

The Training Passport

As a means of stressing that training is a continuous process, each employee is issued with a passport which records their achievement in terms of training and courses. The system also involves a very structured set of guidelines relating to promotion, which helps employees to consider career development.

Appraisal and Promotion

A system of **appraisal** records factors such as individual sales figures and the accuracy of paperwork produced by the individual. Employees are encouraged to assess their own achievements and to talk about their own specific areas of interest. Promotion within the company is encouraged and there is a development programme of courses for supervisors with the potential to become managers. These courses cover areas like **budgeting**, interviewing, and conducting disciplinary procedures.

Attracting New Staff

The company has particularly targeted women who might be considering returning to work. Some may worry about working in an industry where technology has advanced rapidly in recent years, so the company must address this problem. It was felt that the personal skills of more mature trainees would enable them to handle face-to-face contact with clients with confidence.

Key Terms

appraisal – assessing the contribution an employee has made to the work of the department or company.

budgeting – planning how much should be spent on different department or company activities.

◇ *Exercise* ◇

Training in giving presentations might be valuable to employees with various levels of responsibility in a company.

Below is a list of general guidelines about giving presentations which a trainer wishes to put across to a group of trainees:

Steps for effective presentations

1. Think about your audience carefully.
2. Tailor your presentation to the character of your audience.

3. What are the benefits to them?

4. Prepare for awkward questions – what objections will the audience have?

5. Rehearse adequately – use notes but try not to read a speech.

6. Use imagination in visual aids.

7. Make sure your presentation tells a logical story.

8. Keep it short – 10 to 15 minutes is ideal.

9. Speak up.

10. Speak slowly.

11. Face your audience.

12. Be natural but resist informality.

13. Check papers and equipment before a presentation.

14. Distribute handouts only *AFTER* a presentation.

Plan a training session which would put these guidelines across in a manner which is both interesting and calculated to improve the practical abilities of the trainees.

Future Developments

Travel arrangements within large companies are likely to become more centrally managed, with more thorough policies and more effective reporting ensuring that each journey brings value for money. In order to ensure priority treatment larger companies are increasingly setting up travel **implants** within their own premises. These offices are wholly dedicated to providing an efficient and economic service for all company personnel required to do business travelling.

Changes in Europe

The volume of business travel to Eastern Europe has grown rapidly since 1990 and the Business Travel Unit has to be sure it can meet the requirements of such travellers. East European countries are rapidly establishing commercial contacts with Western Europe.

The arrival of a common currency in Europe would dilute some of the company's foreign exchange business. However, it seems very likely that the ECU will exist alongside other European currencies initially, with its value being quoted separately against each national currency. If a single common currency were to replace individual ones, the company could become heavily involved in selling ECU traveller's cheques. In addition, some 70 per cent of American Express business is concerned with inbound American visitors dealing in dollars and dollar traveller's cheques, so a major part of the foreign exchange service will remain.

Holiday Sales

Increasing interest in long-haul destinations is to the advantage of a company like American Express, aiming for the top end of the market.

However, as the Haymarket office is dependent for much of its business on inbound American visitors, the staff must work hard to retain these American customers. Rising London hotel prices and the lack of air-conditioning during hot weather are two factors which may contribute to more mature American visitors basing their United Kingdom holidays outside the capital.

Technological Development

American Express are planning to develop a computer system linking all their offices around the world. This would enable customers in any American Express office to receive up-to-date travel and financial information. Another aspect of technological change which will probably affect most travel offices in the future is the potential of satellite ticketing. This should eventually make it possible to install machines into which customers can insert cash or credit cards in return for airline tickets. The customer would still have to telephone the travel office to make a reservation, but would be saved the task of going to collect the tickets or having them delivered.

Key Term

implants – offices of a smaller company based within the premises of a larger one.

◇ Exercise ◇

The following extract from an article about tourism technology hints at some of the developments which might take place in the next decade:

Will we see simple printers in hotel bedrooms which, at the touch of a button, produce an itemised bill to be scrutinised over breakfast rather than at the front of a check-out queue? Will we see magnetically encoded cards swiped through readers at ports and airports rather than the sorry coupons and boarding cards of today? Will carriers, governments and other concerned parties work together to acquire and install the technology required to achieve integrated air traffic control systems for the benefit of the passenger? Will the travel industry find ways of allowing smaller airports to equip themselves with the technology required to permit all-weather landings and obviate at least some of the causes of airport congestion?

In what ways do you think the following activities may be affected by technological advances in the next decade:

a) choosing and booking a holiday?
b) paying for goods and services while travelling overseas?
c) passing through airport customs and passport controls?
d) evaluating the success of business travel?

◇ *Discussion points* ◇

1 What features of window displays are most likely to attract your attention?

2 What essential information would a travel counsellor need to take down in order to take a reservation from a client over the telephone?

3 What particular design features can you suggest which would make it more difficult to forge a traveller's cheque?

4 Why do you think the demand for US dollars remains fairly steady all year round?

5 Do you think people should be allowed to claim expenses for entertaining business guests?

9 Studland Bay and Poole – Industrial Development

Introduction

In 1974 the Countryside Commission designated the Purbeck Heritage Coast as one of 30 areas in England and Wales worthy of protection because of its outstanding natural beauty. This was part of a national project aimed at conserving the undeveloped character of coastal areas, reconciling the sometimes conflicting needs of locals and visitors, and enhancing the potential for enjoyment and understanding of such areas. In practical terms this means providing information through leaflets and display boards, organising guided walks, clearing and waymarking footpaths, building stiles, fences and steps, and clearing up litter. The Purbeck section of the Dorset coast, running from the shore of Poole Harbour to Osmington, has long been known for its superb views, spectacular cliffs, fine beaches, good walks and variety of wildlife, making it a popular area for tourists.

Old Harry Rocks

Walking and Wildlife

The area attracts people with an interest in walking and in wildlife. The Dorset Coastal Path begins at Poole Harbour and passes through

Studland, Swanage and Weymouth on its way to Lyme Regis. It passes by or through several important **nature reserves**, homes of a number of rare varieties of flora and fauna. Some of these, such as the Swannery at Abbotsbury, have made considerable efforts to market themselves as visitor attractions.

Summer Congestion

Areas of outstanding natural beauty are constantly under pressure from the volume of visitors they receive. More than a million visits are made to Studland Bay each year, largely because it maintains an unspoilt sandy beach on the edge of some spectacular and varied countryside. The lack of accommodation in smaller beach resorts like Studland means that most of the visitors come on day visits by road from the south-west of England or from nearby towns. The strategic location of car parks is one method of dispersing crowds, and the planned siting of footpaths and signposts is useful in reducing congestion.

The Beach as an Attraction

The great majority of visitors wish to do little more than spend a day on the beach. The sandy beach and safe bathing make it a desirable destination for families with young children. Apart from how easy it is to get there, and in summer there can be substantial queues of traffic to Wareham and beyond, the factor most likely to influence the number of visitors is the weather because there is very little to do on wet or cold days.

Facilities for Visitors

Access to the majority of beaches is free and the landowners, mainly local authorities but in the case of Studland Bay the National Trust, have to decide whether to provide facilities for visitors. These may include car parks, cafés, toilets and shops. A rubbish collection service may also become necessary. Popular beaches may appoint a beach inspector whose responsibilities will include managing the effects of increasing numbers of visitors. Studland benefits by being owned by the National Trust as this considerably reduces the likelihood of unacceptable new building development around the bay.

Reducing the Risks of Accidents

Most popular beaches employ wardens in the summer to guard against accidents. They keep in contact by radio and are generally able to call on the assistance of rescue boats. Fire is a particular risk in the heathland areas adjacent to the beach at Studland, which become very dry in the summer. Although visitors sometimes set up barbeques on the beach, fires of any sort are banned in the vicinity of the heathland area.

Rubbish Disposal

The summer months see a vast rise in the amount of cleaning up which is needed on British beaches. The most common measures used to deal with this problem are the provision of litter bins and notices threatening offenders with prosecution. The task of collecting, compacting and disposing of the rubbish, which requires an investment in staff and equipment such as tractors and trailers, is costly. The compacting process is necessary because of the sheer volume of what is collected.

A Fragile Coastline Environment

Coastlines are particularly susceptible to **erosion**, which can be accelerated by large numbers of visitors walking in vulnerable areas. Studland Bay contains a sand dune system which has attracted scientific interest, and close by is the largest area of continuous lowland heath in Dorset. Lowland heath has been rapidly diminishing since the 1950s, when farmers first began to develop large areas of the heathland. In more recent times housing developments have replaced further significant areas of heath. Heathland is important because it offers a unique wildlife **habitat**. For example, all six of Britain's native reptiles – the smooth snake, the grass snake, the adder, the sand lizard, the common lizard and the slow worm – can be found in this habitat.

Studland Bay from the air

Protective Measures

Sand dune systems can be protected by fencing them off so that the public has no access. This also allows the marram grass, which binds the sand in place, to seed itself naturally. Dunes can also be protected by specially constructed walls of board, with marram grass being replanted by hand. Stone walls are often used as a means of halting coastal erosion.

Storm Damage

Storms can also severely affect coastlines. Apart from the effects of flooding, trees can be blown down leaving areas of subsoil exposed. This rapidly leads to further erosion if people walk over the exposed areas. Wire mesh can be used to protect the ground, giving grass and flowers the chance to establish themselves.

Bye-laws

Beaches are often subject to local **bye-laws**. These may forbid people to remove plants from the beach. They may also include powers to control the use of vehicles in the area. Fines for disobeying bye-laws remain fairly low, but wardens of National Trust sites are empowered to evict people if their behaviour can be proved to be unacceptable.

Key Terms

nature reserve – an area within which plants and animals are protected from harm.

erosion – wearing away under the effects of wind, tides, ice and rain.

habitat –usual living place or surroundings.

bye-laws – laws introduced by local authorities, applying only to the area they control.

Nature Conservation in the Poole and Studland Area

The Nature Conservancy Council was established by Act of Parliament in 1973 'for the purposes of nature conservation and fostering the understanding thereof'. In addition to the 200 or so designated National Nature Reserves, there are over 4,000 sites which have been identified by the Council as Sites of Special Scientific Interest (SSSIs). Poole Harbour is a Site of Special Scientific Interest, largely because it acts as a nesting and feeding ground for up to 20,000 waterfowl during the winter, including internationally important populations of black-tailed godwit and shelduck. The lowland heathland on the Studland peninsula has been designated a National Nature Reserve and is also a Site of Special Scientific Interest. The area supports a number of rare species of flora and fauna, including the sand lizard, the smooth snake and the Dartford warbler.

Martin Auld, the Project Manager for the RSPB Action for Heathland Project

The Studland Shoreline

The bay at Studland stretches from the southern edge of the main shipping channel out of Poole Harbour to the spectacular chalk stacks, known as Old Harry Rocks, at Handfast Point. The chalk stacks represent the edge of a chalk ridge which was once joined to the Isle of Wight. The stacks demonstrate the collapse and retreat of the coastline. The smaller of the chalk stacks, Old Harry's Wife, is being worn away by the sea and will eventually collapse.

The Sand Dune System

While the Purbeck cliffs retreat, the sand dune systems are advancing. Marram grass gradually binds the sand until the dunes become stable, but they remain subject to erosion by people walking over them, as well as by wind and sea.

Beach Life

Although it is not very evident when walking along the sand, the shoreline contains much life. Sand is too unstable for seaweeds to grow but creatures such as lugworms, masked crabs and hermit crabs live beneath the surface of the sand. The sand acts as protection against predators, and keeps creatures such as shellfish moist at low tide. On the edge of sandy beaches there is generally a line of seaweed and other debris left by the high tide. This material rots and so provides food for flies, maggots and small creatures such as sand hoppers. These creatures in turn provide food for birds such as the ringed plover. Other birds commonly seen at Studland include those relying on a fish diet, such as common and sandwich terns, and those, like oyster catchers, which feed on creatures buried in the sand. Many sea birds nest in the cliffs which run from Handfast Point towards Swanage. Most of these, like the familiar herring gulls, live on fish and so would be seriously affected by any major sea pollution.

The rocky areas of Studland Bay are dominated by seaweeds, which are a source of food for periwinkles and limpets, and shelter for shore crabs. Many of these creatures can be easily destroyed. For example, turning over a rock and not replacing it is likely to kill the living things which are exposed.

◇ *Exercise* ◇

Read these two extracts from newspaper articles, the first about the Royal Society for the Protection of Birds and their concern about the diminishing heathlands, and the second about the effects on wildlife of the protected Ministry of Defence land at Lulworth on the Dorset coast.

240 years ago there were nearly 40,000 hectares of Dorset heathland, but today there are only 5,512 hectares left. The rate of decline this century has been twice that of the last century, and part of the reason is that heaths are no longer used by people for grazing, turf cutting and gorse and heather collection. This use kept them in a well managed state, but as it declined, so the heaths began to change, with trees and gorse invading much of the remaining areas of heathland so that the normal mosaic has been lost in several areas.

The RSPB is concerned by this heathland decline because of the rare species such as the Dartford Warbler and Nightjar, which depend on this habitat for their survival. So with BP's support, the project will, over the next four years, set out to manage heathland sites by removing self-set trees and bracken, encouraging the heather and gorse, and maybe even introducing grazing once again to suitable sites.

Lulworth marks the western boundary of the MoD's 7,000-acre Purbeck patch, out of bounds except for most weekends and school holidays.

Although much of the land is scarred by tank tracks and cratered by shells, the army's presence has also been a force for conservation. Its wide margins of safety have meant that enormous tracts of countryside, including hedgerows, uncultivated grasslands and woodlands, have been saved from intensive farming, forestation and probably caravan sites. Birds and animals thrive in these DMZs (Designated Military Zones), so much so that the army now has a problem keeping deer out of its sights.

Either in small groups or as one large group, use ideas from the two articles and any other resource material you can find to debate either of the following motions:

a) 'We believe that the greatest chance of survival for our native wildlife is for it to be left to develop in its own natural way.'

b) 'We believe that our native wildlife can only survive now if carefully managed and protected environments are created for it.'

◇ *Exercise* ◇

This is a map of Musto Bay, a fictional Dorset beauty spot, as it was in 1945:

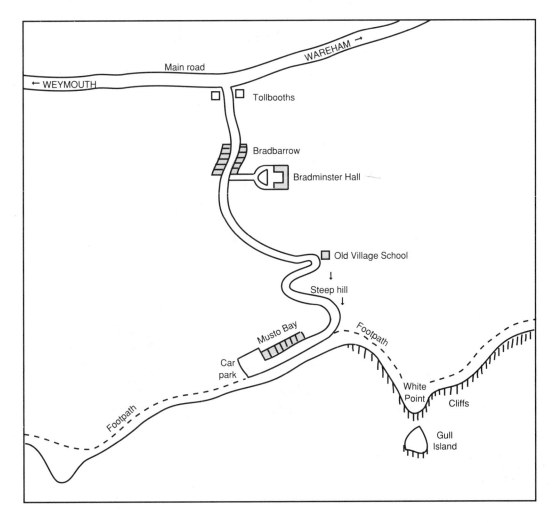

What impact on the area do you think each of the following events would have had?

1948 Chivers Tours includes a one-hour stop on their daily coach tours from nearby Weymouth

1955 A youth hostel is opened in what was the old village school

1964 The cliff path at White Point collapses into the sea and a party of walkers narrowly avoids a potentially fatal accident

1970 The Nottingham catch fly, a rare plant whose sticky leaves often entrap insects, is discovered growing on the cliffs

1972 The narrow road through the village of Bradbarrow is widened

1983 Musto Bay is featured in a *Sunday Times* article entitled 'England's Undiscovered Beauty'

1988 The toll charges on the Bradbarrow Road are doubled

1989 Planning permission is granted for a restaurant and country club on the site of Bradminster Hall.

Discovery of Oil in the Purbeck Area

Kimmeridge Bay

Although large areas of Britain are now covered by exploration licences, Dorset is the only region in which significant new **oil reserves** have been brought into production. The earliest discovery of oil in Dorset was at Kimmeridge, just along the coast from Studland, where shallow wells were sunk more than 50 years ago in the hope of discovering significant supplies. Early finds were limited by the fact that the wells were drilled to a depth no greater than 2,000 feet. In 1959 a well was sunk which remained the most productive single onshore well in Britain until Wytch Farm oil wells near Wareham began to operate.

The 'Nodding Donkey' pump at Kimmeridge

Wytch Farm

In 1974 the Gas Council, drilling near Wytch Farm at a depth of 3,000 feet, discovered reserves of oil then estimated at 30 million barrels. Production began in 1979, using four wellsites initially to produce a thousand barrels of oil a day. By 1983, when British Petroleum (BP) took over as operator for the Wytch Farm site, this quantity had quadrupled. Extracting the oil as fast as possible is the economic premise on which oil companies rely. However, they need to monitor oil fields carefully because extracting the oil too rapidly can result in geological changes which severely inhibit the process of extracting the remaining supply.

The Oil Beneath Poole and Studland

The first oil reservoir to be discovered in the Poole and Studland area, the Bridport Reservoir, was 3,000 feet below sea level. In 1979 a second reservoir, called the Sherwood Reservoir, was discovered at a depth of 5,200 feet. Exploratory wells eventually established that the total reserves were somewhere in the region of 200 million barrels. The size of this discovery suggested that the field might continue to produce oil commercially for 25 to 30 years.

Appraisal Drilling

In 1985 Dorset County Council granted permission for the drilling of up to four **appraisal wells** on Furzey Island, an island within Poole Harbour. British Petroleum had purchased this land from a private owner. Consultations took place over major issues such as the visibility of the site, its effect on air and water quality, the chances of spillage, the consequences for the area's wildlife habitats, and the particular inconveniences likely to arise during construction. During the period of the construction of the wellsite and the appraisal wells it was agreed that there would be no weekend working, that lighting and noise levels would be subject to agreed limits, and that secure boundaries around the site would be constructed and maintained.

Transporting the Oil

The best method of transporting oil from Poole Harbour was a subject which created considerable debate. The Poole Harbour Commissioners supported the use of tankers but others felt that this method carried the highest risk of serious spillage. Rail traffic to and from the oilfield would have had to be increased to 20 trains a day in each direction to carry the oil, while using the road system out of Wytch Farm would have involved putting further pressure on places which were already traffic bottlenecks in the summer months.

The Wytch Farm site

A pipeline seemed the most obvious solution, travelling either west to Weymouth or east to Southampton. Southampton, an existing oil port, seemed a preferable location, with better road, rail and sea access than Weymouth, but to get there the pipeline would have to cross the New Forest, for many years a popular haunt of tourists and a protected environment for plants and wildlife. Approval was eventually given, but many stringent conditions had to be met. The route ran mainly to the south of the New Forest on arable land, and took a number of detours to avoid the cutting down of trees. The trenching into which the pipe was sunk was kept as narrow as possible, which further reduced the possibility of damaging trees and plants. Once the pipeline had been laid the topsoil was replaced and the land replanted so that it resembled its original state.

Key Terms

oil reserves – the quantity of oil in a particular area which could be extracted from the ground.

appraisal wells – wells sunk in order to judge the extent of the oil reserves in a particular area.

◇ *Exercise* ◇

Read this extract from a newspaper article discussing the laying of the pipeline between Wytch Farm and Southampton:

Three of the most important conservation areas crossed by the pipeline were lowland heath sites. Special construction methods were developed, and the scale of these operations made them some of the most ambitious heath crossings ever undertaken.

On Creech Heath, for example, 600 wooden mats were laid to form a temporary road, and nearly 3,000 sq m of heather turf were lifted, stacked and replaced, and the site then irrigated to ensure the survival of the turf.

One of the more complicated aspects of the operation has been identifying the existing agricultural drainage systems, many of them laid down at the time of the early 19th century Enclosures Acts, and replacing or reconnecting them where they were severed by the pipeline.

"Some of the existing systems are so old that they had become very inefficient," said pipeline drainage officer Stuart Duncan, "and in the majority of cases it has been our policy to install completely new drainage systems to which the old ones have been connected.

"One of the problems has been the lack of proper drainage records, and this has meant relying on information gathered from inspection of the pipe trenches following excavation."

Ultimately, affected land-owners are to be presented by BP with comprehensive plans of the new drainage systems installed along the pipeline route, which in many cases include information on old, existing systems which was previously not known.

"We shall be continually monitoring the route for signs of drainage defects in the months ahead," said Stuart, "and will take action as required."

Landowners and occupiers need not worry in the long term, as BP accepts responsibility for land drainage along the pipeline route in perpetuity.

The route will be regularly patrolled on the ground and fortnightly by helicopter to ensure that no building work or tree planting takes place which could damage the pipeline. There will be no restriction on normal farming practices.

All this means maintaining close contact with the 216 land-owners and occupiers involved and with county, district and parish councils and other authorities.

"We have had a lot of co-operation from owners and occupiers during the laying of the pipeline, and we hope this rapport will continue," said senior lands officer for the pipeline, Rob Clarke.

a) Identify three problems which the extract says were encountered by the oil company in laying and operating the pipeline.

b) Explain in your own words the measures which the company took or intend taking in order to overcome these problems.

Offshore Exploration Wells

The knowledge that the Sherwood Reservoir extended eastwards under Poole Bay meant that permission had to be obtained for exploration wells to be drilled in offshore positions. After a further period of consultation this permission was eventually given, and appraisal drilling during the winter of 1988–9 confirmed the extent of the reserves, somewhere in the region of 100 million barrels. The oil-bearing rock extends some six kilometres out under the sea.

Bringing the Oil Ashore

The major concern for those living in the area was how the oil was to be brought ashore. There have been major advances in drilling techniques in recent years, and deviated wells, drilled at angles of up to 60 degrees, enable the oil to be brought to the surface a considerable distance away from its source. However, the size of the Sherwood discovery means that the oil cannot be extracted from the existing land sites. A more easterly wellsite was proposed, possibly offshore. Pumps would be needed, because the reservoir pressure is low. Studies suggested that the best location for a wellsite would be somewhere in the area bounded by Studland, Sandbanks and the Poole Rocks.

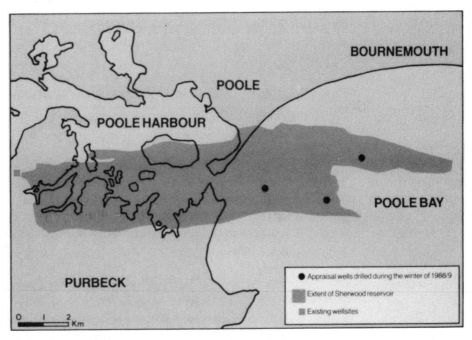

The location of wellsites

An Onshore Wellsite

An onshore wellsite, one of five possible methods proposed by BP for extracting the oil, would have had some advantages. It would be easy to screen the site from view by means of tree planting, fences or walls. It would also be relatively easy to construct the site so that any oil spillage could be contained. A pipeline to the existing facilities at Wytch Farm would be needed, but an onshore site would reduce the distance to be covered. However, in order to enable the maximum quantity of oil to be extracted, a site close to the end of the Studland peninsula or on the

Sandbanks peninsula would be required. Wellsites generally need ten acres of land, and neither the National Trust land at Studland nor the residential area of Sandbanks was thought to be appropriate. Although an onshore wellsite would be the cheapest option for the oil company, summer traffic congestion in the area would hinder the operation. Consultation with the statutory authorities and interest groups firmly ruled out an onshore wellsite solution for the development.

An Offshore Island

The construction of an offshore island always seemed a more likely solution. The same degree of screening and protection against spillage could be incorporated into the design. Although the drilling mast would be visible from the shore, the site most favoured by BP is two kilometres out to sea, so the drilling noise would be less of a problem and traffic to and from the site would be less evident than with a land site. The proposal suggests constructing the island in shallow water, and it was necessary to commission studies to find out what effect this would have on **sediment** patterns and tidal flows. An offshore island would require a pipeline to the shore, but this could be trenched into the seabed.

An offshore island

A Concrete Gravity-based Structure

An alternative to constructing an offshore island is to build a concrete, gravity-based structure which could be floated into position and then **ballasted** down onto the seabed. Although this structure could be smaller than the offshore island, it would rise higher out of the water. The nuisance factor in construction would be avoided as the structure could be built elsewhere. The amount of traffic and noise nuisance would be similar to that created by the island development. The major

A concrete gravity-based island

disadvantage of this plan is that the appearance of the structure would be difficult to disguise. As with the island development, the possibility of changes to sediment patterns would need research. Both schemes would also require negotiation with local fishing interests to ensure that navigation remains safe and that fishing activity is disrupted as little as possible.

A Wellhead Platform

The construction of a concrete or steel wellhead platform could be completed away from the area. The platform itself would be relatively small but would need the frequent presence of a jack-up drilling rig to drill and maintain the necessary wells. Although the platform would not be strikingly visible from the land, the height of the drilling rig would make it very evident and its appearance could not be easily disguised. These constructions also involve a higher risk of oil spillage into the sea. Two structures of this kind would be needed to extract the oil, both requiring 500-metre safety zones excluding navigation and fishing operations. Helicopters would be needed for access, and pipelines would be required both from the platform to the shore and to link the two structures.

A concrete wellhead platform

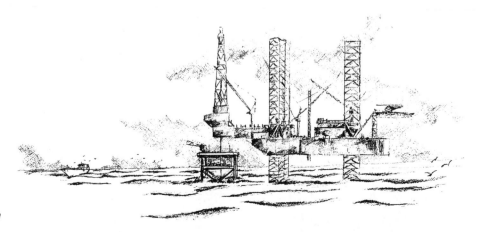

A steel wellhead platform

An Underwater Wellhead Construction

An underwater wellhead construction involves disturbing a wider area of the seabed because between four and six silos would be needed to house the wellheads. It would be virtually impossible to provide any significant anti-pollution containment measures and minor spillages caused during maintenance would enter the sea directly. As with the wellhead platform, a jack-up rig would be necessary to drill and maintain the wells. This construction would also require additional facilities to bring the oil to the surface.

Bringing the Oil into Production

All of these proposals were put to the Standing Conference on Oil and Gas Exploration in the English Channel. In addition, consultations were held with other voluntary and statutory bodies representing the interests of harbour authorities, conservation groups, fisheries associations, and tourism and recreation organisations. These included:

♦ Dorset Tourism Liaison Panel
♦ Southern Tourist Board
♦ Poole Tourism Service
♦ Bournemouth Department of Tourism
♦ Christchurch Tourism Office
♦ Swanage Town Council Tourism Office
♦ Poole Yachting Association
♦ Royal Yachting Association
♦ Poole Yacht Racing Association
♦ United Kingdom Offshore Boating Association.

A working group of local authority officials and BP representatives was set up to investigate the alternatives and put forward recommendations. The offshore island proposal was eventually agreed upon. BP has commissioned a series of environmental studies aimed at minimising the environmental effects of the development. Planning permissions and government consent will be subject to the company providing acceptable answers to environmental concerns. They have now placed a bill before Parliament which seeks approval for the offshore island construction. Even if the parliamentary bill is enacted this does not commit anyone to the development, which would still be dependent on satisfactory permissions being granted and on financial sanction being given by BP and its partners. It is unlikely that commercial production from the offshore sector of the reservoir will be possible before 1995. It is also unlikely that any construction work could begin before 1992.

Key Terms

sediment – sand and mud deposited on the bottom of the sea.

ballasted – weighed down with heavy material to prevent unwanted movement.

◇ *Exercise* ◇

Read the following extracts, taken from a public document produced by BP in January 1988, in which they gave details of their plans for offshore drilling in Poole Bay, just to the east of Studland:

There will only be one rig in the Bay at any one time. On most days the rig will be clearly visible from the coast, and from many locations around the Bay it will appear much the same as before. However, since the proposed drilling locations are closer to the shore the rig will appear larger than before when viewed from these nearby areas. Once drilling is completed the rig will be removed from the area.

Since the wells in block 98/6 will be drilled at locations over 1 mile from the shore it is unlikely that any activities on the rig will be heard by residents or people on the beach.

...The design of the rig is such that all deck drainings which could possibly contain oily water will not be discharged into the sea. Sewage will be treated before discharge, and other effluents such as cooling water will be carefully returned to the sea via a discharge pipe. The discharge of these effluents will need the consent of Wessex Water Authority and they will be monitored to check that the quality of discharges remains acceptable.

... The drilling programme will avoid the busy tourist period during the summer months, and so will have no effect on the tourism trade in Bournemouth and nearby coastal areas. Controls on discharges as described above will ensure that the beaches are protected and bathing water quality is not impaired.

... The presence of a drilling rig is not likely to affect fish stocks, and the aqueous discharges will have no detrimental impact on fisheries generally.

In groups, role-play a meeting of local residents to discuss the plans. You can decide on your roles, but they should include a local hotel owner, a local fisherman and a mother at home with young children.

Monitoring the Environmental Impact

Photographic Studies

Once the drilling of appraisal wells in Poole Bay was underway, BP set up a range of studies to monitor the effects of the drilling. The visual impact of the drilling rig had been assessed originally by the use of photographs from a number of coastal vantage points onto which impressions of the rig had been superimposed. Further photographs were taken of the actual rig, though the drilling all took place during the winter months, thus minimising the effect on tourism.

Noise Levels

Noise levels were measured at five locations along the Bournemouth–Poole seafront, both before and during drilling. The results suggested

*The rig drilling an
appraisal well*

that noise levels from wind, waves and traffic were generally higher
than the noise level from the drilling rig, which was consequently rarely
audible from the coast.

Analysis of the Drilling Mud and Cuttings

The **drilling mud** and **cuttings** produced from the appraisal wells were
the subject of detailed scientific analysis because they were found to
contain hydrocarbons. The analysis revealed that this came from the
deepest part of the wells and, because it was closely combined with rock
particles, was felt to represent no danger to marine life.

The Seabed

Divers checked the state of the seabed before the rig was put in place. During its operation they regularly checked the effect on sediment around the rig legs, and also made certain that no debris remained once the rig had been removed. The pile of drill cuttings was regularly monitored and its shape and area recorded. The sediment around the rig was tested for the presence of minerals such as copper, lead, zinc, barium and arsenic. Although some changes in the populations of various creatures and plants on the seabed were observed, these were thought to reflect natural variations rather than the effects of drilling.

Wildlife

Before the drilling began concern had been expressed about the sand eel colony on Hook Sands, which provides food and bait for the commercially important bass fishing in the area, as well as being part of the diet of seabirds such as puffins, razorbills and guillemots. Sand eels burrow into clean sand at night and it was feared that the presence of drilling mud might prove harmful to them. A survey showed that catches remained consistent during and after the appraisal drilling.

BP also contributed funds towards a survey to be carried out by the Nature Conservancy Council on the distribution and abundance of seabirds in the English Channel and the southern Irish Sea. A local study has also been commissioned to look at the numbers and locations of seabirds in Poole Bay, in particular the red-breasted merganser, grebes, seaduck and auks.

In places where the Wytch Farm–Southampton pipeline crossed sand lizard and smooth-snake colonies, the Nature Conservancy Council licensed a 'trap and release' scheme whereby the reptiles were collected and released in a suitable environment elsewhere. On the well-site at Arne the reptile population was monitored and some habitat-creation work was carried out.

Saltmarsh Restoration

Where the pipeline crossed the Wytch Moor saltmarsh, the land was carefully reinstated. This meant removing and preserving the saltmarsh turves until they could be relaid. A modified industrial vacuum cleaner was used to collect seeds from the area so that the pipeline corridor could also be reseeded with sea asters, sea spurry and saltmarsh grasses.

Key Terms

drilling mud – fluid material pumped down the inside of the steel drilling pipe to cool the drill bit and to bring samples of rock to the surface.

cuttings – the fragments of rock extracted by the drilling process.

◇ *Exercise* ◇

Write a summary of the main conclusions which can be drawn from the results of the noise monitoring measurements shown below:

(a) BACKGROUND NOISE LEVEL MEASUREMENTS PRIOR TO RIG OPERATIONS. 2 OCTOBER 1988 AND 28 OCTOBER 1988

Location	Time		Statistical Analysis (dBA)			L_{eq} (dBA)	Comments
	Start	Duration (mins)	L_{10}	L_{50}	L_{90}		
1. Pavilion Car Park—Poole Head	0100	30	37.0	35.0	33.5	36.9	Very quiet with gentle wave noise. No passing vehicles. Wind occasional gusts to 1 m/sec (2.10.88)
2. Cliff Road	0100	30	46.0	44.5	43.0	51.3	Gentle wave noise. One passing vehicle. Constant wind speed 1 m/sec occasional gusts to 4 m/sec. Peak noise from vehicle 72 dB(A). (28.10.88)
3. Branksome Chine Car Park	0135	30	56.5	53.5	41.0	54.6	Occasional vehicles passing on road and entering car park. Pronounced wave noise. Peak noise level from vehicles 60 dB(A). (28.10.88)
4. Argyll Gardens	0015	30	52.0	42.0	39.0	51.1	Wave noise occasionally discernible passing vehicles in West Overcliff Drive. (2.10.88)
5. East Overcliff Drive	2340	30	53.0	41.0	37.2	52.3	Traffic passing on road and noise from distant traffic discernible. Wave noise not noticeable. (2.10.88)

Weather Conditions
2.10.88:   Wind NW occ 1 m/sec, neap tide with light cloud.
Temperature 10°C.
28.10.88:   Clear, moonlit light
Temperature 15°C.

(b) NOISE LEVEL MEASUREMENTS DURING DRILLING OF 98/6E. 17 NOVEMBER 1988

Location	Time		Statistical Analysis (dBA)			L_{eq} (dBA)	Comments
	Start	Duration (mins)	L_{10}	L_{50}	L_{90}		
1. Pavilion Car Park—Poole Head	0230	15	45.5	44.0	42.5	44.3	Very light wave noise. Occasional brake/drawworks noise just discernible.
2. Cliff Road	0210	15	48.0	46.5	45.0	46.9	Wave noise predominating with occasional noise from brake/drawworks just discernible.
3. Branksome Chine Car Park	0155	15	53.5	51.5	50.5	52.7	No discernible noise from rig.
4. Argyll Gardens	0120	30	48.5	46.0	44.0	49.3	Slight wave noise with one passing vehicle (peak noise level 69 dB(A)). No discernible rig noise.
5. East Overcliff Drive	0045	30	50.5	44.0	42.5	49.8	Some slight wave noise with rig not discernible.

Weather Conditions
Light cloud occasional wind gusting to 1 m/sec
Temperature 12°C.

dB(A)—An internationally accepted unit for the measurement and assessment of environmental noise.
Typical noise levels on this scale are as follows:—
    20 dB(A)—Remote countryside on a still night.
    40 dB(A)—Living room.
    60 dB(A)—Office or restaurant.
    80 dB(A)—Kerbside of a busy street.
L10—Level of noise exceeded for 10% of the time period under consideration.
L90—Level of noise exceeded for 90% of the time period under consideration.
L_{eq}—A notional steady level which over a given period delivers the same energy as actual fluctuating sound.

Oil Spill Contingency Plans

Risks of environmental damage caused by oil spillage are greatest at the initial stage of drilling when the oil pressure is at its highest, although the risks involved in transporting oil must also be taken into account in any oil development. An oil spill on land is relatively easy to contain, but oil can move rapidly and disperse over a large area if it reaches water. The distance of any spillage from emergency equipment will also determine the speed of its containment. Surface tidal currents will affect the directional movement of any spillage at sea.

Wellsite Safety Features

The original Wytch Farm development incorporated oil-proof ditches surrounding the site to catch any leaks from valves or pipes. On sites close to the water's edge inflatable booms were used to prevent any oil running off into Poole Harbour. All the drilling sites have a mobile trailer fitted with a range of equipment designed to carry out a rapid clean-up operation to prevent any oil finding its way into rivers, streams or the harbour itself. The wellsites are also operated in such a way that all equipment is carefully monitored, and separate sections can be quickly and independently closed down in an emergency.

Emergency Provision

Equipment designed to cope with any major spillage is on 24-hour standby at a number of locations around Poole Harbour and along the oil pipeline to Hamble. If a spillage were to occur the oil company could call on the help of other services such as Wessex and Southern Water Authorities and Dorset County Council. There is also a major emergency service based in Southampton, called the Oil Spill Service Centre. Established in 1981, largely by BP themselves, this organisation now holds some £7 million worth of equipment and has experience of dealing with oil spills in a variety of environments around the world. Regular exercises, often unannounced, are carried out to test emergency procedures.

Measures to Contain Offshore Spillage

During the offshore appraisal drilling an oil pollution control vessel remained on standby at all times. This ship carries equipment for containing oil spills and pumping recovered oil into tankers. It also carries dispersant spray systems which can divide oil slicks into tiny particles which will disperse easily. The Bournemouth/Poole beach area was provided with a container of equipment to be used in the event of an offshore spillage.

Insurance

BP's insurance cover would enable them to pay the local authority for the use of its emergency services. They are also insured for any direct damage which an oil spill might cause. Hotel owners may argue that a major oil spillage would cause people to cancel bookings and so deprive them of their livelihood. However, BP is not insured against these losses, arguing that it is impossible to assess accurately the reasons for all cancellations and also that others, such as taxi drivers and shop-keepers, could make similar claims for loss of trade which would be just as difficult to assess.

◇ *Exercise* ◇

A hotelier writing in a trade newspaper made the following comments:

... the oil has been there a long time, it is not needed at the moment, why not leave it there until it is really needed? ... The oil industry is the only industry that can put us, the tourist industry, out of business in 24 hours and for many years ... BP will earn 2.8 billion over 25 years ... by comparison Bournemouth alone will earn 15.8 billion in tourism over the same period, employing many more than any other industry...

Write two letters to the newspaper, one from a representative of a local conservation group and one from a representative of the oil company, commenting on the hotelier's remarks.

The Future of Studland Bay

Environmental Concerns

The Nature Conservancy Council expressed the view that, despite the agreement to restore land crossed by the pipeline to its original state, some damage was likely to be permanent. They were also concerned that discharges into the sea should continue to be carefully monitored. The wildfowl in Poole Harbour and the colonies of cormorants, kittiwakes, guillemots, fulmars and puffins nesting in cliffs along the coast west of Swanage would be particularly vulnerable in the event of any oil spillage, however slight this risk might be. Local current and tidal patterns would need to be recorded as they may change as a result of constructing an artificial island. The effect on the level of sediment in the surrounding sea water also needs continued observation. Feeding and roosting habits of birds in the area might be disturbed by increases in boat traffic and construction work.

Future Sources of Energy

The issue of future energy sources will have an impact on places like Studland. The oil there may last for 25 years, but in the next century the world's supplies will cease to meet the demand. More attention is being paid to the massive energy generated by wind and tides. They represent potential sources of most of our future power needs, but this carries environmental implications. Harnessing wind power would involve the construction of windmills which would be impossible to disguise. Many areas where the winds are strongest, such as the west of Scotland, are also areas containing much highly-valued landscape. Use of tidal energy would involve constructions such as the dam which it was suggested could be built across Morecambe Bay. Such a construction would not only completely alter the visual appearance of the estuary but would also severely affect the habitat of many birds, shellfish and plants.

Visitor Management at Studland Bay

Studland Bay will face a number of issues in the future apart from the proximity of offshore oil drilling. If it is regarded as important to preserve some of the best examples of unspoilt natural environments in Britain, they will need to be carefully managed. This will mean management of tourists as well as the landscape and wildlife habitats. The introduction of traffic controls and road toll charges or admission charges to areas of outstanding natural beauty could become essential for their survival.

The Impact of the Offshore Oil Development

The impact of the construction of an offshore island near Studland Bay may take some years to evaluate. The supply of sand in the bay is important in preserving the appearance of the coastline. The presence of an offshore island might affect currents and sediment movements in the bay, and its construction would involve the dredging of marine sand and gravel for infilling the island.

◇ *Exercise* ◇

Imagine you are standing on Studland Beach in the summer of the year 2015.

  Write two descriptions of what you might see, the first reflecting successful management of the area in the intervening years and the second reflecting what might happen if environmental issues were not effectively tackled.

◇ *Discussion points* ◇

1 Is the continuing problem of litter a sign of laziness or of a lack of interest in the appearance of our surroundings, or are there other causes?

2 How important is it that rare species such as the sand lizard should continue to be found in Britain?

3 Had you been present at the consultation meetings held prior to the appraisal drilling, what questions would you have wished to ask BP?

4 Can you suggest any methods of disguising a concrete or steel wellhead platform?

5 To what uses do you think the information revealed by a survey of seabirds could be put?

6 What kind of planning would there need to be before holding an exercise to test emergency oil spillage procedures?

10 *Tourism Concern*

Introduction

Mass tourism has grown rapidly since the 1960s, and as a result many European coastal resorts have been developed, particularly in countries like Spain. This has undoubtedly brought economic gains, but high-rise hotels now crowd the coastline, and major problems include congestion and the antisocial behaviour of some young tourists. The number of tourists visiting destinations like Spain has fallen as a result. This has been accompanied by a growing interesting in **long-haul** destinations. More regular **charter flights** to places such as Goa and Thailand have meant a reduction in the air fares, and this has encouraged many tourists to look further afield. As many of these new destinations have both fragile economies and fragile environments, organisations like Tourism Concern aim to protect the interests of the **host communities**. They do not wish to see short-term economic benefit followed by the social, cultural and environmental decay which rapid tourism development can bring about. Tourists purchase an experience highly dependent on people and landscapes, and their presence should not be a threat to the landscape and its people's traditional way of life.

Tourists buying souvenirs

Economic Benefits

Governments in many parts of the world have seen tourism as a means of creating employment and generating income. Not only are jobs in hotels, restaurants and transport created, but also those who supply food, goods and services benefit. However, it is not always easy to assess how much foreign visitors will spend at their destination, and it is even more difficult to calculate how much of the profit will be received by the local people. The large sums required to develop hotels and transport systems often come from the countries which the visitors originate from, and much of the profit from such developments is returned to the original **investors**. Increased employment may be only seasonal and is not necessarily well paid. In some countries tensions can develop between generations when the younger people neglect traditional skills and education and, by working in hotels and restaurants, earn more than their parents and grandparents.

Social Conflicts

The arrival of mass tourism in new destinations can create a number of other social tensions. The younger people in the host community are often attracted by the dress and behaviour of the tourists. They lose interest in the traditional way of life of their own people because they want to adopt the lifestyle of the tourists. In societies where modesty and respect for older people have been highly valued in the past, such changes of behaviour among the young may result in a breakdown of the social structure and value system.

Threatened Cultures

Tourists sometimes choose to visit Third World destinations because they wish to escape from the noise, dirt and pressures of an industrial society. They may feel they are escaping from a very materialistic world into a society which is purer, where closeness to nature is preserved and age-old cultures are kept alive through art and **ritual**. The prospect of returning home to the culture they were escaping from encourages tourists to take photographs and buy mementoes, hoping that this will prolong their experience. The real consequence of this desire for souvenirs and photographs is often to place pressure on the local people to produce souvenirs and to perform such things as ritual dances. Artistic objects and ritual dances no longer exist solely to meet the needs of the local community on festive occasions but must meet the continuous demands of the tourists.

Environmental Damage

Many landscapes are seriously threatened by a growing number of visitors. Among the consequences may be the gradual erosion of land adjacent to popular footpaths, the cutting down of trees to provide more ski slopes and the disruption of popular wildlife habitats such as those of the African game reserves. It is not only Third World countries which suffer from a tourist presence. Buildings such as the Leaning Tower of Pisa and the Parthenon have been closed to tourists, and in cities such as Florence the only way to get an uninterrupted view of the streets and squares in summer is to arrive very early in the morning.

Methods of controlling erosion in the Yorkshire Dales: reconstructing footpaths using gravelled steps bordered by stone walls, putting ladders over dry stone walls, and asking the public to avoid eroded areas.

Responsible Tourism Development

Action to combat the adverse effects of tourism can be taken at a number of levels. Governments could choose to restrict the number of tourists admitted to sites, and the number of sites to which tourists have access. Local communities could challenge more effectively the less acceptable kinds of resort development, or offer alternatives which would involve less disruption. A growing number of tour operators have accepted the view that they should contribute towards the preservation of the natural resources and habitats from which they benefit. They may either fund environmental projects directly or promote responsible tourism by means of guide books or videos suggesting what is appropriate behaviour at different destinations. Travel journalists may also play an increasing role in changing public opinion by balancing their descriptions of new and exotic destinations with articles pointing out the impact of tourism.

Key Terms

long-haul – requiring a long aeroplane flight, usually in excess of eight hours.

charter flights – flights booked for a particular purpose such as transporting holiday-makers to a specific destination.

host communities – the local inhabitants of regions receiving visitors.

investors – individuals or companies providing money so that a development can be built or established.

ritual – a ceremony, often of religious and cultural significance to the participants.

◇ *Exercise* ◇

As a group, collect a varied selection of your own holiday photographs and divide them into the following categories:

♦ buildings of interest
♦ scenery and landscapes
♦ leisure activities.

Choose a photograph from each category and ask the person who took it to describe all that they remember of the scene shown in the photograph.

Discuss whether the photographs reflect these memories, and how they might have been taken in order to give different impressions.

Origin and Brief History of Tourism Concern

Tourism Concern was conceived in mid-1988 as a counterpart to a number of European groups working on tourism issues, particularly in relation to the Third World. Its first intention was to provide information to people who shared an interest in protecting the interests of host communities, so that they could keep in touch with developments. This information included notice of relevant conferences and articles, and individual causes of concern were publicised. Activities were added as funding allowed so that, for example, September 1989 saw the publication of the first newsletter to be circulated to Tourism Concern members.

The members of Tourism Concern come from varied backgrounds. Some became involved because they have travelled extensively; others are trainers and educators overseas. A number have a professional interest in tourism, either as **academics**, journalists or employees within the tourist industry. Some of the members are drawn from the host communities of Third World tourist destinations.

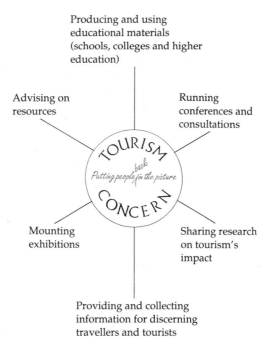

Producing and using educational materials (schools, colleges and higher education)

Advising on resources

Running conferences and consultations

Mounting exhibitions

Sharing research on tourism's impact

Providing and collecting information for discerning travellers and tourists

Tourism Concern activities

Worldwide Links

Tourism Concern is part of a network of organisations all over the world, with whom there is a constant exchange of ideas, resources and information. The founder of the network is the Ecumenical Coalition on Third World Tourism which is based in Bangkok, Thailand. Since 1981 the ECTWT has been drawing attention to the effects of tourism on the world's poorer countries. It is supported by churches in the Caribbean, Latin America, Africa, the Pacific and the Middle East. Other overseas groups involved in this network include the Centre for Responsible Tourism, based in the United States, and Equations, an organisation based in Bangalore in India.

Promoting Responsible Tourist Developments

Not all of Tourism Concern's activities involve the negative effects of tourism. They also research and publicise forms of tourism which benefit host communities and the environments in which they live. It is recognised that the tourism industry cannot be changed unless those with concerns about its effects are willing to enter into a dialogue with those involved. For this reason Tourism Concern is represented at conferences and **seminars** about tourism, as well as at trade fairs and exhibitions.

Publicity

Since its formation, Tourism Concern has had coverage in the national press and in regional newspapers. A small leaflet explaining the structure, activities and aims of the organisation has been published. As a result of a project involving staff and students from Marjons College, Plymouth, a modular exhibition about Tourism Concern was developed and displayed for the first time on a stand at the Daily Mail Holiday Show in February 1990. Tourism Concern has also been represented at seminars and conferences organised by the English Tourist Board and the Tourism Society, and have contributed to a special stand at the Berlin International Tourism Fair, organised by the European group Tourism with Insight.

Key Terms

academics – people who are professionally employed in the detailed study of a subject.

seminars – discussion groups examining an agreed subject of study.

◇ *Exercise* ◇

The design below is the logo adopted by Tourism Concern:

a) What message does it convey to you?
b) What alternative design can you suggest which would convey a similar message?

Four Destinations Giving Cause for Concern

1. Mexico

Mexico has always attracted visitors, especially from North America. Acapulco is perhaps the best known of its beach resorts, but recently a number of modern beach resorts have been constructed at places such as Cancun and Cozumel. Tourism Concern recently drew attention to the building of a new resort at Huatulco, about 300 miles south-east of Acapulco.

The area of Huatulco includes an 18-mile stretch of the Pacific coast, made up of nine separate bays. Good beaches, a mountainous background and constant warm temperatures are all factors likely to make the area attractive to tourists. Oaxaca, the state in which Huatulco lies, was identified by the Mexican government as being sufficiently poor to warrant a boost to its economy.

An Acapulco Hotel

Land Purchase
Compulsory purchase of land by the government meant that families dependent on fishing for many generations were rehoused in the newly-constructed tourist town, La Crucecita. Newspapers reported that the government fund set up to purchase the land and resell it to developers paid the original occupants very little for their land, but it was resold to developers at hugely inflated prices.

Proposed Development

Planning permission has already been obtained for developments in all nine of the bays, including the construction of five-star hotels, residences and golf courses. In La Crucecita a disco and a marina are already under construction. Although its population at the beginning of 1990 was a mere 800, the plan is for the bays of Huatulco to support a population of more than 300,000 by the time the development is completed. The Mexican government sees potential employment as a major reason for the development, estimating that it may eventually create 100,000 jobs.

Descriptions of the Huatulco Development

The Tourism Concern newsletter includes a section entitled 'Juxtapositions' in which extracts about particular tourist destinations from newspaper articles, brochures and reports are set alongside each other so that readers are invited to draw their own conclusions. The information about the Huatulco development is placed next to brochure extracts advertising holidays in the area. The use of words like 'relaxing', 'secluded', 'hideaways' and 'unspoiled' in the brochures assume a different significance when placed alongside more critical newspaper articles. One brochure concedes that new buildings will occupy much, though not all, of the coastline in the area, but suggests that these buildings will 'grace' the bays.

Conflicting Brochure Information

A number of brochures about Mexico suggest that visitors should not attempt to buy local goods without haggling over the price, saying that this is both customary and expected. Tourism Concern printed a leaflet in their newsletter which had been produced by a number of Mexican workers and was intended for distribution among tourists. It pointed out that prices quoted for goods are what visitors should expect to pay. Sellers needing food for the day may be persuaded to lower their prices but they will have to recoup this loss the following day. The leaflet also explained that giving tips is usual in Mexico and is an important part of the income of those employed in the service industries.

Environmental Implications

At some point in the future water shortages are likely to affect both tourism development and the local community in Huatulco. Wildlife is also threatened. The area has been an undisturbed habitat for deer, eagles and turtles for centuries. However, the developers do plan to create an **ecological** reserve where the bougainvillea, laurel trees, almond trees, palms and buttercups can flourish.

Key Term

ecological – involving the study of plants and animals in relation to their environment.

◇ *Exercise* ◇

Read the brochure extract below about shopping in Mexico:

> Mexico is a gift hunter's paradise. Not only does everything look cheap to start with, by the time you've haggled for a while the value can be simply incredible. Look out for local crafts and handiwork – ceramics, silverware and jewellery, woven woollen goods and blankets (serapes), leatherwork, hammocks and the obligatory sombrero. Even if you don't buy, a visit to the market is an experience that no-one should miss.

a) What impression do you think the writer hoped to create by using each of the following words:

paradise, cheap, value, incredible, obligatory?

b) Rewrite the paragraph in the style you think a Mexican seller of crafts and handiwork would have chosen.

2. *Kerala, Southern India*

The state of Kerala lies on the south-west coast of India, facing the Arabian Sea. The beach resort of Kovalam was recently constructed, including luxury bungalows and a five-storey hotel. The resort is only a few miles away from Trivandrum, the state capital, which received its first tourist charter flight in 1989. A British company operated flights in and out of Kerala, contributing to an 18 per cent increase in the number of visitors to the state compared to the previous year.

Cultural Traditions

Many of India's visitors are attracted by its fine buildings, such as the Taj Mahal and the Jaipur palaces, and its distinctive cultures. Kerala has strong cultural traditions of its own. For example, during April or May each year a festival known as Trichur Pooram takes place. Generally coinciding with a new moon, the festival is characterised by a procession of elephants decorated in brightly coloured and jewelled coverings.

Elephants line up for the Trichur Pooram Festival

The Tourism Department in Kerala organised a re-enactment of the Trichur Pooram Festival, as well as a separate event in Trivandrum which was given the title 'The Great Elephant March'. This elephant march gave tourists the opportunity to ride the smaller garlanded elephants, and also included a tug-of-war between an elephant and hundreds of local people. Local groups argued that these activities completely undermined traditional values and that imitation festivals held at the wrong time of year were meaningless. Despite these views, and the fact that the Great Elephant March was poorly supported, it seems likely that the event will be repeated, with an effort to advertise it more widely.

Managing Existing Resources

Tourism Concern print a leaflet which is produced in Kerala and given to tourists there. This argues the case about the devaluation of local culture quite forcefully, but lays much of the blame on the state government rather than on the tourists themselves. It suggests that Kerala had all the resources to maintain a stable agricultural and industrial economy. It asserts that such resources have too often been spent on imported **consumer goods**, and too little has been done to protect the supply of essential foods and power sources. Rising unemployment is one consequence of this disregard. The leaflet blames the state for forcing the people to debase their own culture in order to secure income from tourism.

Key Term

consumer goods – goods available for people to buy.

◇ *Exercise* ◇

The brochure extracts below describe the Ram Lila festival and the temple dances of Khajuraho:

Once every year, in the cool shadows of some ten twilight evenings, the frozen fluidity of the Khajuraho sculptures melts to release the spirit of Dance. Against the backdrop of the temples and their friezes depicting scenes from the ancient text of the Kamasutra, internationally acclaimed exponents of the major styles of Indian classical dance perform their art before you, like the devadasis or handmaidens of God, of old. Even as poetry in stone transmutes to flesh, ethereal images of flesh become immortalised in stone.

...The giant thread that knits the great Indian cultural tradition is the ancient epic of the Ramayana, whose theme recurs in an infinity of ways in classical and folk Indian dance, music, literature, sculpture and even film. Every year, some days before the Indian New Year, the Ramayana, the saga of Lord Rama, the ideal human being, and his wife Sita, the epitome of Indian womanhood, is enacted over ten days in almost every city and village in India in an open-air performance of music and drama called the Ram Lila. In Benaras the Ram Lila takes on particular significance as the Maharajah of Benaras leads the final procession through the ancient streets culminating in the public burning of a mammoth effigy of Ravana, the ten-headed embodiment of Evil, in which the Ram Lila transcends its Hindu origins to become a universal act of faith.

A tour operator has decided to feature two of the following events in a brochure designed to attract foreign visitors to Britain:

♦ a cathedral Christmas service of Nine Lessons and Carols
♦ a Remembrance Day parade
♦ a Harvest Festival service
♦ a pilgrimage to Walsingham.

Write paragraphs about two of these events which, like the Indian examples, emphasise their spectator appeal at the expense of their religious or cultural significance.

3. *Gambia*

The Gambia is a small country on the Atlantic coast of Africa, extending inland along both banks of the River Gambia. On the coast the river meets the Atlantic with a series of sand cliffs and some 30 miles of palm-fringed beaches. Sub-tropical weather and the fact that English is widely spoken made The Gambia an attractive proposition for tour operators looking for new destinations.

In 1965 a Swedish company began operating charter flights in and out of the capital, Banjul, and by 1971 tour operators from other European countries were beginning to fly tourists there. During the holiday season of 1988–9 more than 112,000 tourists were estimated to have visited the country.

A Gambian market

Employment and Income from Tourism

Tourism Concern's Spring 1990 newsletter included an estimate that tourism has created employment for some 6,000 Gambians directly and indirectly. Although some of this employment is connected with the provision of accommodation, transport and retail activities, tourism has encouraged less formal ways of earning a living which are unlikely to be in the country's long-term interests. Visitors have thrown coins from buses to young children. Youths have offered friendship and visits to their homes in return for money and presents. Such gifts are often worth more than the whole week's earnings of older Gambians, which makes these practices divisive.

Effects of Tourism on the Gambian Economy

Gambia is only six hours' flying time from London, which means that relatively inexpensive package holidays there can be put together. The Gambian economy benefits from tourism because 50 per cent of tourism profits go to the government through taxation. However, many of the hotels are owned and managed by foreign concerns, with the result that a proportion of their profits is not invested in the Gambia. The importing of large quantities of food is another drain on the profits from tourism. In the past huge borrowing by the government was used to finance the building of hotels, a policy which would have drastic effects on the national economy if the income from tourism showed any marked decline. However, in recent years there has been a concerted effort to encourage local investment in the tourism development area. The Gambian economy is, apart from tourism, almost entirely agricultural, with most exports being groundnut products. Tourism has provided a broader economic base and now accounts for approximately 90 per cent of the **gross domestic product**.

The Language of Travel Brochures

The picture of the Gambian people which emerges from brochure extracts quoted by Tourism Concern suggests that they are in some ways inferior to their visitors. Words like 'imperfections' and 'rough and ready' are used to comment on the Gambian way of life. Some brochures go so far as to promote The Gambia as a place which offers a primitive experience. Other brochures describe local **handicrafts** in a style which suggests they are tasteless and, by implication, inferior to similar European products. If the attitudes and perceptions of tourists are influenced by this kind of language, there is less chance of the Gambians being treated with dignity and respect.

Key Terms

gross domestic product – the total value of all the goods and services produced by a country (usually measured over the course of a year), minus any income the country earns from investments abroad.

handicrafts – craft objects made by hand.

◇ *Exercise* ◇

The following extract describes sports opportunities for tourists in the Gambia:

Swimming: The estuary of the River Gambia on the Atlantic coast provides miles of magnificent beaches with warm seas throughout the year. Caution is necessary due to strong currents, but the beach at Cape St Mary is safe for both children and adults. **Watersports:** Resorts cater for windsurfing and surfing on the Atlantic coast. **Fishing:** Both sea and river fishing is good all year, particularly line fishing from the beaches. The Gambia Sailing Club at Banjul welcomes visitors. A notable event is the race to Dog Island;

in addition, regattas are organised on special occasions. **Golf:** The Banjul Golf Club has an 18-hole golf course at Fajara near the Atlantic coast. International meetings are organised every year. **Tennis** courts are available at some hotels, while details of the location of other courts are available from the Tourist Information Office or most hotel receptions. Tennis clubs include The Cedar Club near Serekunda and the Reform Club in Banjul. There are also plenty of opportunities for **shooting** in the inland regions.

Bouts (a traditional sport) can be seen on most weekends in Banjul and its suburbs, Serekunda and Bakau. Inter-club **cricket** is played in league matches organised by the Gambia Cricket Association which also organises international matches. A league championship is organised by the Gambia Football Association. **Wrestling** is the traditional national sport, and contests can be watched in most towns and villages.

The Gambian Government want to increase employment opportunities for native Gambians through these sports activities. Discuss how they can achieve this, and make a note of your suggestions in a memo to the Committee for Sports Advantages.

4. *The Dominican Republic*

Columbus discovered the island of Hispaniola in 1492 and, although the part of the island now known as Haiti was ceded to France in 1697, the eastern half of the island, now known as the Dominican Republic, retains a strong Spanish influence. Sugar production provides employment for almost half the population and constitutes 90 per cent of the value of the country's exports.

Before tourism developed significantly in the Dominican Republic, fears were expressed about the safety of the airport. There were also problems with water and electricity supplies, which were subject to interruption. Pressure from hoteliers and tour operators led to the government spending money on improving the airport. They also promised to improve water and electricity supplies, even though this might lead to supplies to local people being cut off before tourist supplies were restricted.

Environmental Problems

Tourism Concern have publicised a plea from the Dominican Federation of Ecological Associations about the millions of trees which have been cut down to enable the construction of hotels and golf courses. Some of these, such as mangroves, are scarce, while others formed essential habitats for native and migratory birds.

The use of pesticides to kill mosquitos and other insects which might irritate tourists has resulted in the pollution of lagoons and inland waters. Coastal waters are affected by the disposal of sewage

*A beach in the
Dominican Republic*

directly into the sea. Coral systems have been irreparably damaged as increasing quantities of coral are removed to make jewellery and handicrafts.

Side-stepping Laws and Regulations

The Ecological Associations claim that the government is allowing developers to ignore laws and regulations in order to encourage the growth of tourism. For example, sea turtles, a protected species elsewhere in the world, are killed so that their shells can be turned into souvenirs, and their eggs and meat can be served up as part of the more exotic dishes for tourists. Crabs and lobsters are caught out of season, with little regard to their size or gender, thus threatening to eliminate them locally. Regulations intended to prevent any tourist development inside the National Park at Montecriste have also been ignored. Permits are officially required to conduct tours, but the Ecological Associations insist that helicopters and outboard motorboats regularly disturb these sensitive environments and do not have permission to do so.

◇ *Exercise* ◇

Below are five descriptions of hotels in the Dominican Republic:

1 An impressive hotel located directly on the beach, the modern Playa Dorada is ideal for those looking for a lively and fun holiday. The accommodation comprises one building with two wings, beside which there is a large swimming pool and sun terrace. With such a good choice of facilities and such an easy-going atmosphere, the hotel has a wide appeal.

2 In a quiet setting, slightly away from the beach, the "colonial" atmosphere of this impressive, traditionally-styled hotel makes it the perfect spot for a tranquil holiday. The hotel is situated on the edge of the Playa Dorada golf course and there is a free shuttle buggy to the beach, about 500 metres away. If you want to enjoy a good choice of watersports, you will not be disappointed as there are

plenty available from the beach. A daily activity programme is organised for the more energetic, otherwise relaxing by the pool is an enjoyable pastime.

3 Built in a nostalgic Spanish-Colonial style, the three-storey buildings which make up the guest accommodation are beautifully set in lush gardens. The pastel-shaded buildings are just across the road from the beach and there is a superb swimming pool and sun terrace. With so many facilities on site, and a daily activity programme, there's plenty to keep everyone occupied at the hotel.

4 Situated in beautiful grounds, this comfortable hotel is built in elegant colonial style and occupies one of the best positions on the Playa Dorada beach. The hotel boasts a

choice of restaurants, three bars, an activity programme and casino. Most importantly, guests will be delighted by the warm friendly service and thoroughly easy-going atmosphere.

5 … a distinguished 19th century-style hotel, offering its guests a thoroughly relaxing holiday, spiced with daily entertainments and a wide choice of cuisine and bars. The hotel has a beautiful, large terrace area which incorporates a freshwater swimming pool. With seven tennis-courts (three of which are floodlit), a tennis shop, coaches and occasional tournaments, this is a particularly suitable choice for tennis enthusiasts. For trips to the beach (under 900 metres away) and the beach club bar, the hotel has regular transport.

Which aspects of each hotel are likely to have affected the local community:

a) during the period of their construction?
b) now that they are fully operative?

Responsible Tourism Development

Alternative Tourism

There are a growing number of tourism models which, Tourism Concern argues, show more consideration for the long-term interests of host communities, while at the same time offering a worthwhile experience to tourists. These schemes are often described as Alternative Tourism. However, many people feel this term is unclear and that it fails to make allowance for the fact that different kinds of tourism may be equally appropriate in different destinations. What is viewed as a desirable alternative to existing tourism in one location may be quite undesirable elsewhere.

Green Tourism

Green Tourism is a concept which originated in France many years ago, and contrasts with White Tourism (based on snow resorts) and Blue Tourism (based on sea and lakeside resorts). The French, however, now use the term 'Rural Tourism' because the term 'Green Tourism' is an inadequate general term for the most desirable kinds of rural tourist development. The term Rural Tourism has become associated with countryside and small community developments. The term has limited use, because it suggests that non-rural tourism is incapable of taking due consideration of the environment.

Sustainable Tourism

Studies of the damaging effect of the expanding skiing industry in the Alps in the 1970s led to the idea of Sustainable Tourism. The intention of Sustainable Tourism was to provide an experience for the tourist which went beyond a superficial encounter with the culture and life of the host community. By shifting the emphasis away from the mass spectacle towards smaller, more widespread activities, the idea was to stimulate the local culture gradually and to enable it to develop in a way which might avoid the debasing effect of regular public performances in tourist 'honeypots'.

Sustainable Tourism needs considerable resources directed into tourist management and into the conservation of a wide range of landscapes and cultural products, whether these be dance, music, art, food, tradition or language. Tourists can be managed by traffic restrictions. Access to popular sites can be confined to forms of transport like rail and bus, where the numbers can be strictly limited.

The Role of the Media

If travel articles and television programmes were to focus on a wider range of destinations, some people would be persuaded to try less well-known destinations. They could also be encouraged to use a different, more environmentally friendly means of getting there. Yet without some overall strategy there is always the risk that such encouragement will simply spoil locations which were previously little known. The travel writer, Eric Newby, planning a television series about 'Hidden Europe' is reported to have said, 'I wonder if we really ought to be doing this. If we do, it won't be hidden for long – and that will be our responsibility.'

Responsible Tourism

In 1989 a seminar on Alternative Tourism, organised in Algeria by the World Tourism Organisation, defined Responsible Tourism as:

> … relating to all forms of tourism which show respect for the host's natural, built and cultural environments and the interests of all the parties concerned, including hosts, guests, visitors, the tourist industry and governments.

The term Responsible Tourism represents a reaction against mass tourism, laying emphasis on the individual experience. The most often-quoted examples of Responsible Tourism usually involve small, independent tour operators who concentrate on small accommodation units, generally owned locally. However, the fact that Responsible Tourism is for the most part small-scale means that only a limited number of tourists can experience it and therefore it can only bring limited economic benefits.

An example of Responsible Tourism is the Locus Project, based in Aberfeldy in Scotland. This project provides tourists with a choice of tours, each linked to a theme. Local people provide information and accommodation at times which are convenient to them, so that there is plenty of opportunity to manage the movement of tourists. Staying with local people gives visitors the opportunity of acquiring more than just a superficial knowledge of the region.

Nepal by Bicycle, started by Surendra Thapa in 1983, offers tours of Nepal. The company brochure says, 'our major objective is to get you acquainted with the people of Nepal, their hardships and problems, their struggle for survival in an endangered mountain world. And we take great care to show you how, as a tourist and a cyclist, you can understand and contribute positively to help these people survive'.

The Festival of the Countryside was an attempt to halt the population movement away from central Wales. Conservation groups joined with the local community to plan a programme of rural activities within the region. Snowdonia was the best-known attraction in the area but the Festival aimed to disperse visitors by stressing the appeal of other places such as Cardigan Bay and the Brecon Beacons. A number of featured events aimed to raise the public estimation of the distinctive nature of Welsh culture and language.

Snowdonia

◇ *Exercise* ◇

The English Tourist Board recently published the following list of tips for visitors:

Either think up some scenes for a short film intended to encourage people to become better travellers by following this advice,

or plan a poster designed to encourage children to follow one or more of the tips.

Issues Tourism Concern will Continue to Address

Economic Benefits

An information sheet produced recently by Tourism Concern highlights the economic advantages which tourism can bring, both within facilities servicing tourists and in industries and commercial enterprises benefiting from increased local spending. Tourism also enables smaller countries to build up reserves of foreign exchange. These reserves are important because they enable the purchase of a wider range of services and goods from abroad at better rates than if the countries were only able to use their own currency.

Tourism Concern is also determined to point out examples where the apparent gains are greater than the real ones. Much of the wealth created by tourism in Third World countries may remain with the **multinational companies** owning the hotels and tour operators. A 1982 study of the Seychelles, for example, revealed that some 50 per cent of the income derived from tourism left the country. In the Caribbean, many managerial positions in the hotel sector are held by foreign personnel, and the proportion of foreigners employed in Caribbean tourism in general is estimated at 30 per cent.

The Cultural Impact of Tourism

Customs and traditions may be revived and monuments restored as a result of tourism. Arts and crafts may be revived because visitors want to buy local **artefacts**. However, once cultural products become separated from their original context, their significance to the host community is reduced. Examples can be seen in the shortened ritual dances specially tailored to suit the needs of tourists in Bali, and the mass production of masks and copies of sacred objects in Papua New Guinea.

The Environmental Impact

Tourism development has led to the pollution of land, sea and air in many parts of the world. Beaches have proved particularly vulnerable in places like Barbados where sand is extracted for use in building construction. Many parts of the Mediterranean coast have suffered for many years from unregulated sewage disposal and a lack of any kind of organised litter collection. Until recently trekkers in the Himalayas were cutting down so many trees for firewood that landslides and soil erosion were increasingly evident along popular trails. Steps are now being taken to ensure that trekkers take their own fuel supplies with them.

The Social Impact

The host community may benefit from the recreation, leisure and food services developed primarily for tourists. There may also be improved education and training to advance industrial and agricultural development. However, the presence of large numbers of new visitors can bring tensions. The wealth and material possessions of the visitors may be resented. Their appearance and behaviour may evoke different responses from the host community's older and younger generations. The villagers' way of life may be disrupted by them losing rights of way across land. In the Philippines and in Indonesia whole villages have been cleared to make way for new tourist resorts. Compensation is often inadequate. Among younger people, working as tourist guides or earning cash from making handicrafts has often seemed a more attractive option than completing their education. Prostitution, aimed principally at tourists, has had an extremely damaging effect on communities in Africa, the Caribbean and the Far East.

The Political Impact

If tourism is to flourish in any country, it needs to appear to outsiders as a stable and peaceful place where safety and security can be ensured. As a result, governments may use this need as a means of stifling opposition. The success of a glamorous and prosperous tourist resort may be used by governments to hide the reality of poverty and underdevelopment in other parts of the country.

The Future of Tourism Concern

The current strength of Tourism Concern is its ability to communicate information from a wide range of sources to a varied membership. Representation at seminars, exhibitions and conferences is a valuable means of extending interest in the organisation. Tourism Concern now has to decide whether it should seek to attract a wider audience by investing in professionally produced publicity materials. This would require sponsorship or alternative additional funding. That in turn would raise questions about the source of such funding and whether any interest group funded by industry can remain objective about issues regarded as sensitive by the companies concerned.

Key Terms

multinational company – a business which operates in several different countries.

artefacts – articles made by human workmanship.

◇ *Exercise* ◇

Getting the message about responsible tourism across can be effectively achieved by means of slogans. The saying 'Take only photographs; leave only footprints' offers advice simply but vividly.

Devise five sayings of your own which you think would help to put across the message that tourists and/or tourism developments should be sensitive to economic, cultural, environmental, social and political issues.

◇ *Discussion points* ◇

1 Why do you think churches became involved in drawing attention to the effects of tourism on the world's poorer countries?

2 How many words can you think of which are frequently used in travel brochures to stress the attractiveness of destinations?

3 Can you think of ways in which poor countries can protect their economy against total dependence on tourism?

4 Is it possible, or desirable, to prevent writers giving publicity to destinations which are as yet unspoiled by the arrival of large numbers of visitors?

5 Do you think that British culture and our heritage have been affected in any way by the presence of large numbers of foreign tourists?

Acknowledgements

I am very grateful to all of the following companies, organisations and individuals:

American Express; BP Petroleum Development; Cheltenham Arts Festivals Ltd; International Leisure Group; Ironbridge Gorge Museum Trust; Leisure Sport Ltd; The National Trust; Thames and Chilterns Tourist Board; Tourism Concern; Forte plc

John Bethell; Liz Biddle; Jackie Craft; Lesley Dixon; Katy Foster; Tim Grey; Marie Gould; Barry Halton; Geoff Hann; Steve Hartwell; Clive Matthews; Sue Milne; Ian Minshull; Derek Oliver; Joe Petrou; Kim Sargeant; Alison Stancliffe; Annabel Stratton; Dave Strevens; Mandy Trotter; Jeremy Tyndall; Ann Waple.

Whether they gave me information, advice, guided tours, illustrations or critical comment – it was all much appreciated!

It has only been possible to produce this book of case studies within a limited time frame because the Travel and Tourism Programme has provided sufficient time and encouragement to do so. The Programme, which is supported both financially and practically by the American Express Foundation, the British Tourist Authority/English Tourist Board, and Forte Hotels, is a major UK Education/Industry initiative. It has developed a GCSE course in Travel and Tourism, created packs of curriculum materials and provided in-service training courses for teachers and lecturers. It is a key player in attempts to encourage business to work with schools and colleges in a variety of contexts both inside and outside the classroom.

I would also like to think my colleagues at the Travel and Tourism Programme – Ray Churchett, Catherine Mustoe, Geoff Antcliffe, Ann Henley and Jill Chivers – for their help and support during this project.

John Ward

Picture Acknowledgements

The majority of the photographs and illustrations were supplied by the organisations featured in the case studies. In addition to this, photographs and illustrations have been supplied by the following individuals and organisations:

The British Tourist Association: (bar graph) page 6; The Gambia National Tourist Office page 205; Images of India pages 203; The Mexican Tourist Board page 201; C. Munn page 158(a); Munich Airport Authority page 141; Munich Airport Authority/Erich Lutz page 151; Wales Tourist Board pages 195, 211; J. Ward pages 1, 3, 5, 7, 9, 10, 12, 19, 57, 74, 84, 90, 156, 158,(b), 197; S. Ward 158(c).

The publishers also wish to acknowledge the source of the article on sport in the Gambia, page 207: Information taken from the *World Travel Guide*, tenth edition © Columbus Press 1991 and reprinted with permission. For further information on the publication call 071 729–4535.

Index